D1831860

TRIBAL WOMAN LABOURERS
Aspects of Economic and Physical Exploitation

Tribal Woman Labourers

ASPECTS OF ECONOMIC AND PHYSICAL EXPLOITATION

SUSHAMA SAHAY PRASAD

GYAN PUBLISHING HOUSE

Delhi-110007

GYAN PUBLISHING HOUSE
5, Ansari Road, Daryaganj,
Delhi-110002
Phone: 011-47034999, 9811692060

@ 1988 Dr. Sushama Sahay Prasad

ISBN. 9788121201933

Printed in India :

Published by Mrs. Gayatri Garg for
Gian Publishing House, Delhi and
Printed by Amar Printing Agency,
Delhi

Preface

In the tribal world women contribute to the working force in a more substantial way than the non-tribal world. The forces of modernization at work in the tribal societies have produced a twofold trend. They have created conditions for prolification of occupations for tribal women. More and more tribal women now move from the primary sector to the secondary and tertiary sectors of employment. With the opening of mines and growth of industries in tribal areas large number of women have been drawn into occupations hitherto unknown to them. On account of the operation of a large number of factors, such as the opening of the tribal country, growing industrialization, growth of education and the impact of Christianity, opportunities for diversification of occupation as well as social mobility among the tribal women have multiplied. The building up of roads and development of fast communications have led to a large number of tribal women taking to petty trading, casual labour work and other commercial activities in some parts of the country.

In areas where a lot of constructional activity is proceeding such as in industrial areas in Bihar, Madhya Pradesh, Orissa, women are lifted on trucks from the nearby tribal villages by the contractors. Tribal women are attracted to such employment as it gives them ready cash and trinkets. They also enjoy the daily outing. In many of the industrial centres the employment of tribal women have led to abuses. The freedom enjoyed by the tribal women in their own social system has been mistaken for licence by the alien contractors. Thus economic exploitation is also accompanied by sexual exploitation. This has ultimately led to break up of family ties, erosion of the authority of the village Headman and a general sanction of the traditional tribal social structure. The present study seeks to understand the various social, economic and psychological aspects of the participation of the tribal women in the secondary and tertiary sectors of employment in the Ranchi District of Bihar, where the tribal working women are locally known as *REJA*.

Financial assistance for undertaking this research study was provided to me by the Ministry of Home Affairs (Tribal Division), Government of India. I am indeed very much thankful to my sponsor as without their help this work could not be completed. I owe my profound gratefulness and gratitude to my guide Dr. A. N. Sandhwar, Reader, Department of Anthropology, Ranchi University who kept on encouraging and inspiring me althrough with his scholarly guidance and suggestions. I am also immensely obliged and grateful to my teacher Late Prof. L. P. Vidyarthi for his unstinted cooperation and assistance which helped me complete this work. I cannot forget to record my deep sense of gratitude for Shri S.K. Lal, I.A.S., who in the capacity of the Director of the Bihar Tribal Welfare and Research Institute, Ranchi rendered full assistance and cooperation to me despite his busy schedule to enable me complete the present work.

Verily I deem it my duty to express thankfulness to the tribal *Rejas*, the contractors, the employers and many other informants who ungrudgingly posted me with relevant information during the course of field study.

I am also very much thankful to my in-laws, parents, husband, brothers, sister who helped me constantly to enable me to carry out the research work without much ado.

Last, but not the least, I would express my sincere thanks to Shri Ram Autar Prasad for typing out the whole thesis meticulously.

Hyderabad
May, 1987

Sushama Sahay Prasad

Contents

Introduction

Sexual asymmetry is a universal phenomenon. It is nowhere as carefully developed in nature as among human beings. Constituting a dependency class, women are described as the 'second sex' and the 'second creature' who live on surplus, their very existence being parasitic on the men who rule them. Relationship between sexes is characterized by sympathetic inequalities. The sex of an individual goes beyond inherent biological qualifications. Sex differences represent a social distinction of the highest rank. Women are "burdened with cumulative inequalities as a result of socio-cultural and economic discriminatory practices which until recently have been taken for granted as though they are part of the immutable scheme of things established by nature" (de Souza, 1975: IX). Women, according to Marxist ideology, are enslaved, suppressed and isolated from the public life of the community. Their status involves a form of domestic slavery and in effect legalised prostitution (Dahlstron, 1967 : 172). Female subordination is an essential feature of human life in all contemporary societies, although the degree and expression of male dominance may vary.

One important manifestation of the subordinate status of women is to be found in the division of labour by that provides a cheap and ready source of labour and presents the organization of marginal groups to further their common goals (Andreas, 1971 : 3). The segregated role-pattern prevalent in the societies entails a structural subordination of women to men. Division of labour between sexes is culturally imposed and it ignores individual endowments.

Rural Working Women : The structural subordination of women to men becomes more manifested when the phenomenon is considered in the context of the rural working women. The rural working women present an unenviable lot. They are the unsung heroines, born to die in the backyard of human civilization, carrying on the burden of humanity for a mere pittance. They work in the scorching sun and in the pouring rain. Away from the home they slog breaking the stones at the quarries and doing all drudgery at the mines, factory premises, brick-kilns etc. They earn on their own or supplement the family income to keep off starvation. They do many things more which men do not do. They cook and look after children and do almost everything that men do, go around to fetch grass and fodder all in order to keep the fire of hearth glowing. They even operate the wells to irrigate the land. They sow the seeds, transplant and harvest the crops.

This is the story of the millions of women workers in India's 5,60,000 villages, the unknown soldiers who help keep our economy going, keep the barns to the full and help India occupy one of the premier places by engineering the Green Revolution. According to the 1971 census women constitute 48.2 percent of our population, but their participation in the economic activities is only 13 percent. In developed countries it ranges from 30 to 45 percent. The vast majority of women in India work in the unorganised sector of the economy and as this area is without protective measures and machinery, information about this group is meagre. As many as 94 percent of women workers are engaged in this sector of the economy. Here again agricultural labour and cultivation are the main fields of the economic activity of women. The primary sector (Farming, Livestock, Forestry, Fishing, Plantation and Orchards) provides work to about 83 percent of women and 51 percent of them work as agricultural labourers.

Tribal Working Women : Although the tribal males are still the major bread winners in the families, in recent times the economic contribution of the tribal women has also assumed significant role due to various reasons. With the opening up of mines and growth of industries in tribal areas, large number of women have drawn into occupations hitherto unknown to them. Now women are not only employed inside the mines but also outside the mines.

In the tribal world women contribute to the working force in a more substantial way than in the non-tribal world. While the ratio between male and female workers in the general population of the country is 5 : 1, it is 3 : 1 among the tribal people. Among the non-tribal women 11.9 percent are workers whereas their tribal sisters have 20.75 percent as workers. The comparative figures of the participation rate of the non-tribal and tribal workers in the different sectors of economy are as follows :—

Table—1

Comparative figures of the participation rate of non-tribals and tribal female workers in different sectors

primary sector

Occupational categories	Cultivation	Agricultural labourers	Mining	Livestock, Forestry, Fishing, Hunting etc.
1	2	3	4	5
General Female	29.8%	50.5%	0.4%	2.5%
Tribal Female	42.7%	48.9%	0.6%	2.6%

Secondary Sector

Occupational categories	Household industries	Manufacturing etc.	Construction
1	2	3	4
General Female	4.3%	2.8%	0.7%
Tribal Female	1.3%	0.9%	0.3%

Tertiary Sector

Occupational categories	Trade and Commerce	Transport etc.	Other Services
1	2	3	4
General Female	1.8%	0.5%	—
Tribal Female	0.6%	0.2%	—

Since the tribal economy is largely confined to the primary sector, 90.6% of the female workers are engaged in agriculture as cultivators or as labourers, 2.67 percent in pastoralism, hunting etc. and 0.6 percent in mining and quarring (Sachchidananda, 1978:8-9).

In a society where the forces of urbanisation and industrialisation are under operation, there has been a wide-spread change in occupational system. The traditional tribal economy which rested mainly on agriculture is no longer the only source of income. Profit from trading and industrial work also began. The economy remained no longer exclusively agricultural. It also became mercantile and industrial. Traditionally Chotanagpur, predominantly inhabited by tribals, was a cluster of villages. Like men, women too were mainly confined to agricultural works besides a few other works as well. The women were conspicuously not involved as labourers but the sooner industrialisation set in, the new job patterns for women have become accepted and preferred by most men. The proportion of women in the labour force has increased gradually otherwise women were never attached to any particular type of labour centre.

On account of the operation of a large number of factors, such as the opening of the tribal country, growing industrialisation, growth of education and the impact of Christianity, opportunities for diversification of occupation as well as social mobility have multiplied. The building up of roads and development of fast communication have led to a large number of tribal women taking to petty trading and other commercial activities in some area of the country.

In areas where a lot of constructional activity is being carried out such as, in industrial areas in Bihar, Madhya Pradesh, Orissa, tribal women are lifted on trucks from the tribal villages and nearabouts by the contractors. In the evening they are usually taken back to the villages (Sachchidananda, 1978 : 9). In some cases the tribal women even migrate outside their villages, district and state to some distant places for period ranging from 2 to 6 months for working in the brick-kilns, agricultural fields, tea Estates, etc.

There was a time when almost no industrial workers, skilled or unskilled, were found in any tribal village. In the first phase of industrialisation several villagers complexed. Many of the tribal labourers left for Andaman and Nicobar Islands (Vidyarthi, 1971) and tea gardens of North Eastern India (Kar, 1976), and to several other parts of India. The tribal labourers working in the Forests in Chotanagpur did not find it much difficult to work in the forest of Andamans. They may be safely termed as the modern builders of Andaman as they have been working for several decades in the Forest Department, Public Works Department, Bush Police and Jetty (Vidyarthi, 1971).

Tribal women also feel inclined to go in for such short and long term employment avenues because it provides them ready cash which they prefer spending on clothes, new fashion ornaments, and other items of daily use. Besides the monetary gains, they also cherish the pleasure of daily outing which is actively associated with such occupations. But, in many of the industrial projects, the employment of women have led to several forms of physical and economic exploitations. The freedom enjoyed by the tribal women in their own social system has been grossly mistaken and misunderstood by the aliens and the local non-tribals who utilise the tribal women for their economic gains. Thus economic exploitation unavoidably paves way for physical exploitation : and to be more precise—sexual exploitation. This has ultimately led to break-up of family ties, conjugal relationship, erosion of the authority of the village headman and a general weakening of the social sanctions of the traditional social structure which provides certain distinct status of tribal women.

The Problem

With this background material, the present treatise has endeavoured to throw deeper light into the various facets of the socio-economic and socio-political implications which pertain to constraints of participation of tribal women as wage earners, attitude of employers towards tribal woman labourers, lack of available information in regard to labour laws/facilities etc. among the tribal labourers, the inability to combine work with household and child rearing responsibilities and lack of institutional supports to the tribal women labourers, etc. For providing empirical facts on the various socio-economic and socio-political issues behind the working tribal women in a larger society hitherto unknown to them, a total study of the tribal *Reja* (Woman labourer) of Ranchi has been undertaken.

Meaning of The Reja : Before venturing to proceed to dwell on the total study of the tribal *Reja*, it is quite imperative to clearly explain the meaning of the term *Reja* which forms the core of this study. In the present study the term *Reja* refers to those tribal women labourers who represent the wage-earners class among the tribal communities of Bihar inhabiting the Ranchi district in South Chotanagpur division. They fall in the age groups of 5-10 years to 60 years. Though the word *Reja* commonly refers to those wage earners who are dependent on some semi-skilled Masons, Craftsmen etc. for assisting them in the various odd jobs like fetching water, head-load carrying, mortar making, etc. in the present context, the term *Reja* essentially refers to those tribal woman labourers who work with the contractors or independently at the various labour centres and are engaged in brick-kilns, construction works, transportation of materials, industrial complexes, etc.

Importance of the Study

The problem of raising the status of women in India has many aspects. The constitution and laws have given them equality of opportunity and status. But women have lagged behind in almost every sphere of activity. Planned action to improve the status of Women in the country started with initiation of Five

Year Plans. But a natural plan of action for women has now been prepared for priority areas in health, social welfare, education, employment and legislation.

Many steps have been taken and efforts are continued for integration of women in the total development process in the country and for removing inequalities and discriminations against women. All over the history instances are replete to indicate that women have been and are still being maltreated. Happily with the growing awareness and renewed keenness among all sections of the society, the condition of women has continued to improve. Expanding opportunities of education as well as the various welfare measures introduced particularly after the country attained freedom have given a filip to the process. But the effect of these measures is yet to penetrate into our rural areas. The rural women still suffer from the traditional handicaps. The conditions of the tribal woman labourers (Reja) are still worse. Illiteracy, lack of awareness of local and other redress processes and unscrupulousness of the employers add to their miseries.

In agriculture, the tribal women labourer suffer from sporadic and seasonal employment and also from disparities and discrimination in wages. Tribal women are generally employed on daily wages in sowing, transplantation, winnowing, crushing and harvesting and all jobs commonly rated as unskilled and less-skilled.

Next to agriculture, the tribal women are employed in various industries, trades, services etc. The vast army of unorganised tribal women labour force faces a battery of insurmountable problems accentuated by their vulnerability, acute poverty, pressing needs for themselves and families. These problems range from insecurity of employment, lack of standards of minimum wages, excessive hours of work and absence of welfare amenities and various other forms of exploitation. Some new industries and crafts, in the recent times, have developed in the backdrop of the tribal women labour force, without having been brought under the purview of labour laws. With callous immunity, many of the unscrupulous employers circumvent or openly violate almost all pieces of labour legislation – be they the Bidi and Cigarette Act, 1966, the Inter-State Migrant workman Act, 1979, the Minimum Wage Act, 1948, the Factories and Industrial Disputes Act, the Contract Labour (Regulation and Abolition) Act, 1970, and the like.

The worst victims are the tribal *rejas* who work as daily wage-earners at different labour centres engaged in brick-kilns, construction works, transportation works, industrial complexes, etc. get their employment either by the contractors or direct by the management or owner of the labour centre. They have neither the benefit of Minimum Wages nor the protection of labour laws. The *Reja* as a profession has not only brought significant changes among the tribal society, but it also brought about many more new types of social and economic problems. Different types of peoples from different corners of the district started working together in a new situation. This not only streched the contact but they also were exposed to many new types of situations which brought significant changes in their life and culture. Besides working at the various labour centres in Ranchi district, the tribal *rejas* are sent to some remote corners of the State and out of the state also. A good number of *rejas* are enticed away to remote places on the alurement of some gains, but they had to come back disappointed for they were not favoured with the promised incentives. The *rejas* are often subjected to exploitation either at the hands of their contractors or employers or other associates. The profile of tribal *Reja* is depressing and the lack of inadequate social security and welfare measure has engendered in her feelings of fear, insecurity, alienation and frustration. They are too weak to rebel because of their poverty, ignorance and illiteracy and the employers know how to loopholes in legislation to evade their obligations to exploit them for weakness and how to circumvent the law.

Although there are laws to enforce regular payment and to prevent unfair deduction in wages, provision of regular working hours and leave and holidays, proper environment, drinking water and social security against old age, sickness, industrial hazards, etc. the government files and research works are replete with instances to show that in most of the cases the benefits of these laws or safeguards are being denied to the vast army of unorganised tribal women force i.e. the tribal *rejas*.

The importance and significance of the present study thus, not only lies in unfolding and unravelling the various facts and figures in a systematic way pertaining to the socio-economic and socio-political dimensions of the tribal *reja* in respect of the points mentioned above; but also to suggest the remedial measures for improving the socio-economic conditions of the tribal woman labourers.

Objectives of the Study

The objectives of the present study are as follows :—

(i) To study the constraints of participation of tribal women as wage-earners.

(ii) To study the attitude of the tribal *rejas* towards their employers and vice-versa.

(iii) To show that how the profession of *reja* serves as an economic embslem in the tribal society.

(iv) To study as to how the tribal *rejas* combine their professional work with household activities, child rearing responsibilities, etc.

(v) To know about the changes in attitudes, behaviours, characters and other aspects among the *rejas*.

(vi) To study the various forms of social, physical and economic exploitation with which the tribal *rejas* are subjected, if any.

(vii) To review the existing labour laws in relation to the problems being faced by the tribal *rejas*.

(viii) Finally, to suggest the remedial measures for improving the social, economic and working conditions of the tribal *rejas*.

Hypotheses

The present treatise has envisaged the following hypotheses:

(i) Men and women are influenled by their social and economical values.

Map of Ranchi Town

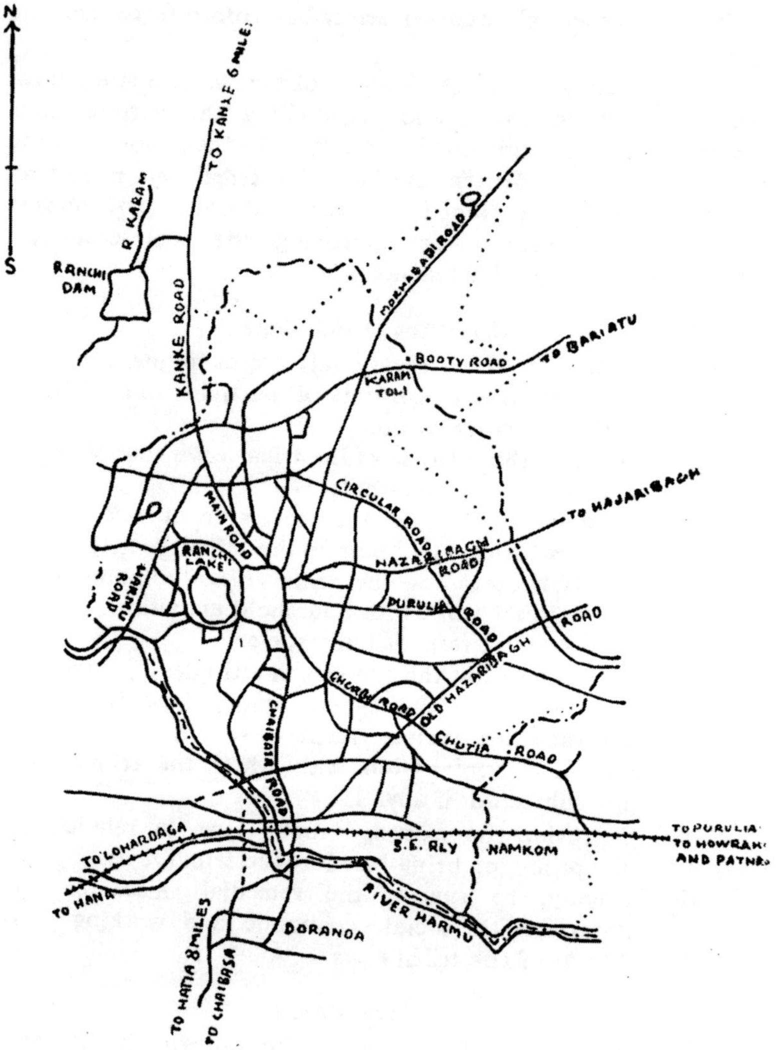

(ii) The family life, the social tradition, the hard instincts, the group prejudices, etc. all exercise their influence on the men and women equally.

(iii) A synthesized growth of social and economic system eventually leads to the emergence of a new socio-economic order.

The Study Area

The persent study is based on the data collected from among the tribal *rejas* of Ranchi district in the State of Bihar. Ranchi is centrally located on the Chotanagpur plateau at a height of 2100 ft. and on the map, it extends between 23° 25^{n} and 23° 25^{n} latitude and between 85° 20^{e} and 85° 23^{e} longitude. The main city of Ranchi according to 1951 census report covers an area of 11.2 sq. miles. This area is acceded, significantly only by Jamshedpur (28 sq. miles) as other cities of Bihar viz. Bhagalpur (11.5 sq. miles), Patna (11.5 sq. miles), Gaya (11.2 sq. miles) have more or less the same area under the municipal boundary.

Ranchi is essentially a linear city expanding from the north to the south. It is bounded on all sides by a number of scattered small villages consisting mostly of the tribal population. Ranchi also is centrally located in the midst of mineralised belt of Chotanagpur and the discovery and exploitation of minerals is one of the main factors in its recent rapid growth. The rich deposit of minerals in Ranchi district has been mainly responsible for the recent establishment of a large number of industrial concerns and owing to these mineral resources Ranchi has become one of the important hubs of industrial development in modern India.

Since the present study necessitated collection of the first hand information on the various socio-economic etc. aspects of the tribal *rejas* working in different occupational categories like construction work, brick-kilns, transportation of raw materials, industrial complexes etc. field work was conducted in various labour centres located at Bariatu, Dhurwa, Namkom, Ratu Road, Kanke, etc. These places are located from Ranchi town at an average distance of about ten Kms. and cover almost all the major labour centres of Ranchi city where the

Map of Ranchi District

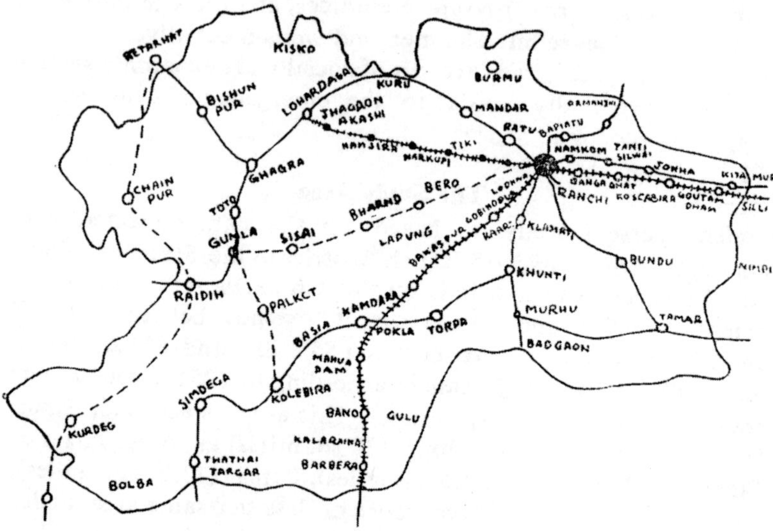

tribal *rejas* āre found working in various a vocations. Apart from the Ranchi town, the datā for the present work have also been collected from the rural areas of Ranchi district. The development blocks like Lohardaga, Kisko, Mandar, Bero and Kuru were visited for conducting field studies among the tribal *rejas* of rural Ranchi. The geographical location of these places has been indicated in the above map.

Research Techniques

Research techniques are the important avenues of collecting, classifying, analysing and interpreting the material and data collected from the field surveys. The present study has involved methods of anthropological and sociological repertory. As regards the materials, the information have been gathered from both the documentary and field sources through various techniques such as observation, interview, schedules, photography, etc. The author has used observations and schedules techniques supported by interviews as basic tools for this research work in the field. Besides these the techniques of case-study and life-history have been used. The whole stuay is supported by a number of case studies and life histories. The names of the persons involved in different cases are fictitious to keep their identity secret. The use of books, journals, periodicals etc. have been quite helpful in this work.

Almost two years' field work at the successive periods was done from November 1978 to June 1979, from December 1979 to May 1980 and from July 1980 to April 1981. Some information were also collected by short visits in the closing months of the year 1981 to supplement the data and fill up the gaps. During these periods 300 schedules have been administered amongst the tribal *rejas* deployed at various labour centres in and around Ranchi town. In regard to selection of units of study, the technique of random sampling was applied with special consideration that each occupational category be represented by minimum samples of at least twenty tribal *rejas*. In this study altogether three hundred tribal *rejas* belonging to five different occupational categories have been included. With a view to knowing the attitudes of the employers and the guardians of the *rejas* towards the working of the tribal women as *rejas*, hundred schedules prepared separately both for employers and guardians, were used to elicit the desired information in this regard.

The field observations were made from different angles, depending upon the situation, sometimes as a participant observer at other times as a non-participant observer, Likewise, controlled and uncontrolled observation simultaneously were found practicable. As aids to observation, notes and photographs were also taken. The interviews were taken with the tribal woman labourers along with their guardians, employers and other associates of different age-groups to know about the attitudes of the guardians, employers, etc. towards the tribal *rejas*. In most of the interviews notes were taken side by side and doubtful information were counterchecked.

In the organisation and analysis of the data collected several steps were taken to be accurate, screening was first done to delete unwanted materials. Through the editing operation, checks were made in the original frame-work of the study and data were collected. In classification, the categories in the proper settings were formed for presenting the data. Thus, the analysis or the creative part of research was done stepwise to draw systematic inferences in a sequential form. The results were finally translated into conceptual language. Income and expenditure have been calculated on the basis of weekly income and expenditure.

Organisation of Data

The whole study is divided into eight chapters excluding introduction. The first chapter dwells on the growth and genesis of the tribal *rejas*. It also deals with the deployment of tribal *rejas* at various labour-centres, their population and distribution at various labour centres. This chapter also covers the phenomenon of migration of tribal *rejas* from their home towns, villages in search of job. After discussing about their population and distribution, the classification of tribal *rejas* has been done according to their nature of works in the second chapter. The second chapter also discusses the various modes of employment along with the causes for acceptance of the wage-earning employment by tribal women. A brief account of their works at different labour centres has been dealt with in this very chapter. The third chapter deals with the relationship of tribal *rejas* with their employers, associates and colleagues, with whom they have to work. The various types of behaviour which the *rejas* experience during their working and non-working hours, and whether the behaviours of their employers and other associates are upto their expectations and vice-versa are the main aspects of this chapter along with the attitudes of the employers or associates towards them. The fourth chapter tries to show the status of *reja* in the family and outside family which she acquires after taking up the job of *reja*. What is her role as an earning member in her family and how far she could become able to raise the standard of living of her family is the point of discussion in this chapter. After having sketched a detailed picture of the economic role of tribal *reja*, the next chapter i.e. the fifth one tries to know about the various role-conflicts among the tribal *reja*s which occur due to their two types of activities. Besides working as a *reja*, the tribal woman has to look after her family also and she has to perform the traditional role of a daughter, wife, sister, daughter-in law, mother and so on in her respective family. She can not make a deviation from her traditional role also and if she fails to maintain a balance at both the levels, she is surrounded by various kinds of streses and strains which are manifested in her behaviourial disposition during the working hours.

Due to different types of work which the tribal women have to do for raising their standard of living and improving their economic condition and trying to adjust themselves at both levels i. e. the working site and the home, marked changes have been seen in their attitudes, belief, behaviours, etc. The changing dimensions among the tribal *rejas* have been dealt with in the sixth chapter along with the sources of recreation which are also changed in the changed context of life.

While working as *rejas* at different labour centres, the tribal women are subjected to various types of exploitations by their employers, associates or other local persons and the tribal women have to face such exploitations becuase of their ignorance, illiteracy, simpleton nature and above all, helplessness and poverty. The tribal women mostly work for the contractors and they also quite frequently go outside their native places to get the job and there they meet with various types of exploitations. The various forms of social, physical and economic exploitations to which the tribal *rejas* are subjected, have been dealt with, at length, in the seventh chapter. Over and above the various labour laws and facilities being provided by the Government to check the labour exploitation have also been critically reviewed in this chapter.

The last chapter deals with the summary and conclusion followed by the appendices and selected bibliography. In this way, an attempt has been made to present a comprehensive picture of the prevailing socio-economic conditions of the tribal *rejas* of Ranchi, which may go a long way in providing much sought relief and bringing about betterment in the socio-economic life of the teeming millions of this tribal belt particularly to that unorganised sector of the *rejas* as a class. Uptill now this unorganised sector has been underestimated, so to say, for they have been denied all sorts of modern facilities, say legislation and the like provisions which would have stood them decidedly in good stead. On the one hand this unorganised sector of the tribal belt of Ranchi has been busy contributing their services towards the progress of the country, on the other, they are ill-treated so much so that they are still unknown to the labour legislation which envisages all sorts of betterment to the labourers.

On the basis of this research work even if slight relief is provided to the female workers termed as *reja* by arousing the present day administration from its apathetic stuper, the efforts of the author would definitely bring about a tangible result.

1

The Tribal Rejas : A Historic and Demographic Profile

Participation of women in economic activity is common in all countries, developed and developing. The extent of their participation depends upon factors too well known to bear repetition. While in the developed countries, many of which are now characterized by full employment, the debate on the extent of employment of women is not keen, and in fact, there is room for more women in the working force, in countries which are marked by labour surpluses, the need for providing employment for women when many men are available for work raises questions which can not admit of categorical answers. It is in these developing countries that incomes by and large are low and the family requires the assistance of an additional earner. Where social conventions do not weigh oppressively against bringing women into paid employment, family income can best be supplemented by a draft on the female population in the working age group (Report of the Government of India, 1969:379).

The tribal woman labourers are also supplementing the income of their families while working as *rejas* at different labour centres in and around Ranchi. In the present chapter an attempt has been made to enumerate a demographic profile of the tribal *rejas* along with their growth and genesis as *rejas*. We shall be trying to analyse the distribution and population of the tribal *rejas* at different labour centres of Ranchi.

Growth and Genesis of Tribal Rejas

From time immemorial it is apparent from a number of instances which have come to light through various journals, periodicals, historical reports, etc. that the women have contributed a lot towards developing of a country. Similarly ours is not an exception to it. Around the country it has been found that women have assisted their male partners in raising resources for the progress of their families by maintaining their separate entity in the field of activities. Thus it goes without saying that no perfections can be arrived at without the participations of males and females alike, be it in agricultural or industrial operations. History is, undoubtedly, replete with such instances besides those of certain epics as well. From the primitive era to the modern age the women have been contributing their mite for the betterment of their kiths and kins so as to occupy a better position in the society they lived.

Industry has grown with the years in India and can be traced back to prehistoric times, even before the development of the Indus valley civilization in the third millennium B. C. palaeolithic activities, of which traces have been found in various parts of India, indicate the existence of primitive industries, the most astounding of which, as far as archaeological discoveries can fathom at present, being the Indian Flake Industry, known as the pre-so n Industry in the pleistocene period. The Soan river was a tributary of the Indus in the Potwar region of Punjab. Flake or chopper tools were manufactured by prehistoric man;whether women helped him to fashion these or not is a matter for conjecture (Piggott, 1950:29).

Though we are not sure as to what part women played in primitive civilisation, they seem definitely to have shared a partnership with men in the Indus culture of about 3000 B. C. Their work seems to have been demarcated from men's, falling into what may be called feminine occupations. In fact, it can be safely said that in Harappa and Mohenjo-Dàro, men delved and women span, the former category of jobs depicting the harder and more masculine, the latter the more feminine occupations which possibly developed into "women's jobs", in factories and domestic life.

In Harappa and Mohenjo-Daro, long before the Aryans came to India, a definite pattern of culture reveals that though women were mainly domestic in their occupations, they were responsible almost entirely for weaving and spinning the clothes which were worn, and took part in the fashioning of pottery and the designing of jewellery. Toy-making, no doubt inspired by the need to give their children something to keep them quiet, was also a woman's job. The arts and crafts of the Indus civilisation were highly advanced, and findings have revealed that they can be linked with the cultural output of the people of Western Asia, especially in the skilled work in faience, tools, vessels, jewels, metalware and household articles. We are even told that men fashioned the pottery and women gave the finishing touches, and this, together with the leather industry, the making of musical instruments, and other simple crafts, formed actually the foundations of the present village industries of India. There is said to have been "standardized technique of production which could control the sizes of bricks, the capacity and types of pots and a system of weights and measures." (Piggott, 1950 : 138).

With the coming of the Aryans in the second millennium B.C. we have much clearer evidence of industries, such as leather work, the making of *gur* and *rab*, and various other activities. We are also on surer ground as to the occupations of women. Indeed, they played no small part in creating utility requisites for their own simple domestic lives and were said to be skilled in arts and crafts. Weaving was known from earliest Vedic times and was mostly done by women, for mention is made in Vedic literature of warp and woof being woven by deft fingers. Sheep's wool was woven and bleached and the Aryans worshipped Pushan, the god of the shepherds, for abundant wool. Carpenters, gold and silversmiths, iron mongers, toy-makers, leather-workers, to mention but a few, all flourished in early Aryan civilisation in India, and though women did not seem to indulge in these occupations, they were certainly responsible for most of their textile output, apart from working in the fields in the easier tasks of transplanting, weeding and reaping the harvest. Women also were known to have studied in the various forest *ashrams* and become *Brahamcharinis.* They were well educated and took part in learned philosophical discourses and wrote hymns. Women even waged war beside their husbands.

In the home, their duties consisted mostly in drawing water, churning butter-milk and making butter and *ghee,* husking and winnowing grain and managing the household finances. A task at which they seem to have been particularly skilled was making of the intoxicant Soma juice, which was appreciated so much by the Aryans that Soma was regarded as a God. We are also told that women understood the plaiting of Mats and sewing, and were familiar with the manufacture of wool which they converted into clothing for their men and animals. Wives were also given direct charge of farm-labourers, slaves and parents.

In fact the women played an active part in their simple pastoral life both at home and in the occupations of the day in the Vedic period, and it is no new venture for them to be termed working women in present day India. Women also were important factors in the administration of their country. Women soldiers were common and Kautilya, the ancient Indian Machiavelli, says that they were armed with bows and arrows. Some ancient sculptures also depict women working at various occupations, some of which are quite masculine in character. The rapid rise of religious dogmas and the invasion of India by foreigners, however, gradually deteriorated their position until they began more and more to rely on the security offered to them in their homes and to content themselves with domestic duties. The increasing strictures of the law-givers also reduced the position of women to nothing more than domestic drudges. The final deterioration of their position came when the Muslims conquered India, and Hindu women were sheltered from their foreign rulers as much as possible. The purdah system of the Muslims also influenced the women of India to keep to their domestic world as much as possible.

In medieval India, therefore, one does not hear much of the activities of women. On the other hand their status became lower and lower until, when the British came to India, the position of women was anything but happy. Many wrongs meted out to them placed them in a pitiable condition, and they were nothing more than mere chattels in the hands of their men and their priests. Neither did British rule alleviate the condition of women to any great extent, because the rulers were afraid to bring about too drastic reforms and to interfere with the religious and social customs of a subject people. Though they did abolish *Sati,* and passed the Sarda Act–not to speak of other reforms which gradually up-graded the position of women–progress was slow. But Christian Missionaries, the Brahmo Samaj, the Arya Samaj and individual reformers whose names are all very well known, beginning with Raja Ram Mohan Roy, awoke a sense of social consciousness which provoked enthusiastic public interest in the welfare of women and children, especially in the raising of the economic standards of women and the right they have of economic independence.

Early in the era of British rule in India an economic situation arose which made it essential for women of the lower income groups to work. The Industrial Revolution in Europe also had its repercussions in India.

"As the technological changes of the industrial revolution transformed the processes of production, the women of the urban proletariate and many of the artisan class were drawn into the factories, Mills and Mines as unskilled wage earners" (Report of the Govt. of India, 1953 : 2).

In Europe, women left their homes for work in factories in large numbers. There was a tremendous economic upheaval. Goods originally made in the home had now to be brought in factories. No longer could women weave and spin their household requirements, as they did before the Industrial Revolution. Likewise in India also, women sought work in factories and industries, though not to such an extent as in Europe. The housewife who worked had to rely on market goods. The cost of living then increased even though woman felt she was better off because she earned a living, no matter how small it was.

Soon, even young children had to seek employment at wages which were appallingly low. It suited entrepreneurs to employ these low-paid hands. *Sardars* were sent out to lure women into factories by promising cash wages. Women, being completely ignorant and wholly gullible, fell easy victims to the bait set for them by entrepreneurs seeking cheap labour.

The Industrial Revolution transferred many tasks hitherto done in the home to the factory, and the family earning were used in purchasing market goods instead of home made goods. To meet this increased cost of living, the wage of the chief earner had to be supplemented, and wives and children began to work. But industry also sought to keep costs and offered low wages to men and supplementary wages to wives and children. "Women thus came to occupy the position of marginal workers in the new economy" (Adyantha, 1954 : 2).

The first wake of industrialisation was felt in Chotanagpur with the exploitation of the coal mining industry in Jharia, Bokaro and Karanpura coal fields in Dhanbad district in 1856 and the installation of Tata Iron and Steel Factory in Jamshedpur in Singhbhum district in 1907. These twin industries of coal and iron marked the beginning of the large scale exploitation of mineral and other industrial resources of Chotanagpur. With the worlds' largest deposit of coal, iron, copper, and adequate quantities of bauxite, limestone, phyllite, chromite, asbestes, graphite, kynite and stealite, Chotanagpur has attracted thousands of local tribals excluding the immigrants from outside to work in the various types of mining as well as mineral based industries (Vidyarthi, 1970 : 5). As a matter of fact the emergence of tribal labour in a sizeable proportion for industrial work is an aspect which is acquiring significance in the country. It gathered momentum since Independence with the location of factories in what were considered traditional tribal belts and with intensive exploitation of forests and minerals. The first consequence of the changes is 'urbanisation' of tribal areas. The 1961 census showed, a significant increase in the population of towns and cities in these areas. With all the consequences of the type referred to earlier, though on a smaller scale, isolated homogenous 'adivasi' communities which looked to agriculture for sustenance, found their lands being acquired for industrial use and a new environment being built with substantial investments flowing in. With such monetisation in the area, the traditional institution—the tribal Panchayat—could help them no longer. Those who still continued to till their lands had to diversify their crops to suit the needs of a growing industrial centre. A study of tribal labour force in the Hatia Industrial complex is quite fascinating. This industrial complex has witnessed the uprooting of twenty-five villages inhabited by 12,990 souls of the uprooted ones; the elderly members of the families preferred to migrate to the other villages, purchased land from the compensation money and continued their traditional occupations. But the young ones took up the challenge of industrialisation (Vidyarthi, 1970). With the advent of industrialisation and urbanisation in the country, a good many structures were seen springing up with the help of a huge labour force in towns as well as in their vicinities. Tribal men and women are both found engaged in greater proportion in the varied labour force (Vidyarthi, 1969).

The day industrialisation and urbanisation started in and around Ranchi, it required huge labour force of different kinds in which new type of peoples were associated and they started giving publicity for the employment through their agents in different parts of the area. With the result tribal people got attracted towards the labour jobs in which cash money started coming. In the beginning men joined first, and women followed them afterward. The entire area started humming up with the bustlings of the labourers engaged in brick-kilns, building constructions, industrial complexes, transportation of materials and the like activities which helped emerging a unique class of tribal female labourers known as *Rejas*. Thus, developed the concept of *Reja* as a profession which is, so to say, a new phenomenon in the tribal life of Ranchi in the first wake of industrialisation as well as urbanisation.

A Demographic Survey of Tribal Rejas

The tribal population of Bihar as per 1971 census, is 49, 32, 767 which is nearly 13 percent of the total tribal population of India and in Bihar out of every 10,000 population 875 persons are reported to be tribals. Over the last 40 years there had been a rise of nearly 57 percent of tribal population of Bihar against 82 percent rise in the residual population. This clearly shows that the overall growth rate of the tribal population during the last four decades is significantly low in comparison to non-tribal population of Bihar.

The females among tribals are more in number than males which is not applicable in case of non-tribal population of Bihar. This feature has been observed in 1961 as well as in 1971. The table-1 presents the sex ratio which is self-explanatory.

Table—1

Sex-Ratio

Sl. No.	Class	No. of females per 1000 males	
		1961	1971
1	2	3	4
1.	Tribals	1014	1004
2.	Non-tribals	992	949

In both the cases the population of female has a decreasing tendency but in the case of tribals the female population is tending to converge to the male population while for the non-tribal population, the gap is becoming wider.

The women folk amongst tribals are known for their participation in economic activities along with their male counterpart. Out of every five workers amongst tribals one is necessarily woman. Their ratio of representation, however, vary from occupation to occupation. While we consider agriculture labour as primary occupation the ratio of male and female workers is 10.00 to 5.65, that is out of approximately 16 agriculture labourers 6 belong to female category. The proportion is highest in construction sector where against 1000 tribal male workers 611 tribal female workers are absorbed. The extent of female workers for 1000 male counterpart for different categories is revealed from the table-2.

Table—2

Tribal Female workers for 1000 Tribal Male Workers (1971)

Sl. No.	Category	Number
1	2	3
1.	Cultivators	145
2.	Agriculture labour	565
3.	Mining, quarrying, Live stock	215
4.	Household Industry (H.I.)	307
5.	Manufacturing other than H.I.	211
6.	Construction	611
7.	Trade and Commerce	238
8.	Transport, storage or communication	185
9.	Other services	237
	Overall	249

Agriculture labour is the most popular and common occupation amongst tribal women. Next to agriculture they are absorbed in cultivation. Thus these two aspects of occupational classifications, jointly provide to the extent of 90 percent of employment to the women folk. The minimum avenue for employment have been provided by the Trade and commerce sector. Analysing the rural population and urban population separately we are confronted with a different situation.

In urban sector although agriculture labour covers the maximum frequency as a single source of occupation, the importance of mining and quarrying, construction and manufacturing industries have more or less equal importance in the field of employment for the tribal women. In the rural sector the percentage of employment under agriculture sector whether as cultivator or agriculture labour goes up to nearly 93 percent. The detail percentage distribution of female workers can be seen in Table-3.

As per 1971 census about 13.84 percent of the female population have been recorded as workers against 55.76 percent for male population. This shows that about 86 percent of the female population are economically dependent or are earning dependent which, however, includes 41.19 percent of the female population whose age are below 14 years.

Table—3
Percentage Distribution of Tribal Female Workers (1971 census)

Sl. No.	Category of occupation	Percentage Distribution Rural	Urban	Total
1.	2	3	4	5
1.	Cultivators	40.92	4.96	39.34
2.	Agriculture labour	50.37	19.18	50.91
3.	Mining, Quarrying & livestock	1.86	13.02	2.35
4.	Household Industries (H.I.)	1.71	1.30	1.69
5.	Manufacturing other than H.I.	1.06	12.89	1.58
6.	Construction	0.14	14.09	0.75
7.	Trade and Commerce	0.15	1.68	9.21
8.	Transport, storage, communication	0.39	6.31	0.65
9.	Other services	1.40	26.57	2.52
	Total :	100.00	100.00	100.00

Population and Distribution of Tribal Rejas

In case of tribal *rejas* as many as 300 *rejas* engaged in different occupational categories were surveyed in course of field study undertaken at different labour centres. According to the survey it was assessed that out of 300 working *rejas* a sizeable number say, 100 (33.3%) *rejas*, were deployed in construction works which clearly indicates that most of the *rejas* prefer to work in construction operations to other categories; whereas next to that the *rejas* at brick-kilns comprise 26.7 percent of the total strength surveyed, meaning thereby 80 out of the total number surveyed, were active at different brick-kilns.

Table–4

Statement showing number of Tribal Rejas engaged in different occupational categories

Sl. No.	Occupational categories	Number of *Rejas* surveyed	Percentage
I	2	3	4
1.	Construction	100	33.3%
2.	Brick-kilns	80	26.7%
3.	Transportation	60	20%
4.	Industrial complex	40	13.3%
5.	Miscellaneous	20	6.7%
	Total :	300	100%

Similarly the working of transportation could attract only 60 *rejas* constituting merely 20 percent of the strength whereas industrial complex and miscellaneous activities as shown in Table-4, could engage only 40 (13.3%) and 20 (6.7%) rejas respectively.

Tribewise Population of Rejas : We have already seen earlier that the *rejas* belonging to different sects or communities of the tribal population have taken to the work of *reja* at different labour centres. The Table-5 indicates that out of 300 *rejas* surveyed, 156 belonged to Oraon community which is said to be the largest contributing community whereas the

Table–5

Tribewise Population of Rejas

Sl. No.	Community	No. of *Rejas* surveyed	Percentage
1	2	3	4
1.	Oraon	156	52%
2.	Munda	97	32.3%
3.	Lohra	20	6.7%
4.	Others	27	9%
	Total :	300	100%

Number of Tribal *Rejas* Engaged in Different Occupation Categories

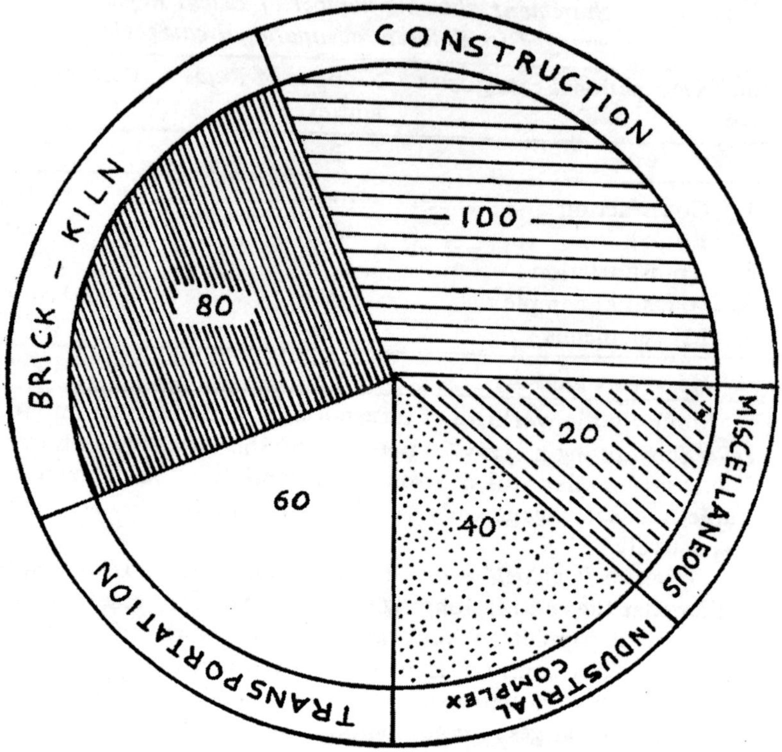

Munda community stands for the second largest having contributed 97 i.e. 32.3 percent. Similarly Lohra and other communities have the credit of contributing 20 (6.7%) and 27 (9%) *rejas* respectively.

Religionwise Classification of Rejas :—Among the tribal *rejas*, while making survey, we could be able to find that most of the tribal *rejas* are Hindu as it is evident from the table-6 that Christian comprises only 4 percent whereas the rest i.e. 96 percent belong to non-christian community as per their numbers being 12 and 288 respectively.

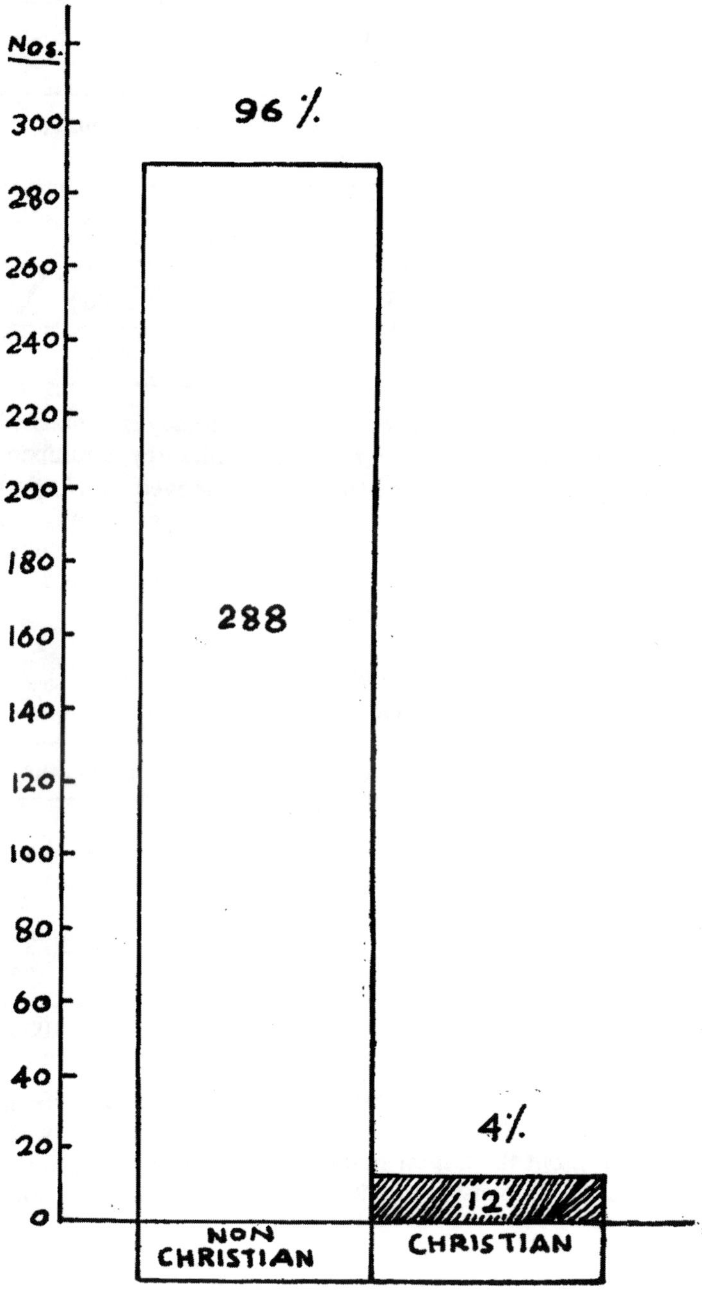

Religion-wise Classification of *Rejas*

Table—6

Religionwise Classification of Rejas

Sl. No.	Religion	No. of *Rejas* surveyed	Percentage
1	2	3	4
1.	Christian	12	4%
2.	Non-christian	288	96%
	Total :	300	100%

Educational Status of Rejas : So far as literacy is concerned it is apparent from the *rejas* surveyed that illiteracy is rampant among them because out of the total rejas surveyed 80.7 percent of them were found to be illiterate and 16.3 percent were so to say literate but not educated upto any standard at all whereas only 3 percent of them can, however, be called educated to some extent. The details have been shown in Table-7.

Table—7

Educational Status of Rejas

Sl. No.	Educational status	No. of *Rejas*	Percentage
1	2	3	4
1.	Illiterate	242	80.7%
2.	Literate without any educational standard	49	16.3%
3.	Educated	9	3%
	Total :	300	100%

Age-group Distribution Among Rejas : At different labour centres tribal *rejas* belonging to different age-groups were found working but the largest number of them was between the age group of 21-25 constituting 24.3 percent and in age-group

Educational Status of Tribal *Rejas*

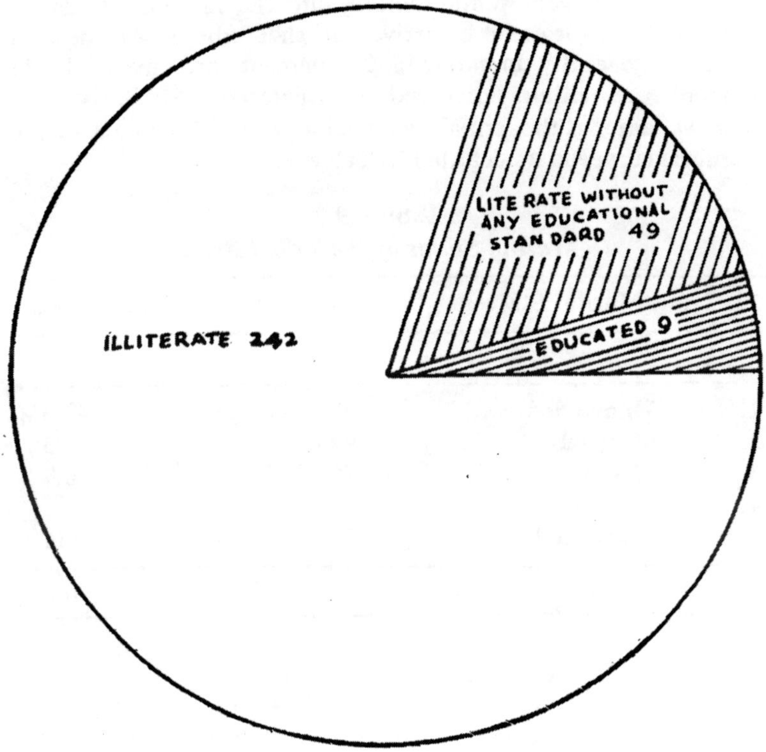

of 16-20, 23.7 percent were found being the second largest number. Likewise from the table-8 it appears that the most scanty number of *rejas* come from the age group of 56-60 which is only 0.7 percent followed by the age group of 5-10 being 1.3 percent whereas only 2 percent belong to the (see Table 8 next page) age group of 51-55. However, different age-groups have been mentioned in the table-8.

Marital Status: While looking into the marital status of the tribal *rejas* it could be arrived at that above 47 percent *rejas* are generally unmarried, 33 percent are married, 11 percent are either divorced or separated. Similarly, the widows among the tribal *rejas* comprise 8.7 percent of the numbers surveyed as detailed in Table-9.

Table—9

Marital Status of the Tribal Rejas

Sl. No.	Marital Status	No. of *Rejas*	Percentage
1	2	3	4
1.	Unmarried	142	47.3%
2.	Married	99	33%
3.	Widow	26	8.7%
4.	Divorced/ Separated	33	11%
	Total	300	100%

Marital Status of Tribal *Rejas*

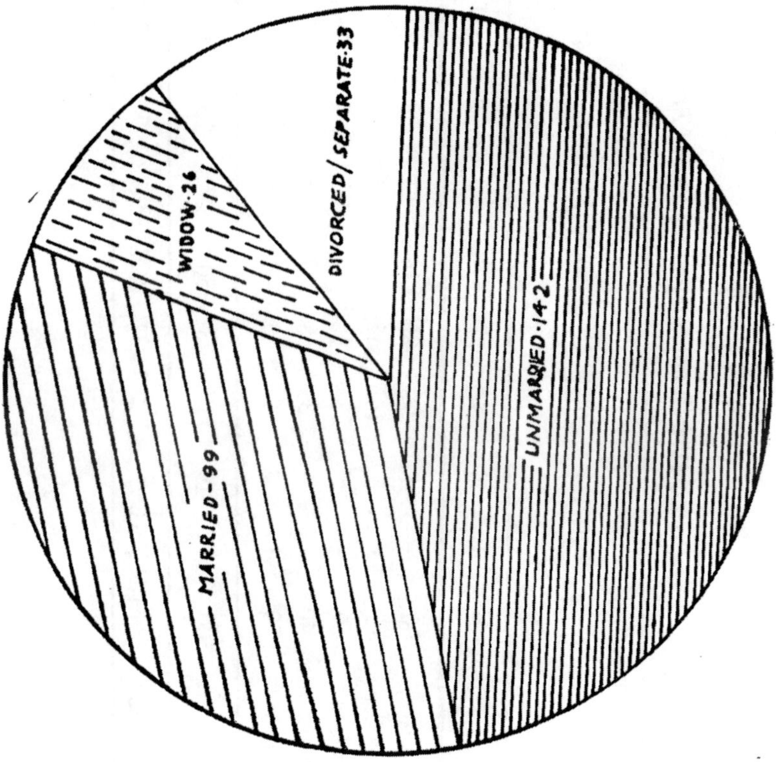

Table—8

Age-Groups Distribution Among the Tribal Rejas

Sl. No.	Occupational categories	Total no. of Rejas	Age-Groups 5-10	11-15	16-20	21-25	26-30	31-35	36-40	41-45	46-50	51-55	56-60
1	2	3	4	5	6	7	8	9	10	11	12	13	14
1.	Construction	100	—	4	22	26	18	12	8	4	3	2	1
2.	Brick-kiln	80	3	8	14	18	20	8	4	2	2	1	—
3.	Transportation	60	—	5	28	18	4	3	2	—	—	—	—
4.	Industrial complex	40	—	—	3	8	7	5	6	4	4	2	1
5.	Miscellaneous	20	1	2	4	3	1	1	2	4	1	1	—
	Total :	300	4	19	71	73	50	29	22	14	10	6	2
	Percentage :		1.3%	6.3%	23.7%	24.3%	16.7%	9.7%	7.3%	4.7%	3.3%	2%	.7%

Table—10

Age-gorup of the Unmarried Rejas

Sl. No.	Occupational category	Total no. of rejas surveyed	No. of unmarried rejas	Age-Groups				
				5-10	11-15	16-20	21-25	26-30
1	2	3	4	5	6	7	8	9
1.	Construction	100	49	–	4	18	19	8
2.	Brick-kiln	80	39	3	7	12	9	8
3.	Transportation	60	40	–	5	20	12	3
4.	Industrial complex	40	9	–	–	2	4	3
5.	Miscellaneous	20	5	1	1	2	1	–
	Total :	300	142	4	17	54	45	22
	Percentage (out of 300)	–	47.3%	1.3%	5.7%	18%	15%	7.3%

Table—11

Percentage of Unmarried Rejas Engaged in Different Occupations

Sl. No.	Occupational categories	Total no. of rejas	No. of unmarried rejas	Percentage
1	2	3	4	5
1.	Construction	100	49	49%
2.	Brick-kiln	80	39	48.75%
3.	Transportation	60	40	66.7%
4.	Industrial complex	40	9	22.5%
5.	Miscellaneous	20	5	25%

It is evident from the table-10 that among unmarried rejas which constitutes 47.3 percent of the tribal rejas surveyed, 18 percent rejas are in the age-group of 16-20 followed by 15 percent which come in the age-group of 21-25. Table-11 shows the percentage of unmarried *rejas* engaged in different occupational categories. It has been found that highest percentage of unmarried *rejas* are engaged in transportation work which is 66.7 percent, followed by 49 percent of *rejas* engaged in construction works, whereas 48.75 percent are engaged in brick-kilns, 22.5 percent in industrial complex and 25 percent in miscellaneous works.

Types & Sizes of Family among Rejas : When we look at the size of family among the tribal *rejas* it has been found that 36.7 percent families consist of 5-6 members which is the highest

Table—12

Family Size Among the Tribal Rejas

Sl. No.	Total no. of families	Family Size/No. of members in the family				
		1-2	3-4	5-6	7-8	9 & above
1	2	3	4	5	6	7
1	300	12	76	110	79	23
	Percentage	4%	25.3%	36.7%	26.3%	7.7%

percentage followed by 26.3 percent of families consisting of 7-8 members as shown in the table-12. Similarly 25.3 percent come in the family of 3-4 members.

Three types of family have been found among the tribal *rejas*—namely, joint family, nuclear family and extended family. More than half of the *rejas* population believe in joint family followed by 29.3 percent of them belong to nuclear family and the rest come from extended families the lowest among the above three types of families as appears from Table—13.

Table—13

Family Types Among the Tribal Rejas

Sl. No.	Types of family	No. of Rejas	Percentage
1	2	3	4
1.	Joint Family	185	61.7%
2.	Nuclear Family	88	29.3%
3.	Extended Family	27	9%
	Total ;	300	100%

Residential Pattern Among Rejas : According to Table-14, it appears that the largest percentage of the tribal *rejas*, that is 51 percent do believe in residing with their parents whereas 23 percent are living with their in-laws, 20.3 percent are living with their husbands and 5.7 percent are living with their relatives.

Table—14

Residential Pattern Among Tribal Rejas

Sl. No.	Occupational categories	Total no. of *Rejas*	*Rejas* living with Parents	Husbands	In-laws	Relatives
1	2	3	4	5	6	7
1.	Construction	100	54	20	20	6
2.	Brick-kiln	80	40	14	22	4
3.	Transportation	60	36	10	12	2
4.	Industrial complex	40	15	11	10	4
5.	Miscellaneous	20	8	6	5	1
	Total :	300	153	61	69	17
	Percentage		51%	20.3%	23%	5.7%

Family Types Among Tribal *Rejas*

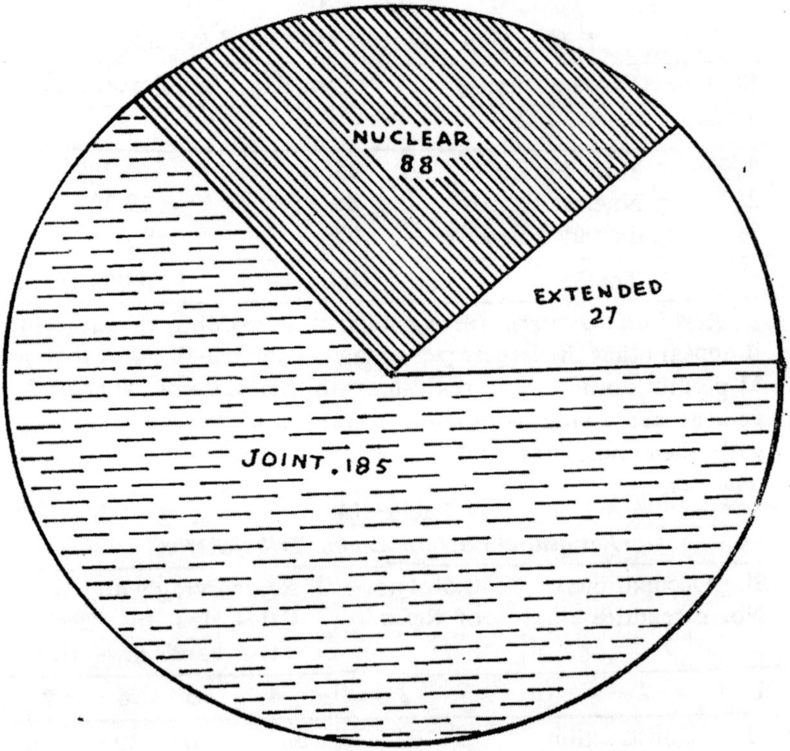

Migrant labourers

This may not be ruled out that the tribal rejas are engaged at different work-sites in the vicinity of their villages, but in order to earn their livelihood they, having been attracted by the prospects at distant places, like Siliguri, Burdwan etc. go there also. Such *rejas* who are not provided with jobs at their own places start finding out some other avenues for the source of their income. In the meantime they are allured by some agents called *sardar* or *sardarni* to go in for earning jobs at distant places, hence the migration. In course of the field study a number of instances of such migrant labourers came to light. Out of the total number of *rejas* surveyed as many as over 33 percent of them were noticed as migrant labourers as they had been to some distant places to work as *rejas* at different labour centres including brick-kilns, tea garden, road construction etc.

The tribals living in Ranchi district are either landless or marginal cultivators. Even the lands possessed by the tribals are mostly infertile and they lack irrigational facilities. Whatever good pieces of agricultural land that exist in the tribal belt of Ranchi distirct, somehow or the other, have been grabbed by the non-tribals. As a result of these constraints not only the marginal cultivators but also the smaller ones can hardly manage foods from agriculture for more than 4 to5 months. Thus in the lean period the tribals mostly eke out their living by working as labourers. Particularly the month of October-November is, out and out, a difficult period for the tribal because they are not only left without any work in agricultural fields but also get their food-stock exhausted. In the tribal societies males and females are equally responsible for earning towards the maintenance of family. But when they find that they are facing difficulties in respect of procuring food to eat at village level, they set out in search of work to places other than their villages. Some tribal males and females not only go beyond the boundary of their village, block, subdivision and district levels but also beyond the State boundaries in order to ward off starvation.

For the tribals of Ranchi winter is a time when they face their annually recurring choice between starvation and brutal exploitation. Man and nature together mock at them during this season, natural calamities drive them out of their villages in the look out for cheap labour. In the tribal belt of Ranchi the land is undulating and acidic and hence the productivity is at the lowest ebb. The agricultural season is short (between June and October) and runs out soon after the monsoon ends. The little usufructs which they have are hypothicated to the *sahus* (mony lenders) against earlier incurred loans. There are no irrigation facilities, electricity or proper roads and thus the tribals can produce only one crop annually at the utmost. And the forest land, which belongs to the government, is also out of bounds for the poor tribals, the government contracts out the forest land to the highest bidder.

Besides this, parts of the tribal belts of Ranchi have been occupied by industrialists and trading communities for commercial interests because the areas are full of minerals and raw-materials. Moreover, entrepreneurs get tax and other reliefs for "developing" these forlorn areas. But for the tribals this has simply meant loss of land and the compensation that has been paid to them amounted to paltry sums. They have also not been favoured with jobs created under the new projects. The tribals can only provide unskilled labour which is supplied by contractors who prefer to bring in labourers from outside because they can be easily manipulated in areas remote and unfamiliar. Besides, the closer of certain mines and factories in Ranchi district drove many tribal-families to face starvation. This scenario, which made the entire area a depot of cheap labour, is ideal for agents, brick-kiln owner etc. who wait to engage such helpless labourers.

Every year around September agents of brick-kiln owners come to the tribal belt of Ranchi in search of cheap labour. As soon as they arrive they establish contacts with *sardars* and *sardarnis*, local sub agents also known as *Arkatia* in the linguafranka of local tribals, who are, sometimes, themselves tribals and have worked for several years in many brick-kilns (there are more *sardarnis* than *sardars* and most of the people recruited from these regions are woman labourers, the *rejas*). These sub-agents, who are paid at the rate of Rs.30 to Rs.40 for each labour, set about contacting the local tribal people. Incidentally, the Munda, one of the largest tribes, call sub-agents *arkatia* which means seller of human beings. Once recruited, the tribals are paid *dadoon* or advance, usually between Rs. 100/- to Rs. 150/-. The *sardarni* accompanies them to the brick-kiln. Once the tribals reach the brick-kiln they are categorised and work begins. The work of carrying bricks from where they are moulded to the furnaces, where they are baked, is usually done by women and children known as *rejas*. Each *reja* receives just enough money to buy about 4 kg. of rice every week. This is normally taken with salt and this is all they have to sustain them through the long period of their hard work. Children (between 8 to 13 years of age) face no better fate. In fact, they are paid less, largely because their output is not as much as that of adults and have to make do with rice and salt as their daily diet.

The trade of *adivasi* labourers through contractors or agents generally pass through three to four tiers. Mostly the contractors trap the tribal leaders for the job who are given some commission. These tribal leaders, generally of the status of Munda Chiefs, known as *Maniks*, command good respect among the tribals. In view of economic stringencies and confidence of their tribal chief (Manik) they agree to go with the contractors for work. These contractors after escorting the tribal labourers upto railway station handover them to some other contractors who take them to the work sites at distant places by train. During journey a strict vigilence is kept on the tribal labourers by the contractors. Generally during the journey the tribal labourers are not supplied with food. On reaching the distant places the labourers are kept confined to a room from where they are taken to the places of work. The condition when these tribal labourers are boarded in the train or bus is no better than the animals which are loaded in either trains or trucks. Sometimes in one bus or on truck about 250 to 300 tribal labourers are loaded for carrying them to work-site. Since the transportation of labourers on the truck is illegal, they are, at times, covered with *tripal* (tarpauline) to avoid checking at the checkposts. At some places the powerful contractors even manage to obtain permit for carrying labourers on buses. Outside the State there are certain strategic places from where the labourers are sent to diffe-

Inter-State Migration of Tribal Woman Labourers

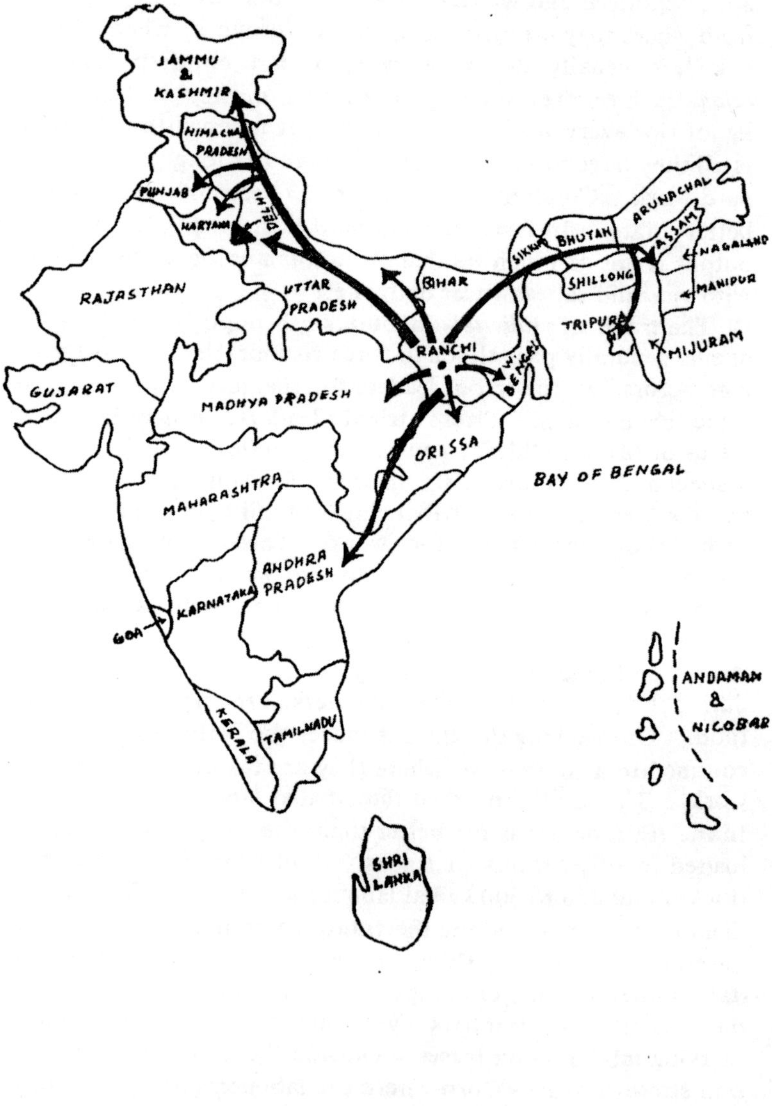

rent places like Siliguri, Hashmira etc. After reaching these places the third contractor or middle man receives them and then take them to different work-sites. On reaching the places of work-sites, these labourers are finally handed over to the real master which is the fourth tier of this labour-trade.

When the labourers have actually reached the working sites they are asked by the employers to construct temporary huts. These labourers generally work for 12 to 16 hours a day. The author has learnt that at some work sites in Punjab and Haryana, the labourers have been given the dosage of *Bhang* (hamp) and *Afim* (opium) with a view to extracting more labour from them. At work sites the labourers are not even paid the minimum wages, not to talk of the remunerative wages. Generally the labourers are employed for Rs. 15/- to Rs. 20/- as *khoraki* for a week. At some places own men of the employers open shops of grocery and labourers are compelled to buy their ration from these very shops. Besides, these tribal labourers, specially the woman labourers—*rejas* are subjected to various kinds of physical, social and sexual-exploitations.

The migrant labourers have to face such traumatic and excruciating experiences during their work at distant places because they fear very much from the powerful contractors or middlemen as they feel that if they report about their woeful working conditions to the Government officials, they would be either oppressed or even killed by the contractors. Most of the migrant labourers are illiterate and ignorant of the places/ Government offices where they have to lodge their complaints. Even the government officials are not being able to fully protect the migrant labourers' sufferings because they are fully tutored by the contractors to tell the inspecting officials that they are happy with the working conditions. And the tribals actually do so because in the event of disobedience of the contractor's directives they may lose the job.

It is evident from the aforesaid facts about migrant labourers that this phenomenon has assumed a significant dimension in the socio-cultural fabric of tribal labourers. Unless some urgent and pragmatic steps are taken by the Government, the plight of migrant labourers will not be redressed properly.

Inter-District Migration of Tribal Women Labourers of Bihar

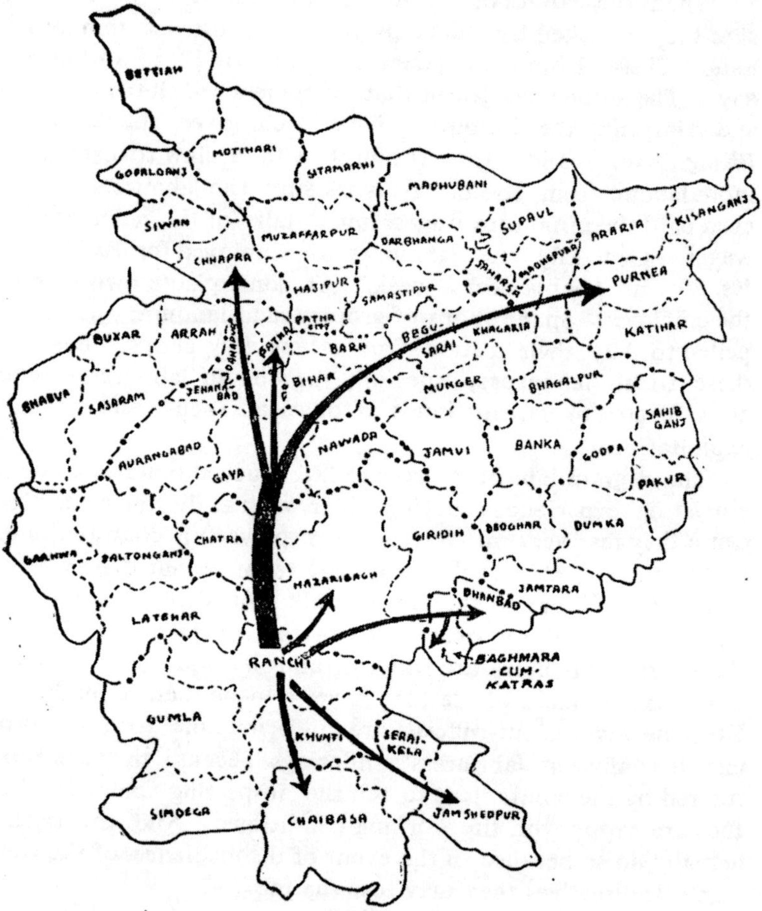

Uptill now we have been discussing about the historical and demographic background of the tribal *rejas* of Ranchi including those of the migrant labourers hailing from this district. In the next chapter we shall switch over to nature of work as well as their working patterns so as to have a complete idea about them in the larger perspective.

2

Typology, Mode of Employment and Nature of work of Tribal Rejas

In the previous chapter we have already made a survey on the tribal *rejas* as to how they have formed a different type of occupational class and how they are involved in the development of Ranchi town in particular and other cities in India in general. They are seen quite frequently at such places where any type of developmental or construction works are going on. It is a common sight to see *rejas* trudging along the country roads of Ranchi in group chating, gossiping towards their destination or the sites of work. Their works may be of different nature. In the present chapter, an attempt has been made to classify the tribal *rejas* on the basis of the different types of work they do, describe how do they get employment, analyse the causes for the acceptance of the work, and how much wages they earn and what is the pattern of their work.

Typology of the Reja

While analysing the types of the work done by the *rejas*, it has been observed that there are different types of job for which the deployment of tribal woman labourers is necessitated. On the basis of the different types of work which the tribal *rejas* select, the following five broad occupational categories can be discerned :—

(i) *Reja* engaged in brick-kilns.
(ii) *Reja* engaged in construction work.
(iii) *Reja* engaged in transportation of raw/building materials on trucks.
(iv) *Reja* engaged in industrial complex.
(v) *Reja* engaged in miscellaneous types of work.

Reja Engaged in Brick-kiln

The *rejas* who are engaged is brick-kilns mostly do the work of loading and unloading the bricks. They have to carry unbaked (*Kuchha*) bricks to the kiln and when these bricks are baked, they have to carry these baked bricks outside the kiln and to arrange them for selling purposes.

Reja Engaged in Construction Work

The *rejas* who are engaged in construction works form second category. Their works are different from those who are engaged in brick-kilns. Construction works may pertain to building construction, road making or repairing, stone quarries, river projects. etc. Whereever such type of work is going on one can see a number of *rejas* standing in a line with their heads wrapped in a dirty piece of cloth against dust, passing bricks upto masons who are building a house. Although neatly clad with a piece of *chadar* tied around their waist these *rejas* are seen carrying cement, lime and mortar in large bowl shaped receptacles (*Karahi*) on their heads.

Reja Engaged in Transportation of Raw/Building Materials on Trucks

The third category constitutes of those *rejas* who are seen moving and chirping on trucks with scarfs on their heads and wrapped in wrappers or bed-sheets which are used by them as protection to their cloths because they have to do the loading and unloading works of bricks, sand, soil, boulders, etc. These trucks are hired by the dealers in bricks, sand, boulders. etc.

and whenever any order is supplied by a company or a dealer, the trucks are pressed into service for delivering the building/raw materials to the concerned parties. The loading and unloading works are done by those *rejas* who are kept reserved exclusively for this purpose in each truck engaged in transportation business.

Reja Engaged in Industrial Complex

The fourth type of *rejas* comprises of those tribal women who are engaged in industrial complexes in the urban or semi-urban areas. In such complexes the construction work of various designs and requirements are carried out quite frequently and the *rejas* are increasingly absorbed in different works such as unskilled labour e.g. in BISCOLAMF, Namkom (Ranchi) the author came across a number of *rejas* who were seen separating sands from lac deposits by dint of certain tools, some of them were also found busy carrying boulders, cement and other materials for some construction works going in its precinct.

Reja Engaged in Miscellaneous types of work

There is a category of such *rejas* who are engaged in miscellaneous types of work. Because of the very temporary nature of their job, the *rejas* have to do other types of work also which serve as a casual occupation for them. The work of brick-kilns generally starts from late October and goes upto May because this period is generally free from rains and, hence, there is no obstacles in brickmaking business. But what happens when the brick-kilns remain closed in rainy season ? It is noticed that in such a lean period most of the *rejas* get engaged in some other casual works. They work as agricultural labourers, maid-servants, etc. They also get employed on occasions such as marriages, birth ceremony, etc. Some of them also start selling vegetables. This is also applicable in the case of those *rejas* who are engaged in construction works, transportation and so on. Table-1 depicts the miscellaneous types of work done by the 20 tribal *rejas* surveyed.

Table—1
Miscellaneous types of Work done by the Tribal Rejas

Sl. No.	Miscellaneous types of work	Number of *Rejas*	Percentage
1	2	3	4
1.	Maid-Servants	7	35%
2.	Vegetable/fish sellers	4	20%
3.	Loading & unloading works in daily market	3	15%
4.	Agriculture labour	4	20%
5.	Ayah	2	10%
	Total :	20	100%

Motivations Towards the Acceptance of Works as Rejas

In the beginning this part of the Chotanagpur Plateau was just a cluster of villages and the peoples' economy was based on agriculture. The staple crop was rice but they also grew a few variety of pulses, maize etc. The tribal people also supplemented their food/requirements by occasional hunting and fishing. Since Ranchi started its journey as a town, by and by, it became a city of migrants. The rate of the migration has been steady because most of the migrants came from the rural areas after having got attracted by the opening of the new offices, industries, business establishments and the like places of employment opportunities. Among the tribal migrants most of them belong to or come from the peasants' or landless labourers' class. Those educated got absorbed in white collar jobs whereas the uneducated and landless lot opted to work in the labour force for eking out their subsistence. In the wake of industrialisation the rural folk also tended towards modernization for which a regular inflow of income was a must which they, however, supplemented by working as *rejas* at different projects. It can be said that the allurement of modern amenities actually worked, more or less, as incentives to extra labours. Tribal women became attracted towards the attraction given by the agents or mediator of the employers either in form of cash or kind. Generally the persons who are in need of labour, give some cash money in advance to them, which serves as an incentive for them. For adjusting themselves in the prevailing condition of society, the tribal *rejas* also want to live a better life, for which they are in need of cash money. When they found that they are able to earn some cash money in this profession, they started getting absorbed in this profession. It is evident from the Table-2 that 74.7 percent tribal women accepted the profession of *rejas* due to family oriented economic reasons. The economic condition of their family forced them to join this profession to support their family, 13 percent came in this profession for the fulfilment of their ambitions, the desire for economic independence, whereas, 4 percent came to use their leisure time. The *rejas* who have joined this profession are of older age-group. They get leisure time because they have other persons in their family to do the domestic works. 8.3 percent *rejas* could not specify their reasons clearly. They accepted the profession of *rejas* either due to economic reasons or due to their desire to earn some money for the fulfilment of their ambitions. Some of them also joined this work by imitating their friends, who were working as *rejas*.

Table—2

Reasons for the Acceptance of Work as Rejas

Sl. No.	Reasons	No. of *Rejas*	Percentage
1	2	3	4
1.	Family oriented economic reasons	224	74.7%
2.	To become economically independent for the fulfilment of their desires or ambitions	39	13%
3.	Desire to use one's leisure time for economic gains	12	4%
4.	Others	25	8.3%
	Total ;	300	100%

Mode of Employment

The rejas who do different types of job at different labour centres can be kept in following categories according to their mode of employment :—

(A) REJAS ENGAGED THROUGH CONTRACTORS
(B) REJAS WHO WORK INDEPENDENTLY

(A) REJAS ENGAGED THROUGH CONTRACTORS :—

The *rejas* engaged through contractors generally prefer to be in the company of their contractors who are ultimately held responsible for finding out new avenues of works for earning their livelihood. The *rejas* engaged through the contractors are either from neighbouring villages of Ranchi or brought from farflung areas of Chotanagpur. At first the contractors seek jobs and then they take up the works with the help of labourers comprising of the *rejas*. In such cases the *rejas* keep on moving from one site of work to another mostly with the same contractors. These contract labourers/*rejas* generally prefer to work with their own contractors rather than running helter-skelter in quest of temporary jobs. If the contractors are offered jobs in places other than Ranchi, either in its vicinity or even at far places, these *rejas* have got to accompany the contractors and on completion of work they again return to their respective villages. In regard to the wage-payments to these rejas the contractors have to pay for their jobs out of what the contractors actually get from the management or the owner of a construction project. In other words it is generally the contractor's wish which ultimately prevails upon the *rejas*.

Here it would be important to mention the mode of employment of *rejas* through contractors at different labour centres.

(i) *Employment in Brick-Kilns* :—The rejas who are seen working in brick-kilns are mostly from the nearby villages. Apart from these, some woman labourers are fetched even from remote villages, who at the end of the day's work are provided with dingy shades as their abodes. Not to talk of Ranchi district only the *rejas* are sent to some distant corners of the State such as Chapra, Purnea, Patna, Hazaribagh, Jamshedpur etc. and out of the State also. It has been observed that deployment of *rejas* from one State to another is on the one hand helpful in establishing the labour force which leads to steady completion of any work. They prefer to employ outstationed labourers than the local one. In case of local labourers they flee away leaving aside their jobs to some other places for even minor gains. Apart from it they may be absent on even small occasion like festival, religious worships, on arrival of some guests etc. which hamper their works. They may not come in time and may go earlier. Whereas the labourers brought from outside the district or State are not in a position to bring about any such hindrance in their jobs. They have to start and close their works on the sweet will of the agents of employers. In recent years very organised type of network of employment systems have been adopted by the labour seekers. It has been observed that there are some persons among these labourers, who have got certain leadership qualities and are able to assemble the tribal labourers. They may be tribal or non-tribal males or females, the males are locally called as "*Sardar*" while female is called as "*Sardarni*". These *Sardars* or *Sardarnis* always remain in contact with contractors. The tribal women who want to work as *rejas* in brick-kilns come in contact with these *Sardars* or *Sardarnis*. On the other hand contractors also remain in constant touch with the *Sardars* or *Sardarnis*. Thus, with the help of the *Sardars* or *Sardarnis* tribal women manage easy employment.

But it has also been found that the tribal *rejas* who are engaged through contractors in brick-kilns are generally sent to the remote places, or those who are working in the brick-kilns of Ranchi and its vicinity are brought from the distant villages of Ranchi district. The rejas from Ranchi villages have even been sent in other States such as Uttar Pradesh, Assam, Tripura, Nagaland, Punjab, Haryana, Andaman & Nicobar, Delhi, Andhra Pradesh, Madhya Pradesh, West Bengal, etc. and a good many dealers in brick-business to their native places in north Bihar to feed various projects undertaken by their relatives. Thus they have got to stay away from their native villages for years together.

While going to Patna by road author had an occasion to see the tribal *rejas* working in some brick-kilns near Fatuha, the outskirts of Patna. Every year a good number of *rejas* of Ranchi go outside the State for working in brick-kilns. In the course of field work the author met with a lady *Sardarni* of Madhya Pradesh, who had brought a number of tribal labourers from there to work in the brick-kilns of Ranchi. According to her, in rainy season when the brick-kilns of these areas remain closed, she gons to Jammu and Kashmir with the labourers because brick-kilns are open there even during rainy season. In Jammu and Kashmir she found the tribal *rejas* of Ranchi doing the job of loading and unloading the bricks.

(*ii*) *Employment in Construction Works*: Mostly those *rejas* who are engaged in construction works prefer to work with contractor and the author has found that same set of *rejas* are engaged with one contractor for a long period. Generally contractors prefer employing the *rejas* of those areas in which the construction works are in progress or being undertaken. To meet the labour requirement, the contractors' assistant, known as *Munshi*, visits the nearby tribal villages and establishes contact with the tribal *rejas* of the village. After having come in contact with the contractor through the *Munshi*, there remains no dearth of work for the tribal *rejas*. At a construction site in the Bihar Tribal Welfare Research Institute situated in Morhabadi (Ranchi) it was found that almost all the *rejas* working over there hailed from the nearby villages of Morhabadi like Sindwartoli, Morhabadi, etc. and the contractor was also a resident of that area. These *rejas* had been working there since last six months continuously. Before starting this work, they all had been working in the construction work of a hostel near this institute under the same contractor.

In the construction work of road making near Ratu Road (Ranchi), *rejas* of nearby village of that area Saparong were working there. But there is no hard and fast rule about this because the *rejas* of one area of Ranchi have been found working in other area also.

(*iii*) *Employment in Transportation of Materials on Trucks*:— The *rejas* are also employed for the transportation of materials on trucks, for loading and unloading purposes of sand, bricks, boulders, etc. through the contractors. There are contractors who are aengaged in the business of these materials and they have their own trucks. When they get order from any company or from those persons who are in need of these items, then the suppliers first arrange to muster tribal *rejas* to supply the materials. For this trucks are pressed into service. The *rejas* are employed for loading and unloading purposes. First of all the driver of a truck tries to collect the *rejas* from their respective villages and bring them to the site. After the work is over these *rejas* are again left by truck to their villages. A set of seven-eight *rejas* are attached with a truck. Generally the same set of the *rejas* are called every time by a owner of a truck. It is observed that they do not work for the another truck of the same company or contractor.. Abdul Raoof, who is a driver in Saluja company at Ranchi since 1962, told the author that he had same set of *rejas* who had been working on his truck for the last 4-5 years. The *rejas* employed in transportation work do not have to wonder in search of jobs because of their equation and faith in the employability and potentiality of their employers.

(iv) *Employment in Industrial Complex* :—Rejas are also employed in the industrial complexes with the help of contractors. These *rejas* are generally engaged by some contractors or contractual companies which assign certain jobs to petty contractors in a bid to hasten the completion of work. These petty contractors maintain a good labour force which comprises largely of tribal *rejas*. The *rejas* are absorbed temporarily in industrial complexes through the contractual companies for doing casual works like head-load-carrying, morter making, water fetching, etc. In sector III of Heavy Engineering Corporation, Dhurwa, Ranchi, there exists a separate maintenance office to manage the occasional requirements of labourers. The maintenance office remains in constant touch with the labour contractors for deployment of labour in the ongoing construction works. etc. within the factory's permises. The *rejas* working in industrial complexes through the contractors have the privilege of rendering duty as per the normal working hours which, unfortunately, is not the case with the *rejas* engaged in other trades.

(B) Rejas Who Work Independently

The *rejas* working independently may also be termed as free-lancers. This type of *rejas* set out early in the morning from their villages in quest of any type of job in the township so as to meet their both ends need. These *rejas* are seen sitting in groups at some strategic points e. g. Lalpur Chowk, Church Road etc. in the township which are frequented with persons in need of *rejas* for the purpose of some works to be completed either in town itself or somewhere in its vicinity. These *rejas* can be used for any type of jobs in view of their capabilities. One can even hire rejas by visiting any tribal village. In villages the tribal women who remain idle, readily agree to work on daily payment in the nearby areas. But only condition with such *rejas* is this that they must return their home in the evening. Besides, the rejas who operate through the contractors also, when out of work, join the company of independent *rejas* at the strategic points where casual labourers assemble in search of work. Such woman labourers who are not employed in a specific centre, work independently wherever they get job, constitute our fifth category of *rejas* who are engaged in miscellaneous types of work as casual labourers. The *rejas* who work independently mostly prefer to work near their respective villages. For example, there are three brick-kilns in Bariatu area of Ranchi—one in the Booty village, one near the junction of Booty Road and Hazaribagh road and one behind the Bariatu Housing Coloney. There are small tribal hamlets near Bariatu such as Baragain, Kishunpur, Booty village etc. A number of tribal women of these villages are engaged in these three brick-kilns and they are not engaged through contractors. When they found that they could easily get job they directly approached the owner of these brick-kilns and started working of loading and unloading the bricks on temporary basis because when they are not satisfied with their works they are free to leave the job and go in search of other job. It has also been observed that school-going tribal girls also work as casual labourers in these kilns.

On casual basis tribal *rejas* also work as agricultural labourers, maid-servants etc. For example, a tribal *reja* called after her daughter's name Sita as Sitiya *Ki maa* (mother of

Sita), works as a maid servant in two or three houses of Bariatu Housing Colony but whenever she gets other job, she starts working there. If there is any construction work in and around this colony she will be seen there loading the *Karahi* with lime, cement etc., or loading the bricks to the mason and so on. If there is an occasion of marriage ceremony, she will be seen there engaged in doing different types of odd jobs.

In BISCOLAMF (Namkom, Ranchi) *rejas* are found not employed through contractor but by the direct approach with the manager. It is evident from the table-3 that 64.7 percent of the tribal *rejas* studied are engaged through contractors in different types of work whereas 35.3 percent are engaged independently.

Table—3

Mode of Employment of Tribal Rejas in Different Types of Work

Sl. No.	Types of work	Total no. of *Rejas*	Mode of Employment: Through contractor	Mode of Employment: Independently
1	2	3	4	5
1.	Construction works	100	87	13
2.	Brick-kilns	80	36	44
3.	Transportation works	60	46	14
4.	Industrial complexes	40	25	15
5.	Miscellaneous	20	—	20
	Total :	300	194 (64.7%)	106 (35.3%)

As depicted in this table tribal *rejas*, who work independently, mostly comprise of those who are engaged in brick-kilns. Out of 80, 44 (55%) *rejas* working in brick-kilns get their job independently. Likewise, *rejas*, engaged through contractors are found mostly in construction works, i.e. 87 (87%) *rejas* out of 100, followed by the *rejas* engaged in transportation of materials, i.e. 46(76.7%) out of 60.

Wage Structure and Incentives

The tribal *rejas* get different wages according to their types of work respectively. As regards the wages of those *rejas* who are engaged in brick-kilns, their work is measured in terms of number of bricks they actually carry in a day, although there is no hard and fast rule in regard to the amount to be paid. In fact it is generally paid at the rate of Rs. 7/- for carrying one thousand bricks. It has been noticed that each *reja* carries either seven or eight bricks in one trip and they hardly earn Rs. 3/- to Rs. 4/- a day which too is not paid daily. Their entire earnings for a week are calculated and payments are made on the day fixed for the purpose. They are even less paid in loading and unloading the baked bricks because for this purpose they have to cover less distance. Hence the rate is also less. They are paid Rs. 4/- for carrying one thousand baked bricks.

Rejas engaged in construction works get Rs. 6/- to Rs. 7/- for a day which they get at the end of the day's work or it also depends upon the will of the contractors. He either makes payment daily or weekly but this is found in the case of those *rejas* who are engaged through contractors otherwise the *rejas* who work independently get the payment at the end of the work.

Those rejas who are engaged on trucks charge Rs. 7/- to Rs. 8/- for loading and unloading work which may continue for days together. But sometimes, there is no work at all for such *rejas*, hence, no income.

Rejas who are engaged in industrial complexes get wages either by contractors or by management. In Heavy Engineering Corporation *rejas* are being engaged through contractors and payments are made to the contractors at the rate of 8.50 per day and it all depends upon the contractors whether he gives such amount to the *rejas* or not. In BISCOLAMF at Namkom *rejas* were paid wages at the rate of Rs. 4/- for working-day and payments are made weekly. If their attendances are found satisfactory throughout a year they also get bonus nearly about Rs. 200/- to Rs. 300/-yearly on the basis of their attendances.

For the *rejas* who work as casual labourers in miscellaneous works, there is no fixed rate of wage-payment for them. The *rejas* who works in agricultural field gets wages at the rate of Re. 1/- for an hour. They work for four hours in a day and get Rs. 4/- for a day but if she gets work for two hours, that is, for half day only then she can earn Rs. 2/- only in a day.

As maid-servants she can earn Rs. 20/- to Rs. 30/- for a month. If she works on different occasions of marriages, etc. she charges Rs. 6/- or Rs. 7/- or Rs. 8/- according to the nature of the works. In fact there is no hard and fast rules about their wages. They are not found aware of the concept of minimum wages prescribed by Government for such labourers.

Incentives Given to *Rejas*

Such type of phenomenon is found among those tribal *rejas* who are taken away by the contractors. Contractors, through the medium of *Sardar* or *Sardarni* try to give incentive in form of *Saree* or some amount of Rs. 10/- to Rs. 20/- as advance (Dadoon) and they give them assurances like regular payment of wages, 8 hours of work in a day, residential facilities, return fare etc. When they get some money as advance, they become attracted towards the job and readily agree to go with them.

Specialisation of Works

As it has been mentioned above that the woman labourers are mostly needed for temporary jobs either through contractors or through the management of some structural companies, it has been noticed that by dint of regular working on such jobs these tribal women specialise themselves in a particular trade. For example, those engaged in brick-kilns for loading and unloading purposes are supposed to be well-skilled in their trade. Similarly, the *rejas* who are engaged in any construction work become specialised in their jobs and same is the case with those *rejas* who are engaged in other types of works.

They do not under go any special training for their respective works. Due to regular working and watching the works of the other *rejas* who are senior to them, they achieve expertise in their works. They do their works so smoothly because they have practice of doing them. Otherwise those who do not have practice, can not manage to arrange nine or ten bricks at a time on their heads. If somehow even she manages to arrange them on head, she cannot move even a step along with the head load. Due to practice, they can arrange these bricks on their heads without any help of others. At certain brick-kilns the old *rejas* of about 65 to 70 years old have been seen supervising the other *rejas* and distributing them *tikli* (token) to maintain the account of their works.

But, unfortunately, the *rejas* specialised in certain works are not paid any additional remuneration for the specialisation of their works. The only benefit which the specialised *rejas* enjoy pertain to convenience in getting jobs. But in terms of wage-payments they are paid according to the rate fixed for all such works.

Working Pattern : A Brief Account

It has been observed that the tribal *rejas* are deployed at different labour centres for conducting different types of work. Their methods of working have been enumerated here as follows :—

Method of Working at Brick-Kilns

The *rejas* who are engaged in brick-kilns, start their work from 8 A.M. in the morning and continue till the sun-set. They also manage some recess time in the noon during which the labour-force quench their hunger. They are observed taking cooked rice with a pinch of salt and some onion, rarely any vegetables. Thus with this meagre amount of food they have to put in untiring labours for the whole day during which they have to do different types of work.

The *rejas* have to generally carry *kuchha* (unbaked or sun-baked) bricks to the kilns. Bricks are laid down by skilled men who are meant for this purpose only and are known as "*pathera*" and their work of laying down the bricks is known as '*Inta Pathna*'. These skilled men are engaged for the entire season and everywhere they are seen engaged in laying the bricks, may be they are either themselves alone or with some other members of their families respectively but the payments are made to them jointly at the rate of Rs. 15/- for laying one thousand bricks. Nowhere the tribal *rejas* were seen engaged in laying the bricks. The *Pathera* finishes his work with the help of his family members like his wife, sister, daughter, daughter-in-law and others. Though they are also called *rejas* they only assist him in his work such as mixing the soil with water and giving that clay soil to him, arranging the laid down bricks in a row and so on. But they are not paid for their works because they are the family members of the *Pathera* and payment is made on joint basis to him. His responsibility lies up to this stage of arranging unbaked bricks in a row for baking them with the help of sun-heat. He is paid on the number of these bricks. If there is rain after this stage, he does not have to bother for it.

The place of laying the bricks or where the bricks are moulded is known as *thagar*. This place is at a distance of about 300 yards from the main furnace of the brick-kiln. At the *thagar* the *patheras* mould only the bricks with the help of wooden moulds meant for this purpose only. These wooden moulds are supplied to the *patheras* by the brick-owners. The owner's name is also carved in this mould so that his name could appear on the baked bricks. The *patheras* are supplied with the paste of wet soil (clay) by their assistants for filling up in the wooden mould. After being filled with clay, moulds are turned over on the ground and thus the *kuchcha* bricks are laid down.

Now the *kuchcha* bricks so prepared by the *patheras* are to be brought in the main kiln for baking. At least seven or eight *patheras* are engaged for laying the bricks in a brick-kiln. There are always heavy demand of *kuchcha* bricks in a brick-kiln because the fire keeps burning continuously inside the kiln, that means once the kiln has started functioning in the month of October, it will remain start until the rainy season and that fire which is burnt at the time of starting, has been burning till its end. Kiln is made in a big area and fire is rolling inside it from one side to another side. If in the half side of the kiln *kuchcha* bricks are being baked, then at the same time in the half side of the kiln the baked bricks are being taken out and *kuchcha* bricks have to be arranged. The area where the bricks are baked remains covered from above, and one can easily move over it. There remains some circular space in the ceiling, which are kept covered with iron lids. One can easily peep inside after removing the lids to see the fire within. The exits are also meant for filling fuel i.e. coal. Specialised persons are deputed to examine the final baking of *kuchcha* bricks. Thus, altogether three different kinds of work remain in progress at a time in a single brick-kiln, firstly, the kuchcha bricks are arranged in one side; secondly, the *kuchcha* bricks are baked in the other side; and thirdly, the baked bricks are cooled in still other side. Since the kiln remains underground, wooden staircases lead to it. To arrange the *kuchcha* bricks in a specific manner in a brick-kiln, specialised male workers are employed, who arrange the bricks in such a way as the fire below may come upto the top, to burn the coal kept above, so that fire may continue upto the whole season.

The tribal *rejas* are employed in the brick-kilns for loading and unloading the *kuchcha* as well as baked bricks. They carry the kuchcha bricks from the *thagar*, the place where bricks are moulded, to the place of baking, inside kiln and hand it over to the specialised male workers who bake the bricks up. The work of tribal *rejas* is measured in terms of the number of bricks they actually carry from one place to another. They get their payment on the basis of carrying one thousand bricks. It has been noticed that each *reja* carries either seven or eight bricks in one trip. Thus, it can be well-imagined as to how much they earn in a day. Even with a level best attempt, they cannot carry even a thousand of brick in a day in view of two main causes :

1. Firstly, they have to cover a considerable distance from the place of orientation of kuchcha bricks to the furnace and moreover, they have to go down through the wooden stair-case.
2. Secondly, they have to remain standing in the kiln upto so much time as is needed by the second person to take the bricks off their head, and simultaneously arrange them in order.

Be as it may, the *rejas* do not fritter away their time otherwise. They do not like talking unnecessarily to others because meanwhile, they could carry several bricks from one place to the other.

Just near the top of the stair-case leading to the kiln, there remains present a special person, deputed by the kiln-owner, to issue the iron-tokens. Sometimes, old *rejas* are also employed for the purpose. The tokens are of various size, and are called *Tikli.* The tokens denote the number of bricks carried, for example, if a *reja* carries eight bricks in a particular trip, she will be given a *tikli* denoting the number eight, and if she could carry only seven bricks in the next trip, she would be given a *tikli* denoting the number seven, and so on. Thus, with every trip, the number of *tiklis* received will go on increasing and the *rejas* keep them securely. At the time of payment at week end, the *rejas* produce the assembled *tiklis* and the total number of bricks carried in a week is calculated. Thereafter, the payment is made at the rate of Rs. 7/- per thousand bricks.

At some kilns apart from the labourers ranging from the age group of 14 to 40 which is a usual phenomenon, some small girls ranging from 8-12 years have also been seen taking to this tough job with one to three bricks on their heads and motives of their works can be attributed to their economic condition that they could earn some money to help their families. They also go to attend the classes of the local schools of their villages respectively but whenever they get leisure time or holiday, come to work in kilns to earn some money.

The *rejas* have to also carry baked bricks outside the kiln, in the same way, as do they carry *kuchha* bricks from outside to the kiln. Baked bricks are arranged according to their different categories. Generally, baked bricks of three categories can be identified in a kiln—categories A, B and C. Category A is awarded to the best baked bricks, category B includes slightly inferior types of bricks, while category C denotes the worst variety of bricks. The bricks are arranged out-side the kilns in accordance with their categories, and this enables a person to choose his desired kind, and to transport it easily. Each category costs differently. The *rejas* also get trained in the identification of categories and sometimes, they themselves arrange the bricks in different categories. However, generally, a person is deputed at the place to guide the *rejas* to keep the bricks as per categories.

During the work in full-swing, the tribal *rejas* out-number other workers in the kilns and they are seen everywhere in the kiln. About 100-200 *rejas* work in a moderate kiln. While carrying bricks, they move in two separate rows. In one row, the *rejas* carry unbaked bricks towards the furnace and in the other, they carry baked bricks outside the kiln.

It has been observed at almost all brick-kilns that they are so much involved in their works of loading and unloading the bricks that they become unaware of their surroundings, what are happening there, who are watching them, etc. Hence it is true in real sense that their full cooperation are responsible for the smooth running of several brick-kilns at Ranchi.

Method of Working in Construction Work

The *rejas* who are engaged in construction works have to do different types of work also. They have to reach at their working places early in the morning near about 8 A.m. They have been observed there carrying the concrete in the *karahi* to the mason, preparing the concrete etc. They can be seen filtering sand, carrying mud and soil, transporting bricks during the work of building constructions. They also do the work of mixing up sand and cement, etc. At that time, they put on long boots coming up to their knees, as are used by the people in rainy seasons, and mix-up concrete—sand and cement—with the help of their boots and axe. Sometimes, a *reja* is assisted in this work by some *coolie* (or male labourer) but normally, two *rejas* do this work together. When the mixture is prepared, two other *rejas*, standing there with axe in their hands, fill up the *karahis* of other *rejas* with this mixture, and also help them place the karahi on their heads. Other *rejas* carry the mixture to the mason. Similarly, some *rejas* carry sands, concrete etc. to the mason, and still others carry bricks to him. The *rejas* are quite well versed in their duty and they easily go to different heights or depths, with large filled up *karahis* kept on their heads.

The *rejas* can be seen cutting long slender iron rods also. One *reja* holds a rod under her feet, places a cutter on the rod and holds it as well while the other strikes over the cutter with a hammer to cut the rod.

The *rejas* also do the work of crushing bricks into smaller chips used for various purposes. During road constructions and repairs, they do the work of spreading stone chips, pouring melten coal-tar, etc. No such work without the *rejas* has been seen in progress at least in Ranchi. Even with their child tied up on their back the *rejas* are usually seen working in full zeal and with full devotion.

The *rejas* employed in construction work usually get their daily wages at the time of going home in the evening. If some *rejas* take money for her breakfast or meal, the same is deducted from her account. The *rejas* come at work in the morning and they work continuously up to noon. They get a break off about one hour in the afternoon during which they take their lunch. Generally the *rejas* carry an aluminium tiffin-carrier with them which contains rice and salt; and sometimes, some vegetables, pulse etc. Those who do not bring lunch in tiffin-carriers, have their lunch or breakfast in some nearby hotel. Sometimes, they take tea, ordinary biscuits etc., talk to one another for a while, and then get ready for the work.

Method of Working on Trucks

The *rejas* associated with trucks do the work of loading and unloading raw thematerials in or out of the truck. Whenever some materials are to be transported through trucks, be it sand, soil, bricks or boulders, the *rejas* are assembled on trucks and are taken to the site. At the site, the *rejas* get busy with the loading of materials. Usually, there remain seven or eight *rejas* on a truck and besides, two to four *coolies* also remain present. For the carriage of baked bricks, the truck drivers park the truck near arranged bricks in the brick-kiln. The *rejas* get prepared for loading bricks in the truck. For this, some *rejas* remain on the truck itself, while others carry bricks to the truck. The *rejas* on truck take the bricks off their heads and arrange them methodically in the trucks. When the loading is finished, they all sit on the bricks, loaded in truck, or stand up on it, and reach the other destination. Thereafter, they get busy with unloading the bricks. Some of the *rejas* get down from the truck and some remain standing on it. The *rejas* above toss the bricks toward the *rejas* below and the latter catch them and place them over their head one by one. After placing 9 to 10 bricks on their head, they carry them to the requisite place and arrange them serially.

Above all the *rejas* have to pack up the trucks with sand, stone chips, brick-chips etc. by carrying these materials on their head loads. Likewise the unloading of sand or stone chips etc. is not that much difficult. The truck is parked at the desired place and the side cover is opened to enable the *rejas* to unload the materials with the help of shovels like instrument.

Besides the above, they have to discharge miscellaneous duties such as picking the grasses from the agricultural fields, or harvesting etc. Sometimes, they also carry vegetables, baskets, etc. in vegetable markets. They also unload vegetables out of trucks and carry it to the market. *Rejas* are also seen working various types of petty jobs in course of assisting the cooks, carrying good articles from one place to another on their heads, and at times they are engaged for cleaning utensils, carrying waters in canisters and buckets etc.

Daily Routine of the *Rejas*

The daily routine of the *rejas* can be divided into two parts : the routine during their holidays and the other on working days. While on the holidays it is needless to say that they get ample opportunity to pass the day according to their own conveniences but just reverse is the case on the working days because most of the period is passed while doing justice to their jobs and only a little of the time is utilised by them according to their wishes.

Daily Routine During Working Days

As to their daily routine on the working days it has been observed that generally a *reja* rises in the early morning because she has to do some domestic activities, which cannot be ignored by her being a female. She has to look after her home, children, husband, parents and other family members, etc. If some other working lady or ladies are present in house, such as, mother, mother-in-law, sister, or sister-in-law, the *rejas* are assisted in their household work by them. But even then, they themselves cover some important household work and then set out for professional work. In that case, the pending work at home is completed by other ladies. If none is present at home, the *rejas* themselves have to do the work at home also, besides their work outside the home. Thus, they have to get up early in the morning and lit the oven. Afterwards they start cooking food for every one at home, and as they have to carry some food for the lunch also, they keep it in their tiffin-carriers. Then, they hurriedly take their breakfast, wash the utensils, and set out for work. Besides doing the work at home, they reach their respective destinations by 8 or 9 A. M. If the working site is near the home, it is well and good, and even if it is far off and there is no conveyance, the *rejas* do not mind footing the distance. Generally the *rejas* get company of the fellow-*rejas* and thus, they go to the working sites from their village collectively. They do their lunch in the break for an hour during day. Afterwards, they wash up their tiffin-carriers and those who are fond of chewing tobacco prepare tobacco, while resting for a while. They take tobacco themselves and do not mind offering it to their colleagues too. They do some gossiping or chatting, comb their hair and if there is provision for taking tea, they take tea, and get ready for the work.

They get free by the dusk on the completion of daily work, and it gets dark by the time they reach home. If the food has been prepared by someone at home, it is well and good, else they have to cook food and serve it to family members. Afterwards, they may pass their time chatting with the neighbours and then they hasten to bed to get up early in the morning.

Daily Routine During Holidays

Generally, the *rejas* are allowed to enjoy one holiday in a week. They are granted leaves on particular days in view of local market or *Haats*, organised in one area on some fixed day. On holidays, firstly the *rejas* finish their pending work, such as washing up clothings, cleaning the house, etc. and sometimes, they also do some sewing or knitting work.

They make arrangements for ration in home and also bring necessary items from the market such as fuel wood from nearby forests and the like. They prefer to go to the market or *haat* generally in the afternoon. Some *rejas* also go to the town to purchase clothings or at times to witness movies also. Thus, after enjoying the weekly holiday, they get ready for their work with a new zeal and vigour.

Thus, while going into the details of their works, working patterns, mode of employment etc. in relation to their day to day routines we arrive at a conclusion that the *rejas* as a class can be motivated and utilised on all sorts of occasions, be it social, agricultural, constructive activities and the like.

3

Interaction Pattern among Tribal Rejas, Employers and Associates

In the previous chapter an attempt has been made to describe several types of work for the completion of which the tribal *rejas* are deployed at different labour centres either through contractors or independently by approaching the owners or managements of labour centres. In course of their different types of work, the tribal *rejas* have to come in contact with various persons because the nature of their works is such that they cannot complete it alone. Hence, they come in contact with different persons who may be their employers, or their other associates such as *munshi*, work manager, truck-drivers, *khalasis*, local people and colleagues, etc. In this chapter it would be relevant to discuss their relationship with different persons they come in contact with in course of their jobs. It would also be important to note what kind of treatment they get from these persons, Though they expect cordial relationship and human treatment from their bosses for efficient working, it has been mostly found that many of them get ill-treatment specially from those who are working at out stations since they are completely under their grip.

The tribal *rejas* have to work very hard for the whole day. They spend their whole day amidst their associates and colleagues. They work at one place for several days or months together and get opportunities to work with the same lot of persons for a long period. Therefore, in such situation what type of relationship they develop and maintain with all of them is the aspect of discussion which we shall be trying to analyse in the present chapter.

Interaction Pattern between Rejas and Employers

Every that person who employs the tribal *rejas* is known as her employer, that person may be a contractor or any body else. That person is very important because due to his help, the *reja* become able to earn some amount. The relationship of the tribal *rejas* with their employers varies according to the different places of their work, which have been enumerated here as follows :

Relationship of the *rejas* with Brick-kiln Owner

In the brick-kilns tribal *rejas* have to perform the work of loading and unloading the unbaked bricks to the kiln or the baked bricks outside the kiln. The *rejas* belonging to different places i.e. outside Bihar, outside Ranchi town and local areas work together. Two types of tribal *rejas* are found in a brick-kiln :

(a) The first type consists of those who have been brought from the distant places with the help of *sardar* or middle man, and

(b) other type comprise those who come from the nearby villages and get the job directly from the owner of the brick-kiln.

In both the cases their employers are those who own the brick-kilns. If they are brought through a contractor, in such case the contractor also levies their own charge on the owner of the kiln and thus their whole responsibilities lie on the owners. The *rejas* who come from distant places, come with the expectations that they will be provided with good places of living, food, clothes etc. Full protection would also be provided to them but it has been found that they are not provided with all those amenities and thus their expectations are shattered. They are kept in the most inhumanly state. Arrangement for their stay is done nearby the brick-kilns. Small huts of bricks covered with the sheets of tin or with straws are provided to them. The doors for entrance are so small and low that one can not enter into them without bowing down; and again, no one sleeps in such huts without legs protruding through the open door. Health, hygiene and sanitary aspects are very poor. There is also a total absence of electricity arrangements in the brick-kilns and the *rejas* have to do their household works at night in the light of lamp or candle.

The *rejas*, who have been brought from distant places, are totally dependent upon their employers because they have to live near brick-kilns and all such facilities which they want for a smooth living, can be rendered to them with the help of the employer only. Generally the brick-kiln owners also prefer the outside labourers to local ones because in the case of outside labourers, they do not neglect their work even on the plea for holidays or so. Brick-kilns are situated at a distant places from the town, so market, shops etc. are not available there. *Rejas* have to cook their food themselves. They are supplied with rice, pulses, vegetables etc. every day. It is called *khoraki*. Its cost is adjusted against their salary. At such places, where market is situated close to their habitation, they purchase edibles themselves. They are paid some money every week for this purpose. They are allowed to attend weekly market from where they make purchases for a week. A man of the employer keeps close watch on them for their security as well as to watch them so that a few of them may not flee away from that place.

It has been found that at every brick-kiln there are some persons deputed by the employer to supervise the *rejas*. Employers do not remain present for the whole day. During working hours, the brick-kiln owners generally come to inspect the work of the kiln. They also inspect the working *rejas* there. *Rejas* have to work at a brick-kiln for the whole season i.e. from October to May; and due to their regular working for several months continuously, their employers recognise each and every *rejas* who work at the kilns. When the work is going on in full swing in the brick-kiln, there a strict relationship is maintained between the brick-kiln owners and the *rejas*, i.e. just of an employee and an employer. Again *reja's* work is measured in terms of the number of bricks she actually carries to the kiln, she ramains busy in her work. She wants to do more trips with the bricks to earn more money. But even if she gets any order from her employer she has to obey him even against her wishes. *Rejas* perform Sundry works of the employers also. They have been seen fetching drinking water for the employer, or serving breakfast to him and his guests. It held true with the author also. The author had several occasions to visit the brick-kilns and every time water, tea or breakfast were offered to her by the *rejas* though the order was given by her employer. Thus, at times, she has to wash the used glasses and plates also. Though the *reja* remains in a haste to complete more trips in a day, even if she gets order by her employer to do any personal work, she can not ignore him because she knows that he is all in all there. If once she becomes successful in pleasing him, she can get more amenities during her work tenure and for this purpose she does everything she can do. Sometimes she goes to work as maid servant in his house. She has to please her employer in every way.

Those *rejas* who do not live there for the whole night show that they hail from the nearby villages, as such have to come in less contact with their employers. They come at their sites of work in the early morning and work there till the lunch break. At lunch break, they go to their respective villages to take their meals. After lunch time is over then they again come to their works. But if the distance of their houses is far and they do not have time to go and come within that short span of time, they carry their meals in tiffin-carriers to the brick-kiln. So, they have got less time to spend free at kiln. At the lunch break, if the employers visit the kiln, they have some opportunity to make contact with him. But their employers recognise each *reja* and also know about the villages to which they belong.

The author had got several opportunities to talk with the brick-kiln owner s and it was found that the kiln owners recog nise each and every *rejas* who is employed at their kilns.

But they care a little for them. As reported at various brick-kilns visited by the author, the employers are more interested in their works, rather than the prevailing conditions of the *rejas*. *Rejas* have to live at desolate place at night so there should be full arrangements for their security and this is the responsibility of the owner of the kiln. But it is not found any-where. It is a risky task to run the work with the help of young girls because it is not necessary that all the persons of the *bastis* (settlements) situated nearby the brick-kilns are good and well behaved. Often it is found that there is a dispute due to the *rejas*. The employers who do not take proper care for them, are sometimes involved in serious circumstances and hence they have to face difficulties. They have to persuade the *rejas* to continue the work. At a brick-kiln situated near the Bariatu Housing Colony, the owner had to face such difficulty when the *goonda* elements of the nearby *bastis* in-vaded the abode of the *rejas* at night and tried to molest them (see appendix no. B-3).

In the brick-kilns, where the *rejas* are provided with accom-modations some other persons also are accommodated. These persons also work at the same kiln as *pathera* (persons who do the job of laying down the bricks) or the persons who do the work of arranging the bricks inside the kiln etc. They are brought from the distant places and are provided with the same kind of huts like that of the *rejas*. *Rejas* have to live with them. In such circumstances, employer has to pay full attention towards all the workers, specially towards the *rejas* so that there should not be complaints from the other persons who live there. The chance of misbehaviour from those workers also cannot be denied.

All the tribal *rejas* surveyed working in brick-kilns were of the opinions that their employers do not bother to care for them or to know about their difficulties. Their total respon-sibility is over when they depute their persons to supervise them. Their real masters are the *munshis* (manager) deputed by the employers. The *rejas* brought from the distant places also used to assemble around the author and narrate the apathetic attitudes of their employers. They told that they had come there to work having full confidence in their employers that they would provide them all the facilities but they found that their employers always shirked from their responsibilities. Actually they do not have courage to raise their voice against their employers because they know that in such case they will be driven away from their work. Hence, they are being exploited by their employers. Employers also do not care to see whether the *rejas* are being paid their wages regularly and correctly or not. They provided all the powers to their *munshis* who serve as mediators between the *rejas* and their *employers*.

Relationship of the Rejas with the Contractors

There is a large category of those *rejas* who are engaged by the contractors either in construction work of different nature, may be building construction, road construction, any river project etc. or in some industrial complexes. Mostly at such labour centres where any type of construction work is going on the rejas are engaged through contractors. Hence the contractors are their the real employers. Such *rejas* move from one place to another with the same contractor and here again due to doing job at one place for a long period they come almost daily in contact of their employers. Their employers also know those *rejas* fully well. The contractor knows to which respective villages they belong; so whenever he gets jobs, he sends information through his men to the *rejas* and the *rejas* report themselves for work under him.

In case when the contractor gets work outside Ranchi, a bulk of *rejas* who are working under him, are supposed to go with him there also. But then it becomes the responsibility of that contractor that after completion of the work, the *rejas* should be reached to their respective villages safely. Generally the contractors try to show that they are providing almost all facilities to their workers for a smooth running of the work. Though there are also some other persons to supervise the works of the *rejas*, the contractors always pay visits at the site and make final inspection of all the works going on there. If the contractor is witty, then there is a chance of his prevailing upon those *rejas* who are good-looking and smart. Such a contractor has been closely observed by the author doing some witty remarks, joking with the *rejas*. In such cases they prefer those *rejas* who are very free and frank in their nature and do not take ill of their jokes, wits and humour and a sort of intimacy develops between the *rejas* and their employers. Sometimes the contractor takes undue advantage of the intimacy when he is able to entice the *reja* to such extent that she goes with him leaving her home and village for good (see appendix no. B-7).

Some *rejas* were heard giving replies to the jokes of their employers but it is not applicable in case of all the *rejas*, only those *rejas*, who have developed their relationship with the contractors have courage to make jokes with them. Such *rejas* are generally good-looking, smart and very frank. Sometimes they are also called at the house of the contractors to do some honusehold works of the contractors.

Sometimes their relationship becomes so intimate that they serve as agents and go on enticing other *rejas* to work for that particular contractor. In other words, such rejas are called *Sardarnis* (see appendix no. B-7).

Though it is a fact that when the *rejas* are engaged through contractors, they do not have to move here and there in search of job, but for maintaining their relationship with the contractor they have to face various situations. Contractors generally take full advantage of them and they are being exploited by them to a great extent. When the *rejas* are engaged through contractors, their wages are paid by them also. They have to depend upon the contractors for the payment and it depends on the will of the contractor whether he makes full and regular payment to them or not. The *rejas* become puppets in the hands of their contractors as such they try to please them. They feel that it is necessary to please them for continuing themselves in the profession. When the *rejas* are engaged in industrial complexes through the contractors, their payments are made to the contractors on the basis of minimum wages fixed for them but the *rejas* are not paid at the same rate. Similarly, there are the instances of less payments in construction works also (For detail, see the chapter—Exploitations of the tribal *Rejas*).

Relationship of the Rejas engaged in Miscellaneous Works with their Employers

We find such types of *rejas* also who are engaged in miscellaneous works as casual labourers. They are employed through those persons who are in need to complete their works. In such situations also *rejas* again remain in contact with their employers and the chances of intimacy develop. But generally the *rejas* are employed to complete the work for a shorter period. Their employers are in a haste to complete their works first as they want to take full works from them. Even though working for a shorter period *reja* has a chance to grow more intimate relationship with her employer if the employer is also interested in it. Out of twenty *rejas* surveyed, who are engaged in miscellaneous types of works, seven *rejas* have been able to get the job of maid-servants and five of them who developed intimacy with the employer are often offered jobs by him. Thus they develop such intimacy with their employers that whenever their employers are in need, they prefer to engage them only if they are available.

It has been found that while working on several occasions for the same employer a *reja* has grown such relationship with him that she starts living with him as maid-servants and she went with him to his native place in north Bihar. After taking her there her employer made her agreeable to marry with a servant at his village home and thus she got married with that servant. After living there for some years, she again returned to Ranchi with her husband and started working as a *reja* here. Her husband, who is a non-tribal, is doing the job of distilling country liquor here. Sometimes, she is also found working as a maid-servant in the house of that employer, with whom she had gone to north Bihar (see appendix No. A-2). This shows as to what extent of relationship they develop with their employer during their schedule of working as a *reja*.

It has also been observed that during their working hours if any accident takes place in which the *rejas* sustain some injuries, may be minor or major, they are carried to hospital by their employers. They make arrangements for their medicine, treatment etc. and this is only possible because of the good maintenance of a good relationship between them. But it is not necessary that everywhere such types of relationships exist between the employers and the *rejas*.

Though the employers are responsible for the well-being of the *rejas* it has been found that the employers afterwards forget them altogether. It is evident from the table-1 that 54.3 percent *rejas* have neutral relationship with their employers. As many as 19 percent of the *rejas* as shown in the table-1 are of opinion that there does not exist a congenial relationship between the *rejas* and the employers because the employers are chiefly concerned with their own ends and they care a fig for the well-being of the *rejas* under them. However there is no denying the fact that 9.3 percent *rejas* admitted that the relationship between them is, more or less, good.

Table–1

Relationship of Rejas with their Employers

Sl. No.	Labour centres	No. of *rejas* surveyed	Relationship with employers			
			Good	Bad	Neutral	Not replied
1	2	3	4	5	6	7
1.	Construction work	100	11	26	48	15
2.	Brick-kilns	80	7	16	45	12
3.	Transportation work	60	3	7	38	12
4.	Industrial complex	40	5	6	22	7
5.	Miscellaneous	20	2	2	10	6
	Total	300	28 (9.3%)	57 (19%)	163 (54.3%)	52 (17.3%)

Interaction Pattern between *Rejas* and Associates

The *rejas* have to pass their most of the time during their working hours among their associate workers rather than their employers because the employers are not present always at the site for the whole day. It is found that in every category of *rejas*, either working in brick-kilns, or in construction works, or on trucks, or in industries or as casual labourers engaged in miscellaneous types of works, they have to live with other associates such as *munshis*, work-managers, truck-drivers, khalasis, local people, etc. *Rejas* remain in more contact with such persons who are appointed by their employers to look after them. Though the employers are responsible for their payments, the payments are done through the medium of these intermediaries who, at times, shirk from doing full justice to the responsibilities towards the poor *rejas*.

The *rejas* who are engaged in brick-kilns are kept under the supervision of *munshis* or managers who happen to be the agents of the employers. So in such cases the *rejas* have more chances to come in close contact with them. Every day, for the whole season of brick-making business, they have to work under them, hence the *munshis* become well-acquainted with the nature of every *reja*. The employer also used to get the payments distributed to the *rejas* through the *munshi*. So *munshi* serves as a mediator between the employer and the *rejas*. Most of them are faithful and loyal to their masters as they are their paid men.

The *rejas* who are engaged in construction works, have to work under the munshi. The *rejas* who are employed in factory for a particular type of work have to work under the supervision of manager, likewise the *rejas* who are engaged in transportation of materials on trucks have to work under truck-drivers and *khalasis*. Besides these, there are other *rejas* and *coolies* (male workers) also among whom they have to work for the whole day. We shall be trying here to discuss their relationship with the different types of their associates as follows ·

Relationship with Munshi or Work manager

It is noticed that wherever the works of construction or brick-kiln is going on, there are some persons, who have been dressed themselves more smartly than many other workers might be wearing *dhotis—kurtas*, fullpants, *Kamij* (shirts) or *paijamas* (trousers)—shirt ect., sitting or standing on a particular place and watching the activities of all the *rejas*.

Because they serve as mediators between the employer and the *rejas*, the *rejas* try to please them also. They do not like any slackness regarding the work of the *rejas*. If any reja shows slackness in her work she is rebuked by them and often some sort of threatening is given to the effect that complaints well be lodged against the *rejas* to the employer, or their wages will be minimised or deducted. So rejas have developed a sense of fear within themselves from *Munshis* or Managers but pretend to show that they are normal and happy with them.

The author has got several occasions to watch the *rejas* working at various construction projects either of building or road, etc. Whenever an attempt was made to consult the *rejas* during their working hours, it was observed that they did not like to talk with the author, not because of their unwillingness but due to the fear from the *munshi*. They simply replied that *munshi* would question them for their delay in work as he remains watching them, more or less, regularly. Thus on such occasions the author had to seek the permission from their *munshi* for talking a bit with them.

Since the modes of payment differ from job to job, the *rejas* engaged in brick-kilns can hardly evade work whereas the *rejas* engaged in other centres can very easily shirk from duty as their *munshis* are not so much whatchful towards them. The *rejas* engaged in construction-works prefer to have unstrict *munshi* rather to strict and disciplinarian one, who may not supervise them very closely. It has been observed that while they are engaged in carrying the concrete or bricks up to the mason they come out of the range of *munshis* eyes, they become slow in their works and start idling away time in chatting, talking among themselves. At a particular site, there remains only one *munshi*, hence it is not possible for him to supervise every one at a time. Suppose the construction work is going on the third floor of any building, then in such case the prepared concrete will be kept on the ground floor and *rejas* have to carry the materials on the third floor, so when they come on ground floor, they relax there but if in that condition they are ever detected by their *munshi* they are rebuked for their lapses in duty. That is why they stress more on pleasing the *munshi* by all means.

Often *munshis* were cutting jokes, passing remarks with the *rejas* to the enjoyment of *rejas* as well. The *rejas* have to compromise with the circumstances because they think if the *munsht* is pleased with them it is well and good, then he should be pleased and kept his mind cool. Once it was seen that a *munshi* was teasing a *reja* by hanging down the *tokri* (basket) from the upper floor of a building and in return outwardly the *rejas* was enjoying the fun though crying "*Maar debau-Maar debau*" (I shall beat you). The *rejas* was also taking interest and was giggling over the *munshi's* behaviour because in this pretext her two purposes were being served—firstly, she was getting time for relaxation and secondly, it was leading towards development of an intimate relationship with the *munshi*. After sometime when she could not succeed in getting her basket, she collected some sands or concrete and threw it on the body of the *munshi* up to his profound delight.

Thus a *munshi* takes personal interest in a particular *reja* having been charmed at her beauty and smartness. Once, while in course of her field-work while talking with a *munshi*, the author's attention was drawn by the *munshi* towards a so-called heroine among the *rejas*. The *munshi* was all the time insisting upon that particular *reja* to come and talk with the author also and the *reja* ostensibly was seen very much delighted over the attachment of due importance by the *munshi*.

It has also been observed that sometimes during the working hours, the *munshi* used to pull the braids of the *rejas*. Whenever any order is to be given to a *reja*, the *munshi* will like to convey it by pulling her braid or caressing her hand. When the *munshi* has developed some weekness towards a particular *reja* he ignores lapses on her part. He does not see whether she is doing her job perfectly or not and his such behaviour for a particular *reja* gives rise to the feeling of jealousy among other *rejas*.

Munshi is also the incharge of those *rejas* who are brought from the distant places and are provided with their accommodations near the site. There they are kept under the supervision of the *munshi*. In such case, if the *munshi* is taking interest in a particular *reja*, he will provide her more facilities with regard to her boarding and lodging. But his such type of behaviour cannot remain hidden from the other workers and thus the *reja* has to face an awkward position among her colleagues.

It has also been observed that a few *munshis* give kind treatments to those *rejas* who are old or handicapped and are not capable to do the strenuous works but being forced by her economic and domestic predicament she has to take to the work of *rejas*. In such cases, they try to help them and generally try to omission or commission in their works. The author had an occasion to meet an elderly *rejas* of about 30-35 years, who was mad to some extent and was engaged in a road construction work. She was deserted by her husband owing to her madness or insanity. She had to live with her parents and elder brother. She had no knowledge of money but she came to work for the sake of being involved in the work. She was working there due to kind nature of the *munshi* and the *munshi* was fully aware with her history and he himself narrated her woeful tale to the author. She was being paid full amount for her whole day work at the personal risk of the *munshi* himself. He was ready to convince his master that although handicapped she was capable of doing work up to his satisfaction. The *munshi* could have easily got her removed from the job but out of sheer compassion he let her continue despite her insanity. He told the author that being an earning member of the family she could be able to get some respect in the family otherwise she would be put in a great difficulty. Nobody would be attentive to her at all.

When such type of cordial relationship develops between the *rejas* and their *munshi* or manager then the *rejas* have no objection in doing some personal works of the *munshi*, etc. In spite of uncongenial relationship the *rejas* have to do their personal works though unwillingly whereas in respect of good relationship they like working without any grudge against the munshi. These personal works relate to washing clothes, cooking and serving food and sometimes massaging of his head or legs besides doing his household works and sundry.

But sometimes, when they see that the *rejas* are in their full control they want to take undue advantages also from them. When the *munshi* or the manager see that in the absence of their masters, they are the masters of the *rejas*, they start to exploit the *rejas* in different manners, even at the cost of the work.

Further it has been observed very minutely that *rejas* have no knowledge of time. If they are engaged to work from 9 A.M. to 5 P.M. with a leisure of an hour in the mid-day, they have to believe their *munshi* or manager in respect of duty times. If the *rejas* ask the manager about the time, he very easily can exploit them saying wrong time. Likewise even if they report on duty before time, they might be scolded by the *munshi* on the plea of late arrival on duty.

If the *munshis* are old, they take more interest in extracting money while making payment to *rejas* rather than in the personal beauty of the *rejas*. Further they are always in quest of some occasions which might enable them to deduct the wages and misappropriate the money thus deducted. (details about exploitation have been discussed in the chapter—Exploitation of the tribal *Rejas*).

Relationship with Truck-drivers/Khalasis

The *rejas* who are engaged in transportation works, have to live in contact with the truck-drivers and the *khalasis* for most of the time. It has been found that a set of seven or eight *rejas* are engaged on one truck for a long period. Whenever that truck is pressed into service for reaching the materials to the working sites, the truck-driver collects the *rejas* who work on that truck and take them to the site where the truck is loaded with materials and the *rejas* do the job of loading the materials on truck. Thereafter the truck is again taken to that place where the materials are to be reached and there the truck is unloaded by those very *rejas*. After the work is over, the driver has the responsibility of reaching all these *rejas* to their respective villages. Every truck-driver has got a *khalasi* who assists the driver. During their regular working tenure, the have *rejas* more opportunities to develop intimacy with the drivers and *khalasis* of the trucks. Once, when they board the trucks, they are on the mercy of the drivers and the *khalasis* of the trucks because they have to go to distant places from their villages with them. The truck *rejas* have more opportunities to develop relationship with the truck-drivers and *khalasis* than of those with the *munshis* who are engaged in brick-kilns or construction works etc. The truck-*rejas* are reported to be attached with the same truck-driver and *khalasi* for more than 6-7 years. But it is not necessary that a *reja* works at a brick-kiln for such a long period or a construction work may prevail for such a longer period.

The truck-*rejas* are always found moving on the trucks, sitting over the materials loaded on it or even standing on vacant trucks, gossiping, chatting, chirping and singing among themselves. They have to cover a long distance for reaching the materials, hence, there is every possibility that they may have to return to their homes at night. In case if the truck gets broke down in the midway and there is no chance of its repair, they have to spend the whole of night on the very truck until the truck is ready to move ahead. In this situation the driver and the *khalasi* have to arrange for their food and protection, hence, they fully depend upon the mercy of the driver or the *khalasi*. There is also possibility of the truck being broke down at such a place where there is no shop or hotel and the *rejas* have to cooperate with the drivers and the *khalasis* until some arrangements are made for food and shelter.

The *rejas* who prefer to work on trucks are of the more enjoyable nature and fond of merry-makings. They try to make their journey more enjoyable and hence they like that their associates also be of similar nature, so that there may not be any difficulty in adjusting with them. As mentioned by a truck driver, the *rejas* always prefer to work on that truck in which driver and *khalasi* are of the same mentality that of the *rejas*. If their mentality is alike, their relationship continues to be very smooth and congenial.

While moving on trucks the *rejas* generally expect favour from the driver and the *khalasi* to move about shopping at some village-*haats* which come across on the way and thus further allow to take country liquor or *hanria*. Truck drivers and *khalasis* generally have no objection to their wishes because they themselves are also fond of drinking *hanria* or country wine particularly when they see that *rejas* are themselves interested in such things.

It has been observed that generally *rejas* of younger age groups prefer to work on trucks because they like to travel here and there. Out of 60 *rejas* surveyed 40 (66.7%) rejas are unmarried and come under the age group of 11-30 years. They have more chances to see and know different places. It has also been noticed that sometimes *rejas* go away with the truck drivers or the *khalasis* not to return again. Once a married *reja* fled away with the driver of a truck and did not return for nearly six months. When she returned her husband did not allow her to live with him. At this she started living alone but she had to forgo her children also. This happened because after developing a very intimate relationship with the driver of the truck, the driver insisted her to go and live with him. But when she went with him she found that she was deceived by the driver. She was in fact in better position at her own home as she was not provided with the promised incentives for better living or more income etc.

Khalasis are generally very humorous in nature and hence cut jokes with the *rejas*. The *rejas* also due to their frank nature do not mind the jokes at all. Their such relationship also extends up to provoking the *rejas* which at time irritate them as well. It has also come to our notice that once *rejas* had to jump out of the moving trucks for the sake of their chastity which was being maligned by the drivers or the *khalasis* (for detail see the chapter—Exploitations of the tribal *rejas*).

During their night stay at lonely places owing to breakdown of trucks, the drivers and the *khalasis* also get chances to exploit the *rejas* because the *rejas* are, so to say, quite helpless there. Truck-drivers are generally non-tribals and they are of opinion that in all cases these tribal *rejas* are of loose characters, and because of such attitude towards the *rejas*, they want to take undue advantages.

Rejas are exploited because of their highly ambitious desires i.e. for the fulfilment of their ambitions, they go in for working on trucks. They also look to their own profits in the sense that while working on a truck even for one trip only they earn Rs. 7 or Rs. 8 and if there are more trips in a day, they can earn even more whereas they have to do less work in comparison to those *rejas* who are engaged in kilns or construction works. Moreover they get the opportunities to move here and there on trucks.

Relationship with Local People

Generally the tribal *rejas* have to work in such localities where they cannot ignore the local people. Suppose the construction work of any building is going on in a colonial area where they come in contact with the local people of that area, or the residents of the neighbouring houses, etc. it has been observed that while working at the same place continuously for several days, a kind of relationship also develops between the *rejas* and the local persons of that area where the work goes on.

Take for example the construction work of a college building going on in the middle of the main town of Ranchi. While working there, the *rejas* get the opportunities to watch the students, staff-teachers of that college. During the period of lunch-breark they can go even outside the college campus in the market area and thus they have opportunity to watch the activities of the other people in the town. The author also got an opportunity to watch them while working in a construction project of a local college and she observed them for days together. It was noticed that while working in that college the *reja* had developed a relationship with the girl students of that college and started talking with them like friends. Whenever the *rejas* wanted to know certain things, they enquired from the students. On the other hand the girl students also recognised them and during their leisure, when they talked to the *rejas*, they were pleased. *Rejas* also got opportunities to watch those students as to how they spoke, behaved and were dressed. On being questioned how they were able to do so hard works, they were found replying that they had developed practice of doing such things for money.

While working in a residential colony, it has been observed

that *rejas* have developed relationship with the servants and the maid-servants of the neighbouring houses, and whenever the *rejas* got their lunch break or some leisure at times due to heavy rains, they were found talking with those servants and maid-servants. If they have to drink water, they are offered water by the servants etc. These servants also were seen passing filthy remarks in respect of the *rejas*.

Once it was noticed that a small girl, aged six years, of the owner of the building where construction work was going on, started talking with the *rejas* and she was so much impressed with the *rejas* that she often likes to remain in their company. Not only this much, the baby started copying the jobs of the *rejas* and used to fill up the *karahi* with concrete, chips etc. This is another instance of relationship between the *rejas* and the girl because whenever the girl came in contact with them, they used to talk or play with her. They further used to teach the baby how to play with stone chips. *Rejas* also develop good relationship with local people while doing their works, such as picking up of the stones from the wheat, or separating stones from the rice with the help of winnowing basket, or sweeping the dirty place, etc. while they get time during their lunch hours after their lunch.

Relationship with Colleagues

The colleagues of *rejas* include those associates who help in doing her job. They include *coolies* (the male labourers) and the other *rejas*. The tribal *reja* have to work along with those coolies and *rejas* and there are chances of development of more intimacy among them because they also hail from the same category and community and their ways of life are almost the same. A *reja* completes her work with the help of these labourers and here it is seen that due to regular working together they all are known very well to one another. Their problems are almost the same and they have to do the same type of works also. These all things lead to the development of intimate relationship among them.

Generally the tribal *rejas* are found involved in their working communities, they do not worry at all for the opinions of other people towards them, they are only interested with their own works which are the only sources of their income. They want to make their works more enjoyable and for this they have to maintain a good relationship with their colleagues in the absence of which their tough work will be proved tougher for them. It would be better to discuss the relationship of *reja* with *coolies* and other *rejas* separately.

Relationship with Coolies: Though the *coolies* are male workers but due to the working in same profession, *rejas* have developed intimacy with them, which later on turned into friendship between them. It has been observed that in case of lot of workers, some of them belong to a particular village and in such cases they have a fellow-feeling among themselves. When the *rejas* have to return to their villages, they are being escorted by those *coolies* who belong to their villages respectively. In such situation *coolies* act their safe guards. They have no fear while working away from their villages because they know that there are some persons of their villages also who will protect them against eventualities. If the *rejas* are being teased by the *coolies* of other village then the coolies of her own village side them. Apart from the feeling of oneness the feeling of casteism also persists among them. If the *reja* belongs to the community of Munda or Oraon then all the *coolies* of that community will favour her.

Sometimes *coolies* were also found quarrelling with the *munshi* or others in favour of *rejas* in case the *rejas* are paid less amount, or are exploited by them in any way. Although there is absence of any type of union among them, the *coolies* sometime act as union-leaders for their right as they were seen claiming their amenities and facilities. When the *rejas* find that the *coolies* are helpful to them and they are of the same profession, friendship automatically develops among. themselves. *Coolies* are found helping them in their works because being male, they are more efficient than the *rejas*. When they see that the *rejas* are in difficulties, they come forward to help them. Such type of friendly relationship helps them in developing a healthy atmosphere at work site. *Rejas* also start taking care of the *coolies* and they behave with one another like close friends. During leisures or lunch-breaks *rejas* go to take their lunch in the company of the *coolies*. They are also seen offering some amount of their lunch to the coolies. They go to take tea or light refreshments with the coolies and thus they all generally live together during leisures.

To what extent the *rejas* are worrried for the *coolies* is evident from an event which goes like this. Once two *coolies* were doing the job of cutting the iron rods and in that job they had to do more work and they were sweating a lot. *Rejas* got sympathetic towards them seeing them working hard. They besides insisting them to take some rest offered them water to drink though the *rejas* were themselves doing hard jobs of carrying the bricks to the upper floor of a building but they were not worried for themselves at all.

Rejas and *coolies* have been found exchanging *khaini* and *biris* among themselves. If the *khaini* is prepared by one coolie or one *reja*, it is distributed among all the *rejas* and coolies who are in habit of taking it. *Coolies* are also seen cutting jokes with the *rejas* and *rejas* are also seen replying to them in the same manner and it is a common sight during working hours. *Rejas* were seen sprinkling water or throwing sand etc. over the *coolies* and *coolies* were also found pulling the *rejas* by the border of *sarees*, or their braids etc. During leisures they are also found sitting and chatting together very comfortably.

It has been observed that during lunch hour, one *cooli* was relaxing on the ground keeping his head in the lap of a *reja* and that *reja* was picking lice out of the hairs of that *cooly*, but none had any objection over it. Their such behaviour reveals that the rejas are free and frank with the *coolies* and they are not afraid of the society or their guardians. In such cases we find a marked difference between their behaviour and the behaviours of other literate persons. In an office or at any other place where the literate persons work and employees will act like them before the public, if they will have to cut a sorry figure. But in the case of tribal *rejas* we find that they have no fear of their guardians because their guardians are only interested in the money which they earn and give to them.

There may be possibility that instead of returning home direct, the *reja* may go anywhere else with a coolie and returns home after some time. In such case she satisfies her guardians by making some excuses for the delay. Sometimes she also goes outside the town to some distant place with a *coolie* in search of work. For such behaviour she may be misled by the cooly because it also happens that due to being simpleton they are more attracted towards the novelty and modern ways of life. And thus they are deceived also. (see appendix No......B. 5)

Relationship with Other Rejas : The *reja* generally maintains a good relationship with other *rejas* with whom she works. The *reja* is always found in group of other *rejas*. It is a common sight to see the *rejas* trudging in group towards their destinations of works, the destinations may be brick-kilns, construction project, etc. They go to their working centres in groups but it is not necessary that at a particular working site all the *rejas* are from the same village, some of them may belong to one village. They only come and return in a group. They develop friendship among themselves because most of their time they pass together and their daily routines are more or less the same. At their working sites they have to work in the cooperation of the *rejas* who do not belong to their village or community but due to being in the same profession and working together they come in close contact with each other and a friendly relationship exists among them. It is not necessary that all the *rejas* belong to same age groups, there may be younger *rejas* and older *rejas* but even though they prefer to live in a group. They do not have feeling of caste, community, age, education, etc. When they come to work, they forget about all these things. Only one thing prevails among themselves, that is their profession, hence, all are equal.

Rejas pass time chatting and gossiping with each other. They have been seen moving on trucks singing together or returning to their villages giggling and singing together. During their lunch hours the *rejas* have been seen taking their meals together. They go to take tea etc. in groups. It has been observed that the *rejas* prefer to go in groups of three or four to the hotel or market during their lunch hour. On holidays, they try to finish their household activities in the company of the other *rejas,* with whom they have developed more intimacy. If they have to purchase the food materials, household materials etc. from the village market, they go there with their friends. Likewise for collecting the fuel from the nearby forest of their villages also they go in company of other *rejas*. They have been seen together in cinema hall or circus etc. in the company of the other *rejas.*

Though they have relationship with all the *rejas* with whom they work but among them also different categories of friendships are found. Generally two or three *rejas* are chums and here the degree of intimacy is veiy high. Everything is freely discussed among them and they always want to live in their chums, group. Even in the group of those *rejas* who belong to the same village, chums are found and there are possibilities of formation of a cliques' group which consists of two or three chums, group and thus all the members of a cliques' group are intimate friends but there are some differences among them. They are not open to each and do not disclose all the incidents of their lives to all the members of the cliques' group. When such type of intimacy has developed among them, they form a group and want to work together also. If any member of that group is engaged in brick-kiln then all the members of that group will prefer to work in that kiln, likewise if one is engaged on truck then she can influence the others to work on that truck and same is with those *rejas* who are engaged in construction works.

It has been observed that they share somethings common in respect of dress, meals etc. When they go to work at distant places from their villages, they have to live together, then they also share huts in common. A group of two or three *rejas* has been found living in the same hut, cooking their food in common, wearing sarees etc. of one another and so on.

But it has also been observed that there are chances of rivalry among them. Sometimes it happens that a particular *reja* of a group has been given preference by her employer or *munshi* or other associates and then more facilities have been provided to that *reja*, such things cause irritation amongst other *rejas* and they develop a sense of jealousy for that particular *reja*. Other *rejas* do observe that in comparison to that *reja* they work hard but even then they are scolded by their employers or *munshi* etc. whereas that *reja* is being overlooked if she shows slackness in her duty. In such cases, it has been observed that other *rejas* are taunting or commenting over that particular *reja*. It has also been observed that inspite of a particular *reja*, a group of smart and good-looking *rejas* has been given preference and then that group will be the subject of jealousy for other *rejas*.

The tribal *rejas* are of very co-operating nature and so fellow-feeling exists among them. If a *reja* is not feeling well then the other *rejas* come to help her in her work. They try to give her rest and become ready to finish the work of her companion also though it matters nothing.

The similar habits beget closeness, no doubt, hence habits of taking tea, *hanria*, *khaini*, *biri*, etc. bring them closer to one another of the similar habits.

Thus, we have seen that different types of relationship exist among the *rejas*, their employers and other associates. As depicted in Table-2, 43% percent *rejas* have neutral relation-

Table—2

Relationship of Rejas with their Associates

Sl. No.	Labour centres	No. of *rejas* surveyed	Relationship with Associates			
			Good	Bad	Neutral	Not replied
1	2	3	4	5	6	7
1.	Construction work	100	22	20	38	20
2.	Brick-kilns	80	11	26	28	15
3.	Transportation works	60	18	10	25	7
4.	Industrial complex	40	5	7	24	4
5.	Miscellaneous	20	3	2	14	1
	Total :	300	59 (19.7%)	65 (21.7%)	129 (43%)	47 (15.6%)

ship with their associates, i.e. neither good nor bad. Hence, we can come to a conclusion on the basis of their relationships that whatever they do, they do chiefly for the sake of money. For getting more money regularly they have to continue in their service for a long period, and for maintaining this continuity they have to please their employers and other associates alike because most of the time they have to work among their companies.

It is also evident that apart from source of income, they think that they have to pass their time in doing the tough jobs of *reja* and they hardly get any time for their enjoyment so they want to find enjoyment also in course of their jobs. For this purpose also, they try to maintain good relationship with all of them.

Opinions of Employers/Associates towards Rejas :—Their employers and other associates feel that the tribal *rejas* are more efficient in regard to their duties hence they prefer to employ them. It is evident from Table-3 that out of 50 employers/associates, 41 (82%) are of opinion that the tribal rejas are more efficient in regard to their works. Whereas 7 (14%) remained neutral. So far as the behaviours of the *rejas* are concerned as many as 36 (72%) of the employers and associates have voted in the favour of their good behaviours as according to them they are of good nature and well behaved also, generally they obey their masters up to full expectations. But equally 14 (28%) of them went against the *rejas* in respect

Table—3

Opinions of Employers/Associates regarding Working Efficiency of Rejas

Sl. No.	No. of Employers/ Associates consulted	Opinions regarding working efficiency		
		Good	Bad	Neutral
1	2	3	4	5
1	50	41	2	7
	Percentage	82%	4%	14%

of their behaviours as well as attitudes (Table-4). But regarding their characters, it has been found that 31 (62%) employers and other associates have developed a conjecture within themselves that the tribal *rejas* are generally of loose character because of their free and frank nature, whereas remaining were of opinion that they are least concerned with their characters as it is out and out their personal matter. Thus the employers have developed a thinking that it is easy to exploit and entice the

Table—4

Opinions of Employers/Associates regarding Behaviour/Nature of Rejas

Sl. No.	No. of Employers/ Associates consulted	Opinions regarding behaviour/nature		
		Good	Bad	Neutral
1	2	3	4	5
1	50	36	6	8
	Percentage	72%	12%	16%

rejas even for minor gains and such presumption of the employers and the associates lead to the exploitation of the *rejas* to a great extent. Table-5 shows the opinions of employers and associates towards the characters of the *rejas*.

Table—5

Opinions of Employers/Associates regarding Characters of Rejas

Sl. No.	No. of Employers/ Associates consulted	Good	Opinions regarding character	
			Bad	Not concerned
1	2	3	4	5
1	50	7	31	12
	Percentage—	14%	62%	24%

The main thing is money and for its earning only the tribal *rejas* have to take to this tough job as their profession where they are also exploited by their employers and other associates. So, now we will try to analyse the role of a *reja* as an earning member in the family in the next chapter. How far she has achieved success in raising her status in the eyes of her family members will be the further point of discussion which follows.

4

The Tribal Rejas as Earning Members in the Family

In the preceding chapter, the relationship of the *rejas* with their employers, associates, colleagues and the like have been dealt with elaborately and it has been seen that their attitudes, behaviou, activities, temperament, etc. differ from individual to individual in view of different jobs, status etc. Since the tribal *rejas* constitute a particular class of working women, their behaviour is somewhat similar to one another barring a little differences which is but natural as to individuals concerned. Before taking to the work of *rejas* the tribal women are, more or less, like innocent, rustic belles but when they are engaged as *rejas* either in brick-kilns or in other works like building construction, road coaltaring etc. their standard of living starts showing a sudden change in course of time and ultimately they are branded in their own society as of higher status as compared to other women population of the same area where they actually hail from.

While observing the general activities of the *rejas* it can be said that the status which they acquire by working as *reja* is more or less responsible to bring about a remarkable change among the *rejas* as regards their social standard, outlook and temperament are concerned. But to know much more about the socio-economic condition of the *rejas* one will have to look into the general way of life of the *rejas* as they have been leading in their respective families. It goes without saying that the *rejas*, before they actually switch over to the job of *rejas*, are just like burdensome in their families. Not to talk of the female members only but even the male members of a family, who are jobless, are also responsible for the burden of a family. But as they are provided with some sorts of jobs to enable them to earn their livelihood, they are regarded as useful as well as beneficial to the families which they belong to.

In the present chapter let us examine critically the socio-economic status of the *rejas*, in their families as well as outside their society, which they acquire by working as *rejas*.

Status in Family

The woman members of a tribal family are treated as burdensome so long they are jobless and do not earn a single farthing so as to help to meet the day to day expenses of their family. The parents or the local guardians often keep scolding or rebuking the female members from the very start of their career to find out some livelihood. Having been thus hard pressed with the antagonising behaviour of their parents, such female members prefer to be engaged as maidservants as well as labourers somewhere with a view to contributing towards their family expenditures. It has been observed that above all a sizeable number of the *rejas* were engaged as domestic servants because the jobs of maid-servants are very easily available in the urban society for which they have not to struggle much. On the contrary some of the well to do families in the society are themselves in search of maid-servants to cater to their domestic chores, hence the employment of maid-servants. It has also been observed by the author while visiting the villages where the *rejas* hail from that prior to the job of *rejas* the female members of families either worked in the fields together with other male members and thereby assisted them in the work of cultivation. Similarly as occasion arises some of the female members moved to the nearby urban environment and got the jobs of maid-servants to which they try to do justice until they are pursuaded by some other agencies to take to the profession of the *rejas*. This sort of pursuasion would have hardly influenced them had they not been allured by the life of the *rejas* which they often see while working. Thus they actually envythe life of the *rejas* and think within the heart of their hearts to get an opportunity to enjoy the life of the *rejas*. As depicted in the table-1, 57.3 percent *rejas* were working as maid-servants prior to taking to the work of *reja*, whereas 15.3 percent were working as agricultural labourers.

Table—1

Types of Work done by Tribal Rejas Prior to taking to the Profession of the Reja

Sl.No.	Types of work done	Number of *rejas*	Percentage
1	2	3	4
1.	Maid-servants	172	57.3
2.	Agricultural labourer	46	15.3
3.	Did not work	56	18.7
4.	Miscellaneous	20	6.7
5.	Not replied	6	2
	Total	300	100%

It has been observed that the tribal girls, who do the job of maid-servants, in course of time become somewhat restless as they grow in age. Before the period of adolescence these maid-servants go on doing their jobs with quite sincerity and perseverance but with the advent of adolescence they become somewhat restless as during this period they get sensitive and well acquainted with the outwardly glamour and charms, of course in accordance with their standard and capacity. Coming in contacts with the civilized population as well as having been influenced and impressed with the charms of urbanization, they begin searching out avenues for more income so as to stead themselves in good stead. In the meantime they happen to come in contact with either the working *rejas* or the intermediaries who are out to find out suitable females to work as *rejas*. These intermediaries or the *rejas* present a very lucrative aspect of life to such maid-servants who have already been in quest of more income. Hence, they prefer to the work of *rejas* rather to ordinary maid-servants.

Now, these types of tribal womeny earning for the jobs of *rejas*, later, present a glowing picture of more income and better status of life to their parents and guardians who immediately consent their female inmates to go in for the jobs of *rejas*. Besides, their guardians or the parents are themselves fully aware of the status of the *rejas*, as such they need not be very fussy on the approaches by their female inmates to work as *rejas*. Thus they are engaged as *rejas* in different labour centres and bring about more income to their families. The parents or guardians of the *rejas* have also no objection because they are supplementing their families with their income. It is evident from Table-2 that 80 percent of the guardians of *rejas* accepted that for they are benefited by the income of the *rejas*, hence no objection, whereas 20 percent of the guardians are of conflicting opinions about the profession of *rejas*. Out of these 20 percent, some of them particularly the fathers preferred their daughters to opt for the work but their mothers did not hesitate in differing from their spouses. Likewise in some cases the husbands of the *rejas* though disliked their spouses to act as *rejas*, pecuniary helplessness debarred them from preventing their wives to take to the work of *reja*.

Table—2

Opinion of the Parents/Guardians towards Working of Their wards as rejas

Sl. No.	Total no. of parents/ guardians consulted	No. of parents/ guardians who are in favour of work	No. of parents/ guardians who are not in favour of work
1	2	3	4
1	50	40 (80%)	10 (20%)

It is needless to say that with the growth of income the status as well as the standard of living grows by leaps and bounds. The female members now the *rejas* start enjoying a better status in her family and likewise her family also gets a better status in the society. Their parents or guardians once annoyed with their female members for their so called inactions and inertia, now give more importance to these *rejas*, sources of income, status and nothing else. Not only this, the entire family of a *reja* tries to keep the source of income always pleased and happy so that the *rejas* may not leg behind in raising the resources for the support of their families. This is why in course of their duties if the *rejas* have to break the social norms or ethics, they are not going to be looked down upon by their families. Moreover, their families like to ignore such rif-rafs for the purpose of keeping the *rejas* ever pleased or for fear of having been deprived with the source of income. As compared to the status of the other members in the families, the *rejas* enjoy definitely better status and virtually they are the guiding forces of their respective families. A time comes when the parents or the guardians become wholly dependent upon the income of the *rejas* for most of the families are unable to meet their annual expenditures with the income from agricultural lands or their own meagre incomes. Naturally they have to be always in tune with their female workers working as *rejas*. On the other hand, these *rejas*, by virtue of their income, are verily the chiefs of their families by whose dictate the entire families move about. At times the *rejas* commnd the rest of their family members and in respect of some important decisions their views are respected most.

Status outside the Family

As a general rule the society does not have a good opinion about the *rejas* particularly in view of their way of life, free mixing with all types of people, freedom of movement whether in the day time or at nights. As to the status of the *rejas* out of their families, the different sections of the society have different opinions about them. (For detail see Chapter III). It does not mean that the probable vices in the life of the *rejas* are not known to their families concerned but circumstances have compelled them to ignore the vices whatsoever and be contented with the virtues only.

Similary the tribal society is fully aware of the evils cropping up in the work of *rejas* but for so many years such things have been prevalent in the society which have now been accepted as dignity of labour only and nothing else. But apart from the tribal societies, who are not subjects to the profession of *rejas*, treat the *rejas* as fallen girls of the society because they are quite opposed to females working together with *coolies*, *khalasis*, drivers etc. and that too in distant road beyond the purview of the guardianship. But the *rejas* have little to do with the objections raised by the non-tribal society as they are hardly concerned with them. These *rejas* after putting in day's jobs get back to their respective families to have a respite in the night and again in the morning they march on to their jobs. Thus they have hardly any leisure to counteract the adverse feelings about themselves in the non-tribal societies.

Role of the *Rejas* as an Earning Member

Actually the *reja* plays a pivotal role in her family just like a "*karta*" in a non-tribal family. She enjoys a very very important position in her family because it is with her own income her family is supported. Her likes and dislikes are given priority in the family and the rest members of her family are always conscious of her pleasures and displeasures so much so that none dares to go against her whims and at times obstinacy. Sometimes it so happens that her guardians or parents, whosoever, have got to bow before her admentine attitude lest she should not deprive them of the facilities. Besides looking to the interest of her family members, the *reja* has to keep herself tidy, active and smart so that her values in the market of the *rejas* remain ever intact.

As regards her role in her family for the betterment of other inmates is concerned she has to look after the interest of her younger brothers, sisters as well as old parents, in-laws, her husband and children alike. She remains concerned for the schooling of her children because in course of time she comes to know of education to children and other aspects for the betterment of the family members. Although working as *reja*, she does not like to put her further generation in the same profession but it is not applicable in respect of each *reja*. It has been observed that those *rejas* who have been in touch with educated families generally like to emulate their ways of life rather than harping on the same old tunes and so they are seen inclined towards imparting primary education to their children. Similarly she has to remain alive to the existing circumstances in the family, say for example, if some of her family members fall ill, she has to get them properly treated and look after them with all possible cares. Thus examining her roles in her family it is concluded that during the hours of need a reja becomes virtually a guardian of her family who is responsible for the well-being of not only herself but the entire family of hers. As it is evident from their items of expenditure (Table-5) that a big amount of their income has been given to their family to meet the minimum requirements of food, shelter etc.

Standard of Living

While studying the standard of living of the tribal *rejas* one will have to examine their living standard in view of their different categories. Standard of living generally depends upon one's income and expenditure and can be judged by income and expenditure on different goods. It varies from man to man and community to community.

It has been found that the tribal *rejas* get their wages according to their nature of works. They work at different labour centres and, generally, they are paid on weekly basis. Table-3 shows the average annual income of the *rejas* working at different labour centres, which is calculated on the basis of their weekly wages. Table-4 shows average per capita income per annum and per capita daily income of the *rejas* engaged in different labour centres. It is evident from this table that the per capita daily income of the *reja* is very low. *Rejas* who are engaged in construction works and industrial complex are earning a sum of Rs. 4.73 as their daily per capita income,

Table—3

Average Annual Income of the Rejas Working at Different Labour Centres

Sl. No.	Labour centres	Total no. of *rejas* surveyed	Total average annual income in Rs.
1	2	3	4
1.	Construction work	100	1,72,800
2.	Brick-kilns	80	80,640
3.	Transportation work	60	95,040
4.	Industrial complex	40	69,120
5.	Miscellaneous works	20	28,800

Table—4

Average per Capita per annum and per Capita Daily Income of the Rejas Working at Different labour Centres

Sl. No.	Labour centres	Total no. of *rejas* surveyed	Per capita per annum income in Rs.	Per capita daily income in Rs.
I	2	3	4	5
1.	Construction work	100	1,728	4.73
2.	Brick-kilns	80	1,008	2.76
3.	Transportation work	60	1,594	4.37
4.	Industrial complex	40	1,728	4.73
5.	Miscellaneous works	20	1,440	3.94

followed by the *rejas* engaged in transportation of raw materials on truck whose per capita daily income is Rs. 4.37. Even the per capita daily income of the *rejas* who are engaged in miscellaneous types of work is more than of those who are engaged in brick-kilns. The per capita daily income of the *rejas* engaged in brick-kilns is calculated as Rs. 2.76 which is the lowest rate of the wage. The reason behind this is that their wages are calculated in terms of the number of bricks they actually carry in a week. They are paid Rs. 7 for carrying one thousand bricks and it depends upon the *rejas* as to how many bricks they can carry in a week (For detail of wage-structure, see Chapter II).

Above all we may look to the standard of living of those *rejas* who are engaged in labour centres in remote villages and not are in the vicinity of any urban population. Such types of *rejas* at the utmost try to copy the ways of life of those non-tribals who are working with them either in the capacity of employer, *munshi* and other associates other than that of the non-tribal communities. By and by, according to their capacity, they like to copy the dress, decoration besides food habits and the like. On off days these *rejas* are seen moving about in the village *haat*, *melas* and looking at different items of dress and decoration within their reach. The same *rejas*, who prior to taking to the job used to move about bare-footed in the market or the *haat*, were seen using plastic *chappals*, glass bangles, imitation of brass or silver made earrings, chains, etc. While on the jobs almost all the *rejas* look alike in respect of apparels they use but on week days the *rejas* differ from one another because of their different categories of working centres.

It is clear from the table-5 that the tribal *rejas* give a major portion of their income to their families. The highest contribution is made by the *rejas* who are engaged in brick-kilns. They contribute 80 percent of their total income to the family, though their income is lesser than those *rejas* who are engaged in other labour centres. But their expenditure on different items like clothes, cosmetics, entertainments, etc. are less than other *rejas* because the brick-kilns are situated in rural areas and the *rejas* have a less opportunity to come in contact with non-tribal population.

Coming to the *rejas* engaged in labour centres located in urban areas, they more or less try to live like non-tribal population but their desires and likes are restricted to their income. No doubt, some of the *rejas* were aware of the latest

TABLE–5

Average Annual Expenditure on Different Items of the Rejas Working at Different Labour Centres

	Labour centres	Total no. of *rejas* surveyed	Average annual income in Rs.	Expenditures on different items in Rs.							Average annual Expenditure in Rs.
				Contribution to family for food, house etc.	Refreshment etc,	Cosmetics	Clothes	Entertainment	Khaini/ Hanria etc.	Others	
1	2	3	4	5	6	7	8	9	10	11	12
1.	Construction work	100	172800	107136.00 (62%)	10368.00 (6%)	8640.00 (5%)	20736.00 (12%)	6912.00 (4%)	8640.00 (5%)	9504.00 (5.5%)	171936.00 (99.5%)
2.	Brick-kilas	80	80640	64512.00 (80%)	1612.80 (2%)	1612.80 (2%)	6451.20 (8%)	1612.80 (2%)	4838.40 (6%)	6451.20 (8%)	87091.20 (108%)
3.	Transportation	60	95040	57024.00 (60%)	5702.40 (6%)	5702.40 (6%)	13305.60 (14%)	4752 00 (5%)	6652.80 (7%)	3801.60 (4%)	96940.80 (102%)
4.	Industrial Complex	40	69120	51148.80 (74%)	2764.80 (4%)	2073.60 (3%)	6912.00 (10%)	1382.40 (2%)	2073.60 (3%)	5529.60 (8%)	71884.60 (104%)
5.	Miscellaneous	20	28800	21600.00 (75%)	576.00 (2%)	1152 00 (4%)	2880.00 (10%)	1152.00 (4%)	576.00 (2%)	1728.00 (6%)	29664.00 (103%)

modes of appliances like powder, snow, boroline and in some cases lip-sticks as well but they are handicapped due to their limited income. Moreover, their status (see Table—5) Page 104 varies from *reja* to *reja* in view of their economic condition as well as family back-grounds. For example, if there are more than one *reja* in a particular family their income is

Table—6

Average per capita per annum and per capita Daily Expenditure of the Rejas Working at Different Labour Centres

Sl. No,	Labour centres	Total no. of *rejas* surveyed	Per capita per annum expenditure in Rs.	Per capita daily expenditure in Rs.
1	2	3	4	5
1.	Construction work	100	1719.36	4.76
2.	Brick-kilns	80	1088.64	2.98
3.	Transportation work	60	1615.68	4.42
4.	Industrial complex	40	1797.12	4.92
5.	Miscellaneous	20	1483.20	4.06

naturally more than that of the family where there is only one *reja*, hence the standard of living will differ from family to family. In some cases it has also been seen that the *rejas* prefer to spend more on their dress and decoration rather than their food habits. It has been found that the *rejas* who are engaged in transportation of materials on trucks, spend 14 percent of their income on their clothes, 6 percent on cosmetics and refreshments, respectively, 7 percent on khaini/hanria etc. and 5 percent on their entertainments. They contribute 60 percent of their income to their families. It goes without saying that the urbanisation has actually left indelible impressions on the minds of the *rejas* as a sequel to which they have become more prone to modern ways of life. As regards the *rejas* who are engaged in construction works, their pattern of expenditure also shows that they spend more amount of their income upon them. They make contribution of 62 percent in their families for food and other domestic expenditure, and rest of the amount they spend upon themselves. The rejas, who are engaged in construction and transportation works, have more opportunities to move in urban areas than those who are engaged in brick-kilns, industrial complexes, etc. and their expenditures on clothes, refreshments, cosmetis, entertainments are more in comparison to other rejas.

The rejas engaged in labour centres in rural areas are fully satisfied with the sources of entertainments whatsoever available in the rural areas such as *melas*, *nautankis* etc. whereas those engaged in urban areas or on trucks delight themselves with latest movies, by occupying even cosy seats in modern cinema houses. But in any case they do not prefer to transgress the normal limits of their life and as far as practicable they believe in balanced budgets.

By going into the details of their standard of life, it has been marked that they hardly believe in borrowing from others which is regarded as a redeeming feature indeed, they actually believe in maintaining income and expenditure alike. In otheir words, they are so much conscious of their physical labours that they try to fulfil their desires by dint of their hard labour and strife. Nevertheless their incomes are so meagre that some of them are barely able to make the both ends meet. So far as amounts of savings are concerned, most of them are hardly in position to save out of their incomes for the future needs. But it may also be taken as granted that they hardly go in meeting their day to day expenses by incurring loans, on the contrary, they know how to adjust their requirements within their own means. Anyway in case of *rejas* engaged in construction works, somehow or the other, they are in a position to save to the extent of only. 5 percent of their income as is evident from the table--7. Further it is also evident from this table that a larger section of *rejas* deployed at other centres are more or less maintaining a deficit budget. It has been seen that generally the per capita income in most of the cases is not in tune with the prevailing needs as a sequel to which they are still living hand to mouth. In view of such meagre per capita income a family can hardly provide capital

Table—7

Saving pattern among the Tribal rejas

Sl. No.	Labour centre	Total no. of *rejas* surveyed	Average per capita perannum income in Rs.	Average per capita per annum expendi ture in Rs.	Annual saving in Rs.
1	2	3	4	5	6
1.	Construction work	100	1728	1719.36	– 8.64(–5%)
2.	Brick-kinl	80	1008	1088.64	–80.64(–8%)
3.	Transportation work	60	1594	1615.68	–21.68(—2%)
4.	Industrial complex	40	1728	1797.12	–69.12(–4%)
5.	Miscel-laneous	20	1440	1483.20	–43.20(–3%)

formation for future needs. In most of the cases the tribal populations are prone to drinking liquors, country wines, rice-beers (*hanria*) and such acts never help anyone forming capital, hence, the tribal population badly lacks in providing providence to their family members. From the very beginning, not to talk of *rejas* only, but the entire tribal population prefers to indulge in extravagance rather to frugality. Tribal *rejas* are also found spending their money on *khaini*, *hanria*, etc., as it is evident from their items of expenditure. The *rejas* engaged in transportation works spend 7 percent of their income on this item, followed by the *rejas* engaged in brick-kilns, who spend 6 percent of their income on this item. The *rejas* engaged in other labour centres are also spending their money on this item. Their other items of expenditure consist

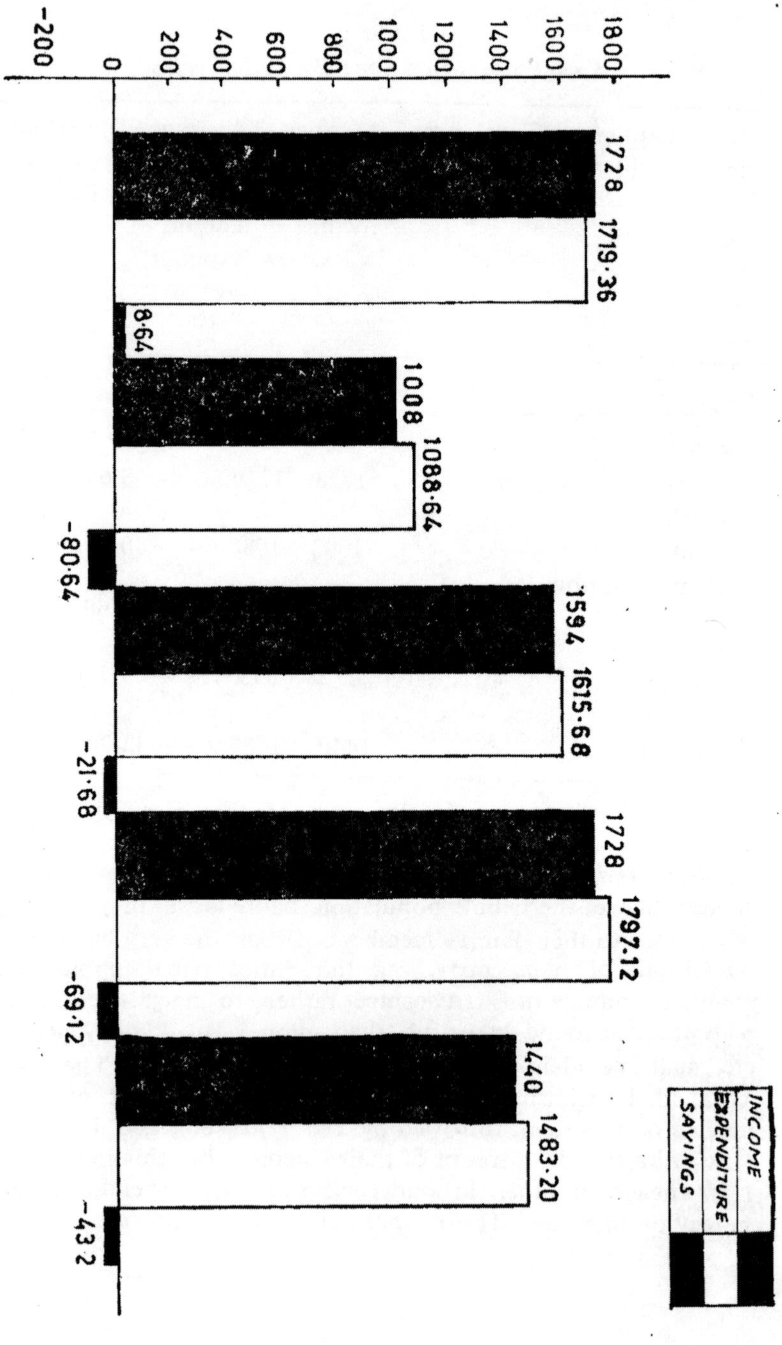
INCOME
EXPENDITURE
SAVINGS
1800
1600
1400
1200
1000
800
600
400
200
0
-200
1728
1719·36
8·64
1008
1088·64
-80·64
1594
1615·68
-21·68
1728
1797.12
-69·12
1440
1483·20
-43 2

of some occasional expenditures on birth, marriage, death, festivals, medicines etc. in their families.

In nutshell it can be concluded that the tribal *rejas* have been shunning altogether the habit of thrift and hoarding.

Dress and Decoration of the *Rejas*

It is evident from Table—5 that the tribal *rejas* spend a good amount of their income on their clothes and cosmetics. It has been observed that they are very much conscious in regard to their dress and decoration. As the concept of rejas as a profession has brought about a new dimension in the society, it is equally responsible for turning the general life culture, tradition, dress, decoration, aesthetic sense etc. in the life of the tribal rejas.

The tribal women before they took to the work of *rejas* were not only ill fed but were ill clad as well. They used to wear utmost coarse clothes as sarees without petticoats and blouses and were in habit of remaining topless but with the flow of income from the profession of the *rejas* their way of life took a sudden change having been influenced by the urbanisation as well as industrialisation. These working women called the *refas* are more or less living like non-tribal population so far as their dress and outfits are concerned. Their coarse sarees have been replaced by synthetic sarees worn on either printed or plain petti-coats together with matching coloured blouses over modern brassiers. The climate of Ranchi and the nearby areas force these tribal rejas to go in for synthetic clothes which are always looking crisp and tidy although braving rains and damp breezes. While dressing themselves with modern items such as ribbons, metal clips while parting and arranging hairs, tugging buds of flowers in their braids, they are very much particular about keeping always a comb to arrange their hairs very often. They are so much prone to modern fashion that they do not go without applying *kaajals*, in most cases matching with their skins, but over and above, they apply attractive as well as projecting *bindi* on their foreheads. Silver chains around their necks together with other garlands of stones and beads besides brass rings on fingers imitating like that of gold rings, often form the items of their decorations. When they are donned with such apparels and ornaments they do not forget to varnish their nails with glowing paints and apply fragrant powder, cheap snow, besides red lip-sticks. Chappals or sandles made of rubber or plastic are often used ' by them particularly when they are out on sight-seeing, visiting cinema houses, strolling in *meals*, marts and markets.

Although indulging in the filthy jobs none of them is seen in filthy clothes or garments, reason being that during leisure hours they clean their cl othes with the help of soaps. And in case of white garments they use indigo and tinopal to whiten them to the maximum and finally get them calendered by the washerman. But in most of the cases they prefer to go in for coloured and printed clothes, mostly synthetic ones which involve less of labour while washing.

While going to their jobs they tie around their loins coarse clothes or bed sheets which help protect their apparels from dust and filths. Similarly, those engaged for carrying loads on their heads, generally protect their hairs or clothes by covering their heads with coarse clothes like towels etc. Not only this, they are so much particular about their hair-style that they hardly allow them to get unruly even if they are engaged in physical labours and during the shortest span of leisure, they take out their combs and arrange their hairs quite afresh to be protected against dust with the help of scarfs, prominently seen around the necks of the *rejas* going on trucks. To summarize it, it can be said that the *rejas* are actually very much particular about their dresses and decorations.

Decoration does not mean decorating one's bod only but the act of decoration holds good in respect of decorating their hearths and homes alike. As far as practicable they try to keep their homes tidy, clean as well as well plastered, be it with clay only. By coming in contact with modern population they have started knowing the importance of cleanliness and are aware of the probable hazards of dirty way of living. The *rejas* who used to rush to the village *vaidya*, quake, *ojha*, now like to go to physicians, doctors and surgeons in the hour of needs. Thus, it can be said that they are now under full the influence of characteristics of modern age as well as modern way of life and like wise their society also is acquainted with these modern amenities although it is subject to availability in view of their capacity to pay for it.

Thus, summing up this chapter, we have examined different aspects of the roles played by the *rejas* in their families besides their social status in their families and in the society in all perspectives. We have also gone through the relevant changes brought about by these *rejas* in their families and society. Their income, expenditure, items of expenditure, dress and decoration have also been dealt with in detail. But the roles that the *rejas* actually play in their families, no doubt, on the one hand, lead to the betterment of entire family members but on the other, they may be responsible for some sorts of conflicts among themselves. The conflicts may be between the *rejas* and their parents as well as among other family members including their husbands, in-laws, brothers, sisters etc. which too shall be studied in the ensuing chapter so as to know the extent of stress and strains emerging out of the conflicts due to their professional activities. Secondly, we shall be coming to a conclusion with regard to their total adjustment with their own family members. Whether the conflict leads to their happiness or displeasures shall also be looked into by examining their attitude towards their members in their families. In respect of some cases the role conflict may lead to family break-up as well but can there not be a mutual understanding among them in case some sort of amicable settlement is arrived at ? However the next chapter, that we are going to deal with, will reflect some glaring instances of role-conflict among the *rejas*.

5

Role-Conflict among Tribal Reja

In the previous chapter we have discussed certain salient features of role of *reja* as an earning member in her family and also about her status as an individual in the society. It was found that for the purpose of totaladjustment in their family and society, the *rejas* have to unavoidably undergo certain stress and strains. Since the *rejas* have got to do certain specific jobs apart from their traditional duties they give way to cropping up the phenomenon of role conflict.

The role conflicts to which the Indian woman is exposed due to her entry into new spheres of life are above all inter role conflicts (Gross, Mc Eachern and Mason, 1957:288). These inter-role conflicts are caused by the acceptance of two (or still more) roles to which, according to definition, different sets of exploitations are directed, which cannot be avoided (Mies : 1980, 163). According to T. Parsons (1951 : 280-283) the conflicting sets of expectations are characterised by the fact that they are considered to be legitimate but the fulfilment of which is impossible in reality. He further explains in the following words :

> "It is necessary to compromise, that is, to sacrifice some at least of both sets of expectations or to choose one alternative and sacrifice the other. In any case the actor is exposed to negative sanctions and, so far as both sets of values are internalized, to internal conflict. There may, of course, be limited possibilities of transcending the conflict by redefining the situation, as well as of evasions as for example through secrecy and segregation of occasions."

This conflict situation exists objectively and is independent of whether the actors subjectively feel the external conflicts as internal frustration. In the present chapter we shall be dealing with these objective conditions as well as of the subjectively felt conflicts and strains in different stages and at various levels through which the *rejas* have to pass. An important question will be how far the tribal *rejas* feel an external conflict situation as also internally frustrating.

When both (or several) sets of conflicting expectations are institutionalised, they appear, according to Parsons, with a claim to legitimacy. This must intensify the ambivalence and the conflict, since one cannot disqualify any of the behaviour types that correspond to the one or the other set of expectations as deviant in the criminal sense (Parson, 176). This state of affairs is to be found clearly in the case of the tribal *rejas* for whom it has been observed that their families as well as profession of *rejas* are institutionalised legitimate role expectations. Among them the professional role of the women is also institutionalised due to economic crisis. Under the pressure of growing economic crisis many families expect of their women that they contribute to the maintenance of the family. This is also true of tribal families. In this way the pursuit of a profession by which woman acquires a *de facto* legitimacy, which results from a situation of economic necessity but which has not yet led to far-reaching ideological and structural changes. This situation is therefore particularly precarious for working women. They must work, but at the same time they must conform to an image of womanhood in which out of home economic activity of woman is considered to be degrading and immoral (Mies, 1980 : 164). The role conflicts of working women are caused not only by contradictory role expectations but more by structural obstacles. She is expected to contribute to maintenance of the family, but at the same time she is also expected to fulfil all family duties and abide by the rules of sex-segregation at her place of work.

The role conflict of working tribal women, therefore, results to a great extent from the clearage between the new social and economic goals and the rigid social structure, above the family structure which stands in the way of realization of these goals. The deviant behaviour of women is determined by the chasm between structures and institutions on the one hand and new social goals on the other.

Parsons concludes that in a situation of conflicting, legitimate and institutionalised role expectations, social sanctions and with that social control are eroded which ought to lead to social change. "Then on the one hand role conflict can be seen as to be very important as a sort of undermining of the motivational basis of an established order which includes the provision of motivationally acceptable alternatives." (Parsons, 276).

Here an attempt has also been made to emphasise that how the tribal *rejas* maintain a balance amidst various types of stress and strains generated from their role-conflicts both at their family level and job level. So far as different types of conflicts in the day to day life of the *rejas* are concerned, one will have to examine the stages at which their conflicts due to their different roles put them in various types of controversies.

Nature of Stress and Strains

It has been found that the tribal *rejas* are deployed at various labour centres in and around Ranchi town, engaged in different types of job. The *rejas* are deployed as full timers that means they have to devote their whole day in their duties. They remain busy in their jobs from morning till evening. It has been observed that the tribal *rejas* meet with various kinds of stress and strains at both levels, i.e., at the family level and at job level. As a matter of fact there are several types of stress and strains which keep the *rejas* always worried but they have no alternatives than to face them with certain amount of boldness otherwise they will have to do away with their jobs.

First of all the author would try to explain these stress and strains generated by their role-conflicts at both the levels respectively, then an attempt will be made to describe their mode of adjustment at different levels.

Conflicts at Family Level

The conflicting role expectations which the tribal *rejas* face are put forward by the persons who are of decisive importance in their family role set. The most important are those who have authority in the family i.e. father, mother, husband, parents-in-law, possibly also brothers and sisters. In nuclear households, mainly father and husband are important for women. They represent the family system externally and watch that the women do not deviate from the culturally accepted norms and behaviour. When a woman shows non-conforming behaviour, the negative sanctions of the larger society are first directed towards these members of the family. For fathers and husbands the family roles of the women have priority before all other roles which they may take up. Role-conflicts will not become manifest as long as the woman agrees to subordinate all other roles to the dominant family roles, i.e. as long as she does not put her profession above her duties as daughter, housewife, wife and mother. As soon as woman stops recognising the unconditional primacy of the family roles, and pursues her extra-familial activities independently of these roles, open conflicts between the woman and her family members are bound to emerge, which causes stress and strains to her.

The female members of the family after taking to the job of *rejas* have to be free from their domestic affairs to a very great extent. The affairs left over by those female members naturally fall back on the other members of that family; over and above their own duties. The other members of their families are none else than their own parents, brothers, sisters, husband, children etc. who have to share the burdens of the extra work abandoned by those switched over to the work of *rejas*.

It has been found during survey that 51 percent of the tribal *rejas* are living with their parents while 23 percent of them are living with their in-laws and 5.7 percent with their relatives. These *rejas* have to face less problem than those 20.3 percent *rejas* who are living with their husband in nuclear family or it would be better to say that the problem faced by them is of different nature than that of those *rejas* who are living with their parents, relatives and in-laws.

There is no denying the fact that generally people have developed a tendency of shirking from their own duties and on the other hand when they have to discharge the duties of some others also, they are a bit emerged within themselves. But because the left over jobs also form the part of the duties towards their own families they have no alternative other than to accept the responsibilities willingly or unwillingly. On the other hand, the *rejas* after discharging the whole day's works when get back to their home they often fall victim to the wraths of their family members arising out of some extra burdens discharged by them on behalf of the *rejas*. Thus the *rejas* have got to forbear such stress and strains for the time being and also for the day to follow when they have to report again for duties at different centres. Such a system continues for months together and the *rejas* have got to be attentive to their jobs despite such stress and strains, for their own as well as the benefit of their family members.

The study shows that about 75 percent *rejas* are facing this situation and they are working under such stress and strains. Out of these 75 percent *rejas*, 33.3 percent are living with their parents, 18.3 percent are living with their husbands, 20 percent are living with their in-laws and 3.4 percent are living with their relatives. Though they are not stopped by their guardians for working as *rejas*, still they have to face the wrath of people. Since the *rejas* are supporting their guardians economically, their guardians do not stop them, on the contrary, they expect traditional roles also from the *rejas* which the *rejas* cannot do full justice to, hence, the wrath of guardians. From the following table-1 one can have a figurative account of the Role-conflict among the tribal *rejas* with their family members.

Table—1

A Figurativ? Account of the Role-conflict among the Tribal Rejas with their Family Members

Sl. No.	*Rejas* living with whom	Total No. of *Rejas*	No. of *Rejas* facing Role conflict	Percentage
1	2	3	4	5
1.	Parents	153	100	33.3
2.	Husbands	61	55	18.3
3.	In-laws	69	60	20
4.	Relatives	17	10	3.4
	Total :	300	225	75

The *rejas*, due to the nature of their job and domestic duties, have to live in somewhat different way in comparison to their other family members. They have to dress themselves in a more tidy way than other non-*rejas* women because while on work they have to be more tidy and smart otherwise they may have to lose their job. In case they look dirty and unsmart their services also may be dispensed with by their employers because every employer has a tendency to engage good looking, smart and well dressed *rejas*. This has been very minutely observed by the author at various working centres visited in course of the research work. In this case it becomes the primary duty of the *rejas* to keep themselves always smart for which they have to spend some more money on themselves which pinches their family members to a great extent, and, hence the scuffles, at times, ensue among their family members. On one hand, the family members of the *rejas* expect good amount from the working *rejas* but, on the other they do not like that the *rejas* should spend more on them on different items of dress and decorations. Such feelings at family levels bring about a tussle among the members of the family which cause a great trauma and mental excruciation. When the rejas feel some difficulties in adjusting with their family members, they start defying the opinion of others in their family and stick to their own wishes and desires which ultimately lead to a great strain on personal level also. The *rejas* with a view to earning more money have got to flout the instructions of their elders in their family also as they pay much more attention to their earnings rather than to the feelings expressed by their family members. But even if they flout or defy the feelings or the opinions of their family members their minds are always haunted with the agonies caused due to stress and strains in the family. It is mostly found in the case of unmarried *rejas* who are supporting their parents. Such *rejas* want to spend some amount of their income on their dress and decoration whereas their parents are only interested in their money, hence, the tussle starts.

Sometimes it so happens that due to certain reasons the *rejas* have got to do some more jobs than their normal working hours due to certain emergencies and as such they are not in a position to get back to their home in time. Had it been a single instance it could be ignored but for days together they have to remain engaged in some extra jobs which do not allow them to return homes in time. It happens in the case of those 33.3 percent *rejas* who are engaged in construction works or with those *rejas* also who are engaged in brick-kilns and transportation of material. The *rejas* who are engaged in building construction works, they have to often work more than the normal period, specially then when they are engaged in casting of the roof of the building. The author has observed them working even at late night also. Likewise, the *rejas* engaged in transportation work are also seen working and moving on trucks at night for meeting the pressing demand of the building materials. At this their family members fly into passion and start hurling abuses on them even despite explaining by the *rejas* the valid reasons for their late return after day's works. But the family members hardly believe them and they start suspecting their integrity and character. Such sort of suspicion causes much stress and strains among the *rejas*.

Conflicts at Job Level

Over and above the conflicts faced at family level, the *rejas* are subjected to stress and strains even at job level also. Instances have come to our notice that the *rejas* have faced much stress and strains even while working at different labour centres. At a particular centre it was seen that a *reja* was looking dejected and dismayed because she was asked to do more labour than her colleague who was alleged to be a favourite of the employer or the *munshi.* When some extra favour is done by the employers to certain *rejas* due to their whims the *rejas* subjected to a step-motherly treatment feel greatly insulted, distressed and disappointed and frustrations engulf them for no fault of theirs. About 80 percent of the *rejas* under study were found to be under stress and strains because of the differential and preferential treatment of their employers with the *rejas* working together. Had they been not affected by such stress and strains they could discharge their duties more freely and efficiently which would undoubtedly go in the interest of fetching more wages.

The *rejas* sometime hardly react to the differential and preferential treatment by adopting a lukewarm attitude by their employers while on their respective jobs but they are so much under the influence and control of their employers that they cannot afford to do anything substantial by way of harming their employer. Thus, their suppressed feelings within themselves grew a good deal of strains among them. At sometimes it has also been observed that some particular *reja* is favoured much by the employers in comparison to the others and the employers, at times, having been pleased with such favourite *reja*, gives some presentation in shape of cash rewards, attractive *sarees* and other kinds of gift items. When this information spreads among other *rejas*, they become much distressed and feel like doing some harms to the employers but they are so innocent and helpless that though willing, they cannot translate their feelings into action. They, no doubt, envy the lots of such favourite *rejas* and sometime in course of their chit-chats they cut some jokes with their colleagues for their privileged position. They might be undergoing agonies and anguish over the unjustified behaviour of their employers but circumstances hardly permit them to react.

It has also been observed that due to arbitrary attitude of their employers, the *rejas* have got to undergo certain stress and strains, for example, if a *reja* has got some urgent work to attend to at her home and if she abstains herself from duty, not only her day's wage will be cut, she is even rebuked for remaining absent. This high-handedness on the part of the employees is enough to arouse strains among them. In some of the cases if the *rejas* have not reported for duty due to some urgent works at their homes, their wages are not only denied to them but they are replaced by some other *rejas*. Thus the insecurity of jobs among the *rejas* is a very important aspect for causing stress and strains at job level. The work of the *rejas* is on one hand no doubt a remunerative one, but on the other, it causes much stress and strains in *rejas* personal life. The working condition itself is such that the *rejas* can hardly always maintain the sanctity of devoted wives, mothers, daughters etc., for they have to be much more sincere towards their jobs, the employers, the headmen etc. rather than their husbands, children and other members of the family. The *rejas* know it well that they can very well adjust with their family members despite certain diversities in their lives but they can hardly pull on with their employers, headmen etc. in adverse situation. So long as the *rejas* are on their jobs they have to abide by the likes and dislikes of their masters. The charm of earning money for the betterment of the family is such that the *rejas* have to forego their own likes and dislikes and yield to the wishes of their employers. Thus this sort of sacrifices of their freedom, independence, likes and dislikes are valid reasons to bring stress and strains in their personal life and often lead towards various types of exploitation.

Conflicts at the Individual Level

The tribal *rejas* have to suffer with stress and strains even at the individual level because all such stress and strains which they face due to their role conflicts at family level and at job level, lead towards the stress and strains at the individual level.

At family level when they find that they are not doing justice with their families they develop sort of guilty feeling among themselves and if they fail to be successful at their working centres, they find themselves in a much depressing situation. Most of the tribal women take up the job of *rejas* due to economic reasons. But in this process they have to accord more preference either to family or job, and naturally between these two, their jobs have got priority. As they prefer to earn some money than to face situation, their economic necessity often leads them towards their exploitation, both social and economic and even physical. Due to ignorance, illiteracy and their simpleton nature and high aspiration, they often succumb to the desires of their employers or contractors. All such behaviour of their masters which they do not expect cause stress and strains in the individual's psychology. In such conditions they try to keep simply mum lest it would be difficult to work as *rejas*.

Process and Extent of Adjustment

We have so far seen that the *rejas* have to sacrifice their wishes, likes and dislikes at the altar of their jobs. This act of theirs must be regarded as the sincere efforts towards bringing about adjustment and adherence to the jobs assigned to them. They not only try their utmost to adjust with their family members only but to occupy a respectful position in their own society as well. Not to talk of all alike but in most of the cases the *rejas* are seen making frantic efforts to effect adjustment either with the employers or with their own near and dear ones. May be in some cases the *rejas* do prefer to adhere to their own wishes, likes and dislikes but it cannot be generalizcd. Examples have come to our notice also that some of the *rejas* who could not adjust either in their families or with their employers, got compelled to leave their hearths and homes as well and eloped with some other unknown persons. But such examples are a few and far between. The causes for such elopement are mostly attributed to their stress and strains at family as well as at individual level rather than to avarice for a new way of life ahead (for detail see appendix No. B-6).

Family Life

So far as their adjustment in family life is concerned, one will have to at first examine the residential pattern of the tribal *rejas*. Some *rejas*, though married, are living with their parents and some live with their husbands and in-laws. In the third instance it has also been observed that some of the married *rejas* are living only with their husbands and children and none else. Thus, one will have to examine all these three patterns of residence for understanding the process and extent of adjustment.

The married *rejas* who live with their parents have to face somewhat more stress and strains in comparison to the unmarried ones. The unmarried ones have to be responsible to their parents anly, but the married ones are accountable to their parents as well as their husbands alike, and, hence, shoulder greater burden, The unmarried *rejas* when subjected to such stress and strains at their family level, somehow or other have to pull on with their family members even under strained circumstances, but the married ones who cannot overcome the stress and strains, think of deserting their parents and living with their husbands at altogether a different place. One can now well imagine the role of conflict in the life of *rejas* at their family level and think of their anguish which at times is responsible to bring about a total break-up in the family if they fail to adjust with their families (for detail see appendix No......... B-4).

Similarly, the *rejas* who are living with their husbands and children alone, are also confronted with various types of problem in respect of adjustment in their family life. Out of 99 (33%) married *rejas*, 61 (20.3%) *rejas* were found living with their husbands and children in the nuclear families. The work of the *rejas*, so to say, is a non-sedentary occupation during which no *reja* can attend to her domestic work. Under the circumstances of heavy work in distant places the children of the *rejas* at home are either looked after by their fathers or by other elder members; may be the elder brothers or sisters. But in such cases it goes without saving that proper care can not be bestowed upon the children in absence of their mothers. Hence, difficulty in total adjustment in their own families. Out of 61 married *rejas* who are living with their husbands, 38(62.3%)*rejas* accepted that they are working as *rejas* after neglecting their home and children. Even though they rise early in the morning to prepare food for their husbands and children, they cannot devote proper time in their look after. They come to their working centres leaving them behind at the mercy of God. In case of small children, the rejas were seen carrying their babies while on way to their work sites and again they carry them back at the close of the day's work. While on the one hand, the *rejas* are inclined to do their jobs sincerely, on the other, their minds are preoccupied with the personal liabilities which they owe to their kith and kins and hence the hardship in respect of adjustment.

Apart from this, owing to their engagements either in their jobs or in domestic affairs, they are sometimes required to attend to some social functions as well. But it so happens that they hardly get time to be present on such occasions which at sometimes prove hurdles in respect of their adjustment to their own society. In their own society also, those who do not take up the job of *rejas*, hardly lay to understand their difficulties. The tribal *rejas* have to work on daily wages and their wages are not so high to enable them to avoid their duties to fulfil their socio-economic obligations, and hence they prefer their jobs to such social functions. But people seldom bother to know the reality and unnecessarily blame the *rejas* (Details of wages have been discussed in the Chapter IV).

Generally all the the *rejas*, though working at different labour centres, get weekly holidays and they try to fulfil all their obligations on that very day. *Rejas*, whether they are unmarried or married, living with their parents or husbands or relatives, try to compensate their week long due works. At that day they work as daughters, wife, mother, daughter-in-law and so on in their respective families.

Coming to adjustment with the family members, husbands, children, parents or in-laws, besides other members in the family, we see that the *rejas* owe certain specific duties towards each of them equally. Because besides being *rejas* they are mothers, sisters, daughters and daughter-in-laws also as such the *rejas* have got to serve all of her family members in different capacities. But when her work schedule does not permit them to do full justice to her responsibilities towards their families they suffer with stress and strains and face difficulties in maintaining proper adjustment in their families. Almost all the family members remain always in tension as a request to which a sort of bickerings are always prevalent in the families.

The husbands of the *rejas*, though employed or unemployed, like to pass some leisure hours with their wives who are working as *rejas* at some centres. Having been fully engaged in their jobs, the *rejas* can hardly please their spouses and thus a sort of tension prevails in husbands and wives which disturbes their family life altogether. It is evident from the table–2 that 11 percent of the *rcjas* studied, are separated or divorced and the main reason behind their divorce was failure in adjusting with their husbands.

Table–2

The reasons and Number of Divorced/Separated rejas

Sl. No.	Number of Rejas	Percentage	Reasons of divorce/separation
1	2	3	4
1.	16	5.3	Lack of adjustability with their husbands due to neglect of household activities.
2.	14	4.7	Suspicion on their character.
3.	3	1	More income than husband
Total	33	11	

It is clear that the actual conduct of the working women in the situation of tension created by conflicting role demands are determined not only by external circumstances, but also as much, if not more, by the way in which they themselves and their family members interpret and evaluate this situation.

The reaction of a *reja* in a conflict situation is therefore dependent, among others, on whether her own ideas, attitudes and concepts regarding her economic activities agree with the ideas, concepts and attitudes of those members of her role set, whose opinion is important for her. For this reason the question of congruence or non-congruence of ideas and attitudes of husband and wife towards her economic activities becomes one of vital importance. Conflicts between husband and wife at the level of ideas and attitudes flare up particularly on the question of priority of professional or family roles of the woman. When the professional roles of women get priority, husbands cannot adjust in such situation and hence the case of divorce comes in light. 4.7 percent of the *rejas* have been divorced due to suspicion on their characters. The deviation from the social norms governing the behaviour of *rejas* in public, especially from the mixing taboo-an unavoidable consequence of the activities of women as members of a profession—has proved to be one of the most critical factors in the garb of contradictory role expectations. The breaking of the mixing taboo is, however, not an isolated factor that in itself leads to conflicts between the women and her guardians, it is rather part of a whole complex of conflicts as we could gather from the various individual cases. It seems that the social prejudice against mixing is made use of mainly by those husbands whose wives have acquired an added dose of self confidence through their independent economic position and do not any more accept, without question, the traditional pattern of authority in the family. Reproaches against the "bad character" of "working wife", against their coquetry and the insinuation that they amuse themselves with their superiors and colleagues are made in such cases, where the husbands have lost the intra-family patriarchal control over their wives. These suspicions against her character are a last means of winning back this control (see appendix No. B-8)

Similary, the *rejas* owe certain responsibilities towards their parents and in-laws which are also expected by either of them to be fulfilled without fail. But having been engaged in their non-sedentary occupation, the *rejas* are not in a position to please them, and, thus, they invite the wraths of their superiors in the families.

While studying this particular aspect of role conflict, it can be well said that the *rejas*, although being the female members of the families, have got to discharge the responsibilities towards their family members just like the male members of the family. The old, the sick, the handicapped all alike expect proper cares and service from the *rejas* as they are more or less treated at par with the male members of the family. In case some other relatives of the *rejas* join them for a while the relations expect some more time towards them by the *rejas* which is not possible in view of their engagements. In such cases their relations, when back to their pavilions, convey their heartfelt agonies at the behaviour of the *rejas*, members of family to other in the vicinity which ultimately tells upon the social status of the *rejas*.

In nutshell, it can be adduced that the *rejas* have to undergo profound stress and strains while making adjustments amidst their family members. This is so because the roles expected of them remain unfulfilled owing to attaching more priority to the economic activities which they become bound to pursue for smooth maintenance of their family. It has been found that the *rejas* who could not maintain balance amidst prevailing stress and strains became mad (for detail see appendix No. B-9).

Despite the stress and strains that the tribal *rejas* have to go in their life, both at family and job level, they have no way out other than to compromise with the prevailing situation and circumstances, unless and until one peeps into the lives of the *rejas* at a very close range, they would reflect a picture of very cheerful rural folk busy, indulging in merry makings during leisures and always chirping like birds, either when trekking the distance or going on trucks. It has been very closely observed that despite various diversities in life, the *rejas* are still happier than any other class of working women. It seems, as if, happiness is the real motto of their life.

In this chapter we have studied the different aspects of role conflicts in the life of the *rejas* at various levels and these levels were examined very critically with an eye to the stress and strains that the *rejas* actually have to undergo in life. It is needless to say that the *rejas* are also just like other teeming millions of our country who have to suffer all sorts of mental tortures termed as stress and strains which affect their total adjustment in their families. we have also seen the consequences arising out of the role conflict either at family or job or personal level which cause unnecessary tension among one another in the family.

Thus after dealing with the role-conflicts in the life of the *rejas*, in the forthcoming chapter we shall look into the changing values as well as the sources of recreation etc. in the life of the *rejas*. The occupational or role conflict, whatever we may call it, has brought about a very remarkable change in the values and recreational aspects of the life of the *rejas* which ultimately is responsible for altogether change in the modes of the living of the *rejas*. Now we shall have to throw light on the changing modes of the life of the *rejas* which they have ultimately adopted by means of their occupation.

6

Some Changing Dimensions of the Tribal Rejas

In the previous chapter we have discussed about the different types of role conflict among the tribal *rejas* and their adjustments with the different members of their family and society. It is clear by now that the *rejas* have to come in contact with various persons in regard to their job. They get opportunities to move in the societies and watch the various activities going on in the town. They come in contact with non-tribal population of the town and the process of acculturation starts. Acculturation refers to that process of cultural contact in which more or less continuous contact between two or more groups results in one groups taking over elements of the culture of other group or groups. It is seen that when a person comes in contact with different types of persons continuously, one will try to learn certain things of others and its impact will be seen on one's personality. The profession of *rejas* is itself an outcome of industrialisation and urbanisation which have been the major factors for bringing about changes in socio-cultural life of the tribals. Professor Vidyarthi (1968) in his excellent survey article on culture change in tribes of modern India has delineated two sets of processes operating in acculturative situations viz., traditional and modern. The former refers to those which are in operation since long and under this are included processes of Hinduisation and revitalization. On the other hand, the modern processes include factors like Christianity, industrialisation, urbanisation, community development schemes, democratic experiments, communication and administration. These two sets of processes may also be termed as intrinsic and extrinisic factors of cultural change. Apart from being tribal belt of Bihar, Chotanagpur also happens to be the industrial heart of Bihar. Because of the availability of natural resources such as coal, iron, mica and other minerals, and also of forests, some significant large scale industries found their base in parts of Chotanagpur. An industry demands a good amount of skilled and non-skilled labour force. The tribals close to an industrial locale fulfil the required need of labour force. This has resulted in large and small scale migration to the industrial places. Industrialisation ultimately gives rise to growth and spread of the urban areas. The latter include development of towns, cities and cosmopolitan areas. With the continuous attack of urban and industrial influence a change is taking place in tribals towards social institution and personal make-up. Due to industrialisation marked changes have occurred in material and non-material aspects of the tribal culture. In the present chapter an attempt has been made to throw light on some changing dimensions of the tribal *rejas*.

Societies, like all phenomena, are influenced by forces that inevitably cause them to change. The humane composition of societies changes over time, technologies expand, material equipment changes, ideologies and values take on new components, and institutional functions and structures undergo reshaping. No society remains completely static because it exists in a universe of dynamic influence, the reaches of which become steadily greater. The tempo and extent of change vary, of course, from society to society. (Anderson and Parker, 1964 : 384).

Among the tribal rejas also marked changes have taken place in both the material and non-material aspects of culture. "The material aspects of culture include those human products that can be experienced with the senses....The wide variety of these material elements may be partially grasped by examining the catalogue of a mail-order house. Here are displayed thousands of individual components of the most materialistic culture which the world has ever seen. The non-material culture includes the group expectations, the folkways, technique ways, mores, values, traditions, and all other psychological elements that arise out of social life. The fundamental basis of culture is found in the minds of men, not in external manifestations. Ideas are the real foundation of culture." (Merrill and Eldridge, 1952 : 42-43).

Changes in Living Conditions :

It has been observed that urbanisation and industrialisation have greatly influenced the living conditions of the triabal *rejas* of Ranchi who chiefly come from the Oraon and the Munda tribes, besides a little from the Lohra community as well. While studying their living conditions it has been noted that the houses of the tribal *rejas* are of traditional styles but many of the items relating to household have got changed. The author had several occasions to peep into their houses and in course of that it could be noticed that there were sleeping cots, and in some cases wooden or iron chairs, factory built umbrellas instead of their traditional umbrellas made of bamboos, kerosin oil tin lamps in place of *dhibris* or *diyas*, metal utensils including buckets were, available in most of the houses. Some of the *rejas* were found more inclined towards fancy goods such as torches, cheap radios, goggles, etc. Most of the *rejas* are now-a-days like glass bangles in place of lac bangles or even their traditional heavy brass ornaments. Not only this, cheap variety of shoes, sleepers, plastic *chappals*, combs, soaps, cream and powder have become almost essential items to be used by them almost regularly. Likewise their dreses and decorations have not remained untouched with the impact of modernisation as a sequel to which they have almost forsaken their traditional dresses and instead they have donned modern dresses consisting of *sarees*, blouses, brassiers, petticoats, ribbons etc. Even in the families of these tribal *rejas* there are some old men and women, who still believe in their traditional way of life, hence they do wear their traditional apparels which are nothing but merely small pieces of clothes termed as loin clothes. But the tribal *rejas* have changed a lot. They have also developed a tendency to wear cheap brass made ornaments like chains, earrings, hair clips etc. On festival occasions these tribal *rejas* remain in gay mood and spend their days in merry-making donning colourful garments. A few of them have started using cheap lipsticks also (details have been discussed in Chapter IV entitled "*Rejas* as Earning Members in the Family).

Similarly a lot of non-material changes have also occurred in the life of the *rejas*. Although this distinction between the material and non-material elements of culture is in one sense valid, the two, in another sense, are so dependent upon each other that the one cannot be thought of independently of the other. These material aspects of culture might be termed cultural instruments, since their use, which is made of such artifacts, is the important consideration. It is largely determined by ideas and values, the non-material aspect of culture. Among the tribal *rejas* changes are reflected in their behaviour attitudes, temperament, etc.

Changes in Behaviour

Prior to becoming *rejas*, the village *belles* used to behave in a very rustic way as if they were quite unfamiliar to the present day society. But soon after their taking to the work of *rejas* they, by virtue of coming closer to all sorts of people, learnt a lot from them and they moulded their ways of life accordingly. Now-a-days they have been observed behaving in more sophisticated ways. When they go to witness movies, or go to hotels, circus etc. they behave like non-tribal population. While discussing about their relationships with their employers, and associates, we have noticed that their employers and associates are of opinions that the tribal *rejas* are well behaved. They behave according to the accepted norms of the societies. Societies operated through their structural components according to norms – accepted standards for individual and group behaviour.

Moreover, it has also been noticed that unlike their parents or some old members in their families the tribal *rejas* speak non-tribal language. Even among their own societies a remarkable change is nothing but their language. Their associates or the employers have now no difficulty in negotiating with them in their own language as the *rejas* have adapted themselves to the changing circumstances by and by. Remarkable changes have also been noticed among the *rejas* in respect of their religious norms also. Those who are in contact with the Hindu society have been greatly influenced by the Hinduism. Even Christian *rejas* are also seen using glass bangles around their wrists and putting vermilion like Hindu ladies. When asked, they replied that being Catholic they have no bar in following the sophisticated ways and styles of the society prevalent around them.

Their behaviour in respect of other cultural activities has also shown much changes. The tribal *rejas* who previously used to dance and sing quite regularly even on non-festive occasions, are now adopting a lukeworm attitude towards their traditional dances regularly. But this may differ from those *rejas* who have still been living far from the din and bustles of urbanisation, for they are still more prone to their traditional ways of life than those living near urban population.

Changes in Opinions and Attitudes

Great changes are also noticed in their opinions and attitudes. Previously they used to hesitate and get shy in coming closer to non-tribals population or even talking to them. Even today in far flung area of Ranchi the author had to face a queer situation when the tribals in that area were seen fleeing away for fear of talking to her. On the other hand the *rejas* residing in that area came forward smilingly and replied up to the author's satisfaction. Marked differences were noticed in the attitudes of the *rejas* in comparison to their other co-villagers.

Attitude towards Modernity: The attitudes of *rejas* towards learning things of modern era have changed to this extent that they are much more fascinated to remain always in contact with non-tribals so as to enable themselves to copy their sophisticated ways of daily life. They try to mould their children as well as other family members according to the modern ways of living. Table-1 shows the different attitudes of tribal *rejas* towards modern ways of life. Most of the tribal rejas are in favour of modern ways of life as 69.3 percent *rejas* voted in its favour. Though their economic conditions

Table—1

Attitude of Tribal Rejas towards Modernity

Sl. No.	Total no. of rejas surveyed	attitudes towards modernity		
		in favour	against	Not replied
1	2	3	4	5
1	300	208	56	36
	Percentage	69.3%	18.7%	12%

hardly permit them to follow all the modern ways and style of life but they do not think it bad. They want to follow it. But 18.7 percent *rejas* are not in favour of modern ways of life wheras 12 percent *rejas* did not reply.

Attitude towards treatment of disease: When they were asked about the treatment of their diseases, majority of them preferred to be treated by doctors. Table-2 shows their

Table—2

Attitude towards Treatment of Disease

Sl. No.	Total no. of *Rejas* surveyed	Go to Ojha/ Indigenous treatment	Go to doctors	Both
1	2	3	4	5
1	300	45	182	73
	Percentage	15%	60.7%	24.3%

preferences of treatment. According to this table 60.7 percent *rejas* prefer doctors to *ojhas* and indigenous treatment, whereas 15 percent *rejas* are still going to *ojhas* and believe in indigenous treatments. There are also some *rejas* who go to the doctors and the *ojhas* both. When they feel that the *ojhas* or indigenous treatments are not capable to cure the disease they rush to the doctors for better treatment. But the majority of them prefer modern ways of treatment, they do not want to take risk in this regard. The *rejas* who are residing in rural areas, working in brick-kilns, etc. have shown the tendency of being treated by traditional styles. Hence, a change has been seen in their attitude. Previously they believed in their old traditional ways to the extent that even in case of sickness or ailments they deemed it proper to go to village *ojha* for treatment but now the situation has changed and they prefer to be treated by doctors.

Attitude towards Education : The most noticeable change among the tribal *rejas* is this that they now believe in imparting education to their children but previously they were opposed to it. We have found that above 80 percent of the tribal rejas surveyed, are quite illiterate even through they are in favour of literacy. Table-3 shows different attitudes of tribal *rejas* towards literacy. It shows that 76 percent of the *rejas* are in favour of education, whereas 15.7 percent *rejas* did not

Table—3

Attitude towards Education

Sl. No.	Total no. of *Rejas*	No. of *Rejas* in favour of education	No. of *Rejas* against education	Did not reply
1	2	3	4	5
1	300	228	47	25
	Percentage	76%	15.7%	8.3%

show their interest in education. They think that education will debar their children to take up the job of labourers, which is their main occupation. When their children would be educated they will prefer to be engaged in white-collared jobs which is of course herculean task. But those whc are in favour of education, think that education will give more opportunities to their children and majority of the rejas are of such opinions.

Attiiude towards Religion : Table-4 shows the attitude of tribal *rejas* towords religion. Though 88.7 percent *rejas* believe in God they are not superstitious. Beliefs that are not based on facts are superstitious. They generally arise out of sheer ignorance and fear of the unknown. The *rejas* who have faith in God say that all things in the world depend on God hence they all are living on the mercy of God.

Table—4
Attitude towards Religion

Sl. No.	Total no. of *Rejas*	No. of *Rejas* believing in God	No. of *Rejas* not believing in God	Not replied
1	2	3	4	5
1	300	265	25	9
Precentage		88.7%	8.3%	3%

Although they have belief in God, they are not seen worshipping idols of God anywhere. As regards this particular aspect they follow their traditional way. *Karma* and *Sarhul* festivals are still observed by them with gaiety just like other tribal population. Besides this, on the occasion of *Dussehra, Dipawali, Holi*, etc. they participate in the festivities ungrudgingly and enjoy the fun mirthfully.

Attitude towards Marriage : As to their attitude towards marriage the table-5 shows that over 91 percent *rejas* admit the propriety of marriage, whereas only 5 percent of them are opposed to marriage, for they prefer to lead independent life rather to be under the clutches of somebody else. Only 3.3 percent smiled out and kept mum over the issue of marriage.

Although there is no hard and fast rule towards the age for the marriage, they prefer to go in for marriage only when they actually come of age as is evident from the table-6.

Table—5

Attitude towards Marriage

Sl. No.	Total no. of *Rejas* surveyed	In favour of Propriety of Marriage	In favour of Impropriety of Marriage	Did not reply
1	2	3	4	5
1	300	275	15	10
	Percentage	91.7%	5%	3.3%

But in some cases they have to abide by the decisions taken by their parents in respect of the marriage of the *rejas* at their childhood. But majority of the *rejas* prefer the marriageable age between 21-25 as it is evident from the table-6 that 59.3 percent *rejas* are of such opinions.

Table—6

Attitude towards Age of Marriage

Sl. No.	Total no. of *Rejas* surveyed	Marriageable Age 10-15	16-20	21-25	26-30	Not Replied
1	2	3	4	5	6	7
1	300	5	58	178	44	15
	Percentage	1.7%	19.3%	59.3%	14.7%	5%

Attitude towards Love Marriage : When asked about their attitude towards love-marriage, 52.7% *rejas* voted in favour of this whereas 32 percent are against love-marriages. 15.3 percent *rejas* remained mum over this issue. Table-7 shows the attitude of tribal *rejas* towards love-marriages. Though 52.7 percent *rejas* are in favour of this, they are also of the opinion that marriage should be performed according to traditional style. Parents' consent should be respected.

Table—7
Attitude towards love-marriage

Sl. No.	Total no. of *Rejas*	No. of *Rejas* in favour of love-marriage	No. of *Rejas* against love marriage	Not replied
1	2	3	4	5
1	300	158	96	46
	Percentage	52.7%	32%	15.3%

Attitude towards Premarital/Extramarital Relationship : It has been found that the *rejas* are very free and frank in their behaviour. They prefer modern styles of life. We have also found some cases of elopement of *rejas* with their employers and associates but when they were asked about their attitude towards premarital and extra marital relationship, a large percentage of *rejas* voted in against of such practices.

Table 8
Attitude towards Premarital/ Extra marital relationship

Sl. No.	Total No. of *Rejas*	No. of *Rejas* in favour	No. of *Rejas* against	Not replied
1	5	3	4	5
1	300	11	232	57
	Percentage	3.7%	77.3%	19%

It is clear from the table 8 that 77.3 percent *rejas* are against of such things whereas 19 percent *rejas* did not reply on this issue. Only 3.7 percent *rejas* are in favour.

Attitude towards Family Planning :— As regards their attitude towards size of family and family planning, majority of *rejas* are in favour of small family. It is shown in the table—9 that 85 percent of *rejas* are in favour of small family whereas only 15 percent of *rejas* are in favour of large family. As

Table—9

Attitude towards Size of Family

Sl. No.	Total No. of *Rejas*	Small family	Large family
1	2	3	4
1	300	255	45
	percentage	85%	15%

many as 72.7 percent *rejas* believe in planning their family as depicted in the table—10. 18.3 percent *rejas* are not in favour

Table—10

Attitude towards Family Planning

Sl. No.	Total No. of *Rejas*	In favour of family planning	Against family planning	Did not reply
1	2	3	4	5
1	300	218	55	27
	percentage	72.7%	18.3%	9%

of family planning because they are of the opinion that the bigger the size of their family the larger will be the prospects of working hands in the family, whereas the *rejas* who are in favour of family planning are of opinion that better education and living amenities can be provided to children and other family members in a small family. However, 9 percent *rejas* were keeping mum.

Attitude towards Divorce/Separation :—When we look at the marital status of the tribal *rejas*, we find that 11 percent of them are either divorced or separated. But when they were asked regarding their attitude towards this particular aspect 59.3 percent *rejas* were found in favour of divorce/separation on reasonable ground. This type of attitude they developed within themselves because of their economic independence. They are of opinion that the old days have changed now and there

Table—11

Attitude towards Divorce/Separation

Sl. No.	Total No. of *rejas*	In favour of divorce	Against divorce	Not Replied
1	2	3	4	5
1	300	178	87	35
	percentage	59.3%	29%	11.7%

is no time for them to be slaves of their husbands. If they are failing to adjust with their husbands, then there is no propriety in living with them. But 29 percent *rejas* believe that divorce/separation is bad, whereas 11.7 percent *rejas* did not reply.

Attitue towards inter Caste Marriage :—Regarding this aspect, 55.3 percent *rejas* have voted against it because they think that they will lose their status in the society. Some of them said that if the male members of society would marry outside their caste, there would be no objection over this but when they would do so, they would be subjected to the Wrath of their family as well as society. However, 21 percent *rejas* do not consider it bad. A large number of *rejas* i.e. 23.7 percent did not want to express their ideas over this issue.

Table—12

Attitude towards inter-Caste Marriage

Sl. No.	Total no. of *Rejas*	In favour	Against	Not replied
1	2	3	4	5
1	300	63	166	71
	percentage	21%	55.3%	23.7%

Changes in recreation :—The betterment brought about in their economic life has also provided them the opportunities to have recreations by way of visiting *Melas, haats*, witnessing movies, circus, etc. alongwith their colleagues and companions. As shown in Table—13, 37.3 percent *rejas* are interested in witnessing movies. Although 35 percent *rejas* accepted that they did not witness movies though they preferred to witness it. They are handicapped due to their economic conditions and also they have no time due to their busy working schedules. Generally the *rejas* who are engaged in construction and transportation works get time and opportunities to go to cinema houses as most of them are unmarried also. They go there in the companies of other *rejas*. However, 27.7 percent *rejas* are not interested in moview.

Table—13

Number of Rejas who Witness Movies

Sl. No.	Total no. of rejas	No. of *rejas* who witness movies	No. of *rejas* who do not witness movies	Not interrested
1	2	3	4	5
1	300	112	105	83
	percentage	37.3%	34%	27.7%

Table—14 shows the number of *rejas* who listen to radios. Now-a-days radios are not uncommon in tribal areas. 32.7 percent *rejas* listen to radios regularly whereas 38.3 percent

Table—14

Number of Rejas who Listen Radio

Sl. No.	Total no. of *rejas*	No. of *rejas* who listenradio		
		Regularly	Sometimes	Never
1	2	3	4	5
1	300	98	115	87
	percentage	32.7%	38.3%	29%

listen to radios sometimes and 29 percent are not interested in listening to radios at all. Generally they prefer to listen to folk-songs and film-songs played on radios.

Generally the *rejas* who are engaged at the labour centres in town area, prefer to visit hotels for their refreshments, meals, tea etc. but reverse is the case in respect of those who are working in rural areas. It is clear from the table—15 that 42.7 percent *rejas* visit hotels when they are engaged at urban labour centres.

Table—15

Number of Rejas who Visit Hotels

Sl. No.	Total no. of rejas	No. of rejas who visit hotel	No. of rejas who do not visit hotel	Not interested
1	2	3	4	5
I	300	128	91	81
	percentage	42.7%	30.3%	27%

Political Consciousness

A lot of questions pertaining to political life of the country were put to them, but, to our utter surprise, they showed sheer ignorance towards the political life of the country. Utmost only a few of them could reply that they belonged to a country which is called *Bharat*. But it was also surprising to note that barring a few, all were quite familiar with the name of Shrimati Indira Gandhi without knowing her designation. As regards casting of votes, as many as 16 percent could say that they had cast their votes without knowing the names of the parties voted for. Thus, it can be said that they hardly are familiar with the political activities as they are chiefly concerned with their duties only. The table-16 shows the percentagewise *rejas* who cast their votes or abstained from them.

Thus examining the different aspects of the tribal *rejas* with regard to probable changes taking place in their behaviour, attitudes, political life, religious beliefs etc. we have seen

Table – 16

Number of Rejas who Cast Their Votes

Sl. No.	Total no. of *rejas*	who cast votes	who do not cast votes	Ignorant
I	2	3	4	5
I	300	48	175	77
	percentage	16%	58.3%	25.7%

that noticeable changes have occurred which can be attributed to the profession of *rejas*. In the next chapter we shall be dealing with various types of exploitations the *rejas* are confronted with.

7

Exploitation of the Tribal Rejas

In course of their working hours the *rejas* quite often come in contact with various types of men and women. These people, while on one hand are responsible to bring about changes in their values and other important traditional features, on the other, they also attract them by virtue of their modern amenities to lead comparatively a more sophisticated and fastidious life. But in order to emulate the life of sophisticated non-tribals, the tribal *rejas* have to undergo certain types of misunderstandings resulting in misgivings also. As a matter of fact the *rejas* have to practically shun some of their traditional ways of life and cultural traits while switching over to the changed style of life. In the preceding chapter much has been said appertaining to noticeable changes in the values, attitudes, belief as well as their traditional ways of living which ultimately lead to marked changes in their sources of recreation and particularly in the context of their professions.

Thus, it is seen that apart from their own culture they develop immense fancy for copying altogether a different life which sometimes causes some sorts of unexpected miseries to the *rejas*. These miseries are nothing but certain types of exploitations which they are subjected to while changing their attitude and style of living.

The present chapter deals with different types of miseries meted out by these *rejas* due to their interaction with different elements in course of their day to day workings. These miseries can be termed also as exploitation because by way of such exploitations the *rejas* actually have to face different types of miseries which may either be physical, psychological, social as well as economical.

According to the Encyclopaedia of Social Sciences (Vol. VI, page 16) the word 'exploitation' is a borrowing from the French and originally means the working of mines or farms or similar enterprises. Its present use in a larger social sense may be traced to the idea found in all periods of the history of western social thought that some individuals, groups, or classes benefit unjustly and unfairly from the labour of or at the expense of others.

Although the term exploitation is not only vast but vague as well, still we have to pinpoint actually those forms of exploitations which lead to a great set back to this upcoming class of the *rejas* in particular. In order to be well acquainted with the types of exploitations which the *rejas* are subjected to, one will have to delve deep into the different states of affairs of the *rejas* which may be typified as follows :

(i) Economic Exploitation
(ii) Social Exploitation
(iii) Physical Exploitation
(iv) Psychological Exploitation

Economic Exploitation

At the outset we are dealing with the economic exploitation of the *rejas* during their involvement in respective jobs. But before looking into the aspects of economic exploitations, we must clarify that the primary objective of taking to a particular type of job by the *rejas* is merely earning of livelihood. One does a particular type of work and thus she or he becomes entitled to some remuneration in lieu thereof. This remuneration may be in cash or kind but here in case of the *rejas*, there is no system of making payments in kinds. At almost all the centres visited it was faund that the *rejas* are being paid in cash only. Maybe the *rejas* working in different labour centres are paid either weekly or on daily basis but there always exists some mischievous practices in it. If such system of payment is carried out in conformtiy with the Minimum wages Act, then there would not be any instance of resentment or dissatisfaction among the *rejas*. But in course of the study at different labour centres it was detected that the employers or the entrepreneurs, seldom maintain a regular system of payments to the working *rejas*. During the author's interview with the *rejas* in regard to wage payment, it was found that their employers often adopt corrupt practices in making payments. Those who are committed to weekly payments to their *rejas*, often fail to stick to weekly payment system and try to make certain excuses for delays in payments. These excuses are as chiefly attributed to non payments of cheques by the banks either due to holidays or some disorders in issuing cheques etc. Since 80 percent of the *rejas* are illiterate they hardly understand such intricacies and have to confide in their employers. But when such occurrences become frequent then the *rejas* have to hatch conspiracy among themselves. In this way the ignorance and the innocence of the *rejas* are exploited to an undesirable extent. Sometimes the owners dupe the *rejas* at the time of payment by saying that while making some purchases of the raw-materials they have exhausted the money they had in hand and hence the delay in payments.

Due to appalling illiteracy and ignorance among the *rejas* they very easily fall prey to the hands of such exploiters. The poor tribal *rejas* not only fall victim of exploiters in terms of inadequate and irregular wagepayment, but they also have to put labours beyond the standard and prescribed working of 8 hours a day. It is really very sad to note that the *rejas* actually start work with the dawn of the day and wind it up in late evening. Such working hours are meted with fruits in terms of wages only once a week. It can now be well imagined as to how much labour these poor *rejas* in fact put in for the purpose of earning their livelihood. And for all this work the remuneration is deplorably low. For carrying unbaked bricks in one trip to the furnace the *reja* receives some *tiklis* (tokens) which are converted in money. As described in the chapter IV, the average daily income of a *reja* working in the brick-kilns comes to about Rs.3.50 which when calculated in terms of per capita daily income, excluding the off days/non-working days, comes to about Rs.2.76. But even this amount is not paid in whole to the *rejas*. Out of the total weekly earning only some money to buy the bare necessities is paid while the rest amount is withheld by the *Munshi* on the pretext to be paid it afterwards. Here the author would like to quote the experience of a *reja* named Mangari :

> "Last year I was working in a different brick kiln. The *Munshi* did not give me my full weekly wages. Instead he used to say, 'Barish Ke samay jab ghar jaoge to dey denge. Abhi sab mat kha jao (when you would go home during the monsoons, I would pay you the balance. Do not spend all the money now)'. But I was never paid that money."

This tactice, on enquiry, was found to be adopted by some working centres with an intention to keep the *rejas* trapped in the job. The owners on the one hand think of their own interest but on the other they go on exploiting the *rejas* by making less payments. However, it is important to mention here that such irregularity in payment of wages is confined mostly among those *rejas* who go outside their parent villages for working in brick-kilns and other trades. This is so because the *rejas* working in the areas closeby to their parent villages offer resistance in the event of non-payment of the assured wages. But, unfortunately, this is not the case with the *rejas* migrating to distant and alien places.

Less Payments : How the owners or the employers, the intermediaries or the contractors are exploiting the *rejas* working under them by making them less payments for their day's long labour is a subject to be probed into from various angles.

The *rejas* engaged in brick-kils, construction works, deployed on trucks as well as industries or elsewhere are paid in different ways. Those engaged in kilns and construction works are paid at the close of day's work on the basis of number of their trips. Since these payments are made to the *rejas* by some intermediaries they do not do away with the temptation of withholding a part of their wages so that the *rejas* may not run away from their clutches. The intermediaries look to their own interest in right earnest. But on the contrary, the less payments to the *rejas* result in their economic exploitation. At times it was also observed that the contractors and the employers fraudulently manage to take extra work from the *rejas* by asking them to work beyond the normal working hours. What actually they do is that they tell wrong time at the closing hours of the work by the *rejas*. The *rejas* hardly understand the meaning of normal working hours in terms of hours and minutes as a result of which they are to work beyond the normal working hours. Though extra work is frequently taken from the *rejas* by their employers, they are seldom paid for the additional labour rendered by them. The amount of payments for working even beyond the normal working hours are arrived at by calculating the number of hours put in by the *rejas* in relation to the normal working hours. In such cases it is out and out decision taken by the employers which ultimately prevails while paying wages to the *rejas*. Thus by taking work beyond the normal working hour, not making extra payment for this, the employers are economically exploiting the tribal *rejas*.

We have already mentioned earlier that besides those *rejas* who are working independently, either in kilns or construction works, there are a lot of *rejas* deployed in various industrial complexes or even in construction works through contractors. These contractors, in such cases, act as intermediaries between the management and the labour force i.e. the *rejas*. Although these contractors insist the managements to make payments on the minimum wages basis, they themselves shirk from making payments to their *rejas* accordingly. The contractors, as a matter of fact, have been adopting the practices of grabbing some portions of the Minimum Wage for the sake of their personal gains and thereby making less payments to the poor *rejas* who are generally ignorant of the Minimum Wages guaranteed to the labourers by the Government.

While conducting surveys in the industrial complexes, the author happened to discuss the issue of Minimum Wages with the Management of Heavy Engineering Corporation and learnt that the Management paid wages to the *rejas* through the contractors at the rate of Rs. 8.41 per *reja* per day as per the prescribed Minimum Wages Act. But when the *rejas* deployed on works at various sites were contacted they made the author understand that they were getting their wages at the rate of Rs. 7/- only per day by their contractors. Thus the less payments of Rs. 1.41 in respect of each *reja* is a vivid example of economic exploitation. The contractors whether supplying labour force either to Heavy Engineering Corporation or other industrial complexes like Mahalaxmi Fibres, Ormanjhi, Marine Diesel (Garden Reach Company), Dhurwa ete. have been indulging in imposing cruelty on the innocent *rejas* by making less payments and thus misappropriating a substantial amount. The innocent *rejas* who work without any protection or affiliation with the recognised trade unions either fail to understand the malpractices of the middlemen in terms of wage payment or fight their genuine causes with the Management/appropriate bodies. And, thus due to the above facts, the *rejas* succumb to the wishes, desires and whims of unscrupulous contractors or middlemen through whom their jobs are assured.

The instance of less payments is similar even in construction site. A *reja* told the author that she was getting wages at the rate of Rs. 7/ per day for carrying materials from one place to another. She further narrated her tale ofwoe at hand of a contractor through whom she was deployed at another construc tion site. She said that for the same amount of work the contractor used to pay her only Rs. 5/- a day. Such type of extraction of money out of the hard earned income of the *rejas* is actually rampant at almost all the working centres where *rejas* are deployed through contractors.

The economic exploitations due to less payment may also be very much vouched from the following instances :

A *reja* named Sanichari working at a brick-kiln near village Irwa (District Ranchi) explained that at around October when the harvesting was over, the *rejas* have no work and the grain that they produced was so little that it did not last them for long. So they set out in search of work otherwise they had to starve. It was at that time that the *Sardarni* contacted them. They were paid some money in advance, and railway ticket were brought. The *Sardarni* accompanied them to the brick-kiln in Kalyani (West Bengal). She further narrated that once they reached the brick-kiln they were categorised and work began. The job of carrying bricks from where they were moulded to the furnaces where they were baked was usually done by them. But when the question of making payments to them arose the so called contractors or the owners altogether denied the amounts of payment what were actually assured to them by the *Sardarni*. Narrating her woeful state of affairs Sanichari told the author that after returning home from Kalyani she would never like to come again in contact with such *Sardarni* or coagents at whose hands she was exploited economically for the whole seasons of her works.

Similarly at BISCOLAMF near Namkom locality in Ranchi some cases were recorded which depict that there was no distinction between the senior and the junior *rejas*. The *rejas* working in this factory, notwithstanding their being literate or illiterate, are paid at the same rate. Even the experienced *rejas* are being treated at par with the new recruits which is a glaring example of exploitation of the *rejas* working on a permanent roll in a factory.

Social Exploitations

while dealing with the social exploitations of the *rejas*, it is important to mention here that as many as 47.3 percent of the *rejas* are unmarried and also the economically active earning force in their respective families. The high frequency of unmarried *rejas* exists because there parents delay or avoid getting their *reja* daughter married in time for fear of losing a substantial income source. Besides, it has also been observed that the society to which the *rejas* belong looks at the *rejas* from scornfull and derogatory angle because the male tribals do not prefer to marry the *rejas* as compared to other non *rejas* tribal girls. Cases have come to notice that the characters of the tribal *rejas* are doubted from the chastity point of view. Secondly, examples have also come to light that the husbands have deserted their wives due to taking of job of *rejas* by them. While on one hand these poor *rejas* are busy attending to their non sedentary occupations for the betterment of their respective families, on the other, they are being subjected to traumatic and excruciating experiences due to social values. In other words the jobs of the *rejas* are very significant from the point of view of prcviding assistance in developing the national economy but the very sanctity of their constructive profession is doubted by the society which can definitely be termed as their social exploitations.

While talking to a *reja* named Bandhan at road construction work between Daladali chowk and Argora the author was informed that Bandhan was actually married to a well to do boy of her own community and both of them were leading a very happy life. She further said that her husband was always busy idling away his time and hence the difficulties in meeting both square meals. Thus finding no source of income Bandhan was advised by some of the female covillagers to take to the job of a *reja* and she ultimately joined the stream of the *rejas*. Bandhan started supplementing domestic incomes, no doubt but she was constantly ıebuked by her husband to give up the job of a *reja*. But she could not obey him on the plea of the shadow of stravation hovering over them. At this Bandhan was given a good thresh and beaten mercilessly by her spouse who took a sigh of relief only after deserting his wife. Narrating this tale Bandhan actually started sobbing and tears trickled down her cheeks. Although an innocent village belle Bandhan went on to say that even at the cost of chastity there are many high ups in the society enjoying high positions but one being a poor *reja* was subjected to such exploitation which is hanging heavy on my head.

According to survey 11 percent of the *rejas* are divorced or separated from their husbands for different reasons. Out of 11 percent, 4.7 percent were divorced on the basis of their character, 5.3 percent were divorced because they were not adjusting in their families and were lacking in household duties where as 1 percent were divorced because they were not mentally adjusted with their husbands. But all of them do not find their fault so much for which they were deserted by their husbands All were of opinion that it is better to earn some money than to die of starvation. The *rejas* who were deserted by their husbands on character basis were of opinion that their jobs are of such nature that they have to mix with different type of persons and to spend more times out of their homes. But what is wrong with this, they used to help their husbands and families economically. But their husbands did not cooperate them and got rid of them. Their family life was also unhappy because they failed to do their family duties upto that expectations their husbands want from them, as it is evident from those 5.3 percent *rejas* who are divorced on this ground. They said that they were doing their duties according to their capacities and were able to maintain their homes to some extent even they had difficulties in such conditions. Their husbands always used to give pressure upon them that they should leave up the work of *rejas* as they are not able to look after their children and home carefully. But these *rejas* were of opinion that they were successful at both places i. e. in their homes as well as their working places, then, why they would loose the income with the help of which they are independent and also helping their families. They had accepted the job of *rejas* for the betterment of their family, to help their husbands but their husbands gave them reward in this way which lead to their social exploitations.

Apart from those *rejas* who have been divorced by their husbands, there are 33 percent *rejas* who are married and 8.7 percent are widow. These *rejas* have to do justice at both ends-at the the family level and at the working level. While doing their duties at both places they have to undirgo various types of stress and strains and there develops a kind of role-conflict within themselves. Such type of role conflict are also found in the case of unmarried *rejas* who from a large category of *rejas*. All such stress-strains and role conflict among the *rejas* lead to a kind of social exploitation for them.

It has been observed that they fail in their duties towards the fulfilment of social obligation, They do not have spare time to move in society for making social calls to their neighbours and relatives. They are not able to attend each and every function of their villages because they do not have time. They get labelled as *Ghamandi* (arrogant) and so on for all such things but they are helpless. Nobody tries to understand them which make them feel disturbed, socially ostracised and excommunicated.

The lifo of even the married *rejas* is not free from stress and strains due to the peculiar nature of that work which pursue as *rejas.* While working as *reja* the tribal women are literally compelled to shun their role or duty as a mother, wife, daughter-in-law and above all the regular domestic chores (a detailed discussion in this regard may be seen in the chapter entitled "Role-conflict among the *rejas*").

Physical Exploitations

The tribal *rejas* are being exploited physically to a great extent. Several cases of physical exploitations, specially those *rejas* who have been working under contractors in brick-kiln, construction work etc. and also those who come from outside Ranchi from different places in India, have been found. It has been observed that tribal *rejas* are taken away to different places in India by the contractors and there they live under the clutches of the contractors, *sardars* or other intermediaries. They live on the mercy of their employers. In Ranchi also, it has been observed that the tribal labourers, both male and female, have been brought from the distant places like Bilaspur (Madhya Pradesh), Mirzapur (Uttar Pradesh) and also from the places within Ranchi district like Bero, Kuru, Lohardaga, etc. to work in brick-kiln. They have been provided their abodes in the form of huts near the brick-kilns and they have been booked for whole season of brick making. Besides the *rejas* working in brick-kilns, all the tribal *rejas* who are working at different labour centres, engaged in different types of work are also subjected to physical explotations. Their physical exploitation consist of various stypes of physical tortures, sexual offences different crimes and so on. Sometimes it leads to suicide and other criminal assaults also. It is evident that the *rejas* have to work very hard from morning to evening. It has been found that the tribal *rejas* consist of different age-groups ranging from 5—10 years of age-group to 60 years. But she has to work hard whether she is a young one, or an adult one or an old one.

Child Labour : Our constitution for protection of child workers. Article 24 lays down:

> 'No child below the age of 14 years shall be employed to work in anv factory or, mine or engaged in any other hazardous employment.'

But it is a common sight to see tribal *rejas* belonging to the age- groups 5—10 and 11–15 years working assidously in brick-kilns, transportation work, construction sites, etc. Such *rejas* working in the form of child labour hardly earn Rs. 10 to 15 a week in comparison to Rs. 20–25 which an adult *reja* earns. During the survey of three hundred tribal *rejas* 7.7 percent *rejas* belong to the age-groups 5—10 and 11–15 years.

At a brick-kiln near Bariatu the author met a twelve years old girl named Parti working as *reja*. She has been working in brick-kilns since 1977. Everyday she carries six bricks at a time, from sun rise to sun set from the *thager* (the place where bricks are moulded) to the furnace, a distance about 300 yards. At the end of the day when her thin, weak body cannot take it any more, she gets rid from her work but wage is not paid to her at the end of the days work because it is paid th on weekly basis. She earns Rs. 15/–to Rs, 20/—in a week for breaking her back for about twelve hours in a day. Parti comes every year from Gumla to work in the brick-kilns of Ranchi, She told the author that at home there was no work and no food, hence she she has to come here to work every year. Her parents reside in the village. Whatever little she saves, she caries it to home at the end of the the season. It is substantial help to her parents. She reported that inpite of hard work, she is not paid according to her work. She further reported that she used to be closely watched by the *Sardar* and he takes work from her according to his convenience. Neither he cares her difficulties nor her age.

He is only concerned with her works. He has no human touch in his behaviour.

It has been observed that the accommodation provided for the brick-kiln workers is not only inadequate but also unhygienic. The *rejas* are quartered in four feet by five feet *Jhopris* (hut) which are about four feet high. No *reja* can sleep in a *jhopri* without their legs protruding through the open door. According to Gangi Munda, a *reja* in a brick-kiln in Namkum.

> "the quarters are so small that every time we enter them we have to stoop. But we cannot complain because we have got work here without which we would have starved."

Besides, there are no proper arrangements for drinking water and toilets. Medical facilities are missing.

The *rejas* who are engaged in construction works have also several complaints. They reported to the author that heavy works are taken from them. The employers want to take maximum works in less time from the *rejas*. They are being always watched by the managers or middle-men who use to rebuke them if they want to take some rest durlng working hours. It has been observed that the *rejas* have to work continuously during working hours and if she shows some slackness in her work she is rebuked by the *Munshi* and given threatening that her wages would be curtailed. According to a news item published in the local Hindi news paper ("Ranchi Express" ,dated 1.3.82) an owner of brick kiln and his *Munshi* were sent to jail by Kanke police for inhumanly treatment with their labourers. They forced their labourers to drink urine and kept them hungry and also tied with ropes. A labourer named Suresh Naik, who used to work there as *Pathera* told the police that the owner of that kiln did not make pay ments regularly and used to take more work from them. The owner, in contrary, was of opinion that the labourers were planning to flee away after taking the advanced payment.

But the greatest humiliation that the tribal *rejas* have to face pertains to sexual exploitation. It is not uncommon for a tribal woman to be locked up and beaten if she refuses to yield sexually to her employer or local toughs. According to

Laru Jenko, President of the Mahila Samaj in Chakardharpur, who was herself a labourer in the brick-kilns of West Bengal.

> "the reality is that nobody bothers about we tribals. The police are hand in glove with the brick-kiln owners and they would not help us even if they could. Though I have not been raped myself, I know what fate the girls have to suffer. I have seen young tribal girls being sexually assaulted by kiln owners. I have also seen how *sardarnis* have forced girls into prostitution. And the *Munshis* and the owners are all alike. They think that we do not have any character and will sleep with any-one for a small favour." (Sunday, 30 May-5 June, 1980).

It has been found that near about 60 percent of tribal *rejas*, who where interviewed, had occasions to work outside the Ranchi. They had gone to work in brick-kilns of different places in the state and outside the state. But all of them found that it is better to work in Ranchi than to go elsewhere because they are not paid such incentives for which they go outside their home towns. Besides the bad behaviours of their employers and other associates, they were subjected to all sorts of exploitations and ill treatment including sexual exploitations. Two *rejas* went to Lodipur (patna) brick-kilns. It was reported that the non-tribal *sardars* used to molest them even in day times and that too before others. In case of resentment, they were threatened with dire consequences, even death. They were not allowed to move freely and were always under survelliance. To add further to misery they were not paid their dues and had to sell off their ornaments etc. for the return journey. The savings during the period of six months came to an average of Rs.200/-. This is why they are not very keen to go out again. They feel that the labour they put are not properly compensated. They will be happy if alternative source of employment is available in their own area. Most of the female labourers, who were subjcctd to torture do not dare to seek help of officials or police due to the threat of the employers or perhaps they feel shame. So no action could be taken.

As narrated by a *reja* named Biran, of Kishunpur village, who had gone to work in the Talabir brick-kiln in Mogra in Hooghly district, the two other *rejas* who accompanied her in the same breck kiln were raped by the conrtactor and they left the brick kiln aften being raped. They had to work in some other brick-kiln also to earn some money for their return journey (For detail see appendix No B-1).

Apart from being raped by contractors or owners, young tribal girls have to face the same fate at the hands of local hoodlums also. It is evident from the case of Laxmi Munda, a 20 year old girl, who had gone to work in Nabagram in Burdawn district from her village Baragain (Ranchi). She was molested by some hoodlums there (For detail see appendix no B-2).

Several tribal women from Bihar are reported to have died of torture, a large number of them have been kept as captive and many raped in Mirzapur district of Uttar Pradesh. The tribals are working as contract labour in Renukoot and Mirzapur. They were taken by some contractors who made them captive in village Kankari under Bina police Station in Mirzapur district. Any attempt to escape results in severe beating. They are kept in miserable condition. They are not paid their wages. They are not even allowed to return to their villages. (The Searchlight dated 27-2-1980).

These tribal women are taken away by the contractors and they are not only economically exploited by these contractors but also physically tortured if they try to protest against the ill treatment of the contractoras. Mr. Shiv prasad Sahu, M.P. (Congress I) has expressed his concern over the large scale traffic of tribal labourers including women in Uttar Pradesh Haryana, Punjab, Tripura and other places of the country every year. Mr. Sahu said that some contractors who are engaged in the labour supply, take full advantage of acute poverty in the Chotanagpur region in Bihar and take the tribal people to these places for work in brick fields and other manual work. About two lakh tribal labourers go to Uttar Pradesh, Punjab, Haryana, every year in lure of better prospect of work but on reaching there, they find that they have been cheated by these contractors. They are not given the money as promised by the contractors in their home towns. These tribal labourers consist of mostly women and unmarried girls. According to Mr. Sahu, there are no trace of several women who go to work every year. He said that abut 30-40 women have disappeared every year from Lohardaga region. Many tribals use to talk to him about their absconding daughters, daughter in-law etc. But the contractors do not give full account of the labourers to the labour department. Hence there is no record of them and the tribal women are economically and morally exploited by them. Mr. Sahu also expressed his apprehension that if the tribal women were being exploited in such a way then there is no surprise that there would be a change in the race of the Munda and Oraon in coming years. He said that the process of taking away the tribal women is more prevalent during the period November to January and most affective areas are Lohardaga, Bero,Kuru, Latehar and chandwa of Ranchi district. (The Ranchi Express, dated 3.4.80 and 5.8.80).

Investigations by the Tripura Government have revealed that some business managers and contractors in the state allegedly tortured tribal women from Bihar and treated their male counterpart as "slaves". According to official sources Tripura Government investigated a series of allegatins of rape on tribal workers and other inhuman atrocities on male labourers at various brick fields in the state. The sources said 30 of such tortured female workers were rescued from some of the brick fields by the police and later sent to their home state. (The Searchlight, dated 5.4.80).

In a special drive, police have rescued 212 tribal labourers including 120 women mostly unmarried, allegedly brought from Bihar to Agartala for the purpose of " immoral traffic" in the state. The Bihar Government has expressed its gratitude to the left front Government in Tripura for its prompt action in rescuing 212 tribal labourers from the clutches of the middle men and contractors and making necessary arrangements for sending them to Ranchi, according to a press release issued by the Commissioner of South Chotanagpur. The release said that the Commissioner's office at Ranchi received information that some tribal labourers of Khunti sub-division of Ranchi district have been 'fraudulently' taken away by some *Sardar* for employment in Tripura where they were being extremely ill-treated. (The Searchlight dated 7.4.80).

It has been alleged that the labourers were living in inhuman conditions and not even being given adequate rations. The woman labourers were being sexually exploited. The workers felt helpless as any attempt to protest resulted in severe beating. On receipt of this information, the left Front Government in Tripura conducted raids in different parts of the State and rescued them from the clutches of the middle-men and contractors. The Tripura Government also made arrangement for airlifting of the rescued labourers from Agartala to Calcutta and from there to Ranchi by train under the escorts of Tripura Government officers. The Tripura Government has instituted criminal cases against the middlemen and contractors involved in traffic of tribal labourers from Ranchi to Agartala.

According to Mr. Biren Dutta. the State's Minister for Revenue and labour, some of the girls were kidnapped from Ranchi area of Bihar and others allured from drought affected areas of the state for good jobs at Barauni or in the Assam Tea Gardens. He said women were being put under confinement in the brick field areas for 16 to 20 months when several of their babies died for want of food and medicine. They were also severely beaten up for attempting to escape. Mr. Dutta also said there was report of mass raping of tribal girls by '*Sardars*'. Their agents, are suspected to be involved in an all India racket, and other antisocial elements in the brick field areas. (The Searchlight, dated 7.4.80).

Not only this, now-a-days magazines, periodicals, news papers and even government publications are replete with instances of physical exploitations to scheduled tribes particularly of the *rejas* deployed in various working centres. These tribal *rejas* because of untold poverty and miseries are seen to have fallen victim to the cruel clutches of the intermediaries or *Sardars* and having been criminally assaulted by the undesirable elements of the society are left at their destiny to lament their lot for ever. Thus according to reports lodged in various police stations in Ranchi and nearabout, information can be had regarding physical, social and sexual torture and exploitation meted out to the tribal *rejas*. According to a similar report a sixteen years old tribal female named Somari Jamoda of village Banka in Chaibasa was enticed by another villager and was ultimately offered to a brick kiln owner named Bistu Babu at village Paskuta in the district of Midnapore where she worked for nearly eight months or so. Thereafter one day she was admitted to a hospital following falling ill. In the meantime what actually came to pass with that tribal girl is a subject to be probed into. But when the information leading to her ailment was, however, reported to her mother by the son of the aforesaid intermediary, she rushed to the hospital at Paskuta and found to her dismay her daughter pregnant. Thus for fear of being ill treated by the society she, however, brought her pregnant daughter somehow to her village where Somari gave birth to a male child.

This information was given to the police attached to the Harijan Cell at Patna by the father of the illfated Somari. He further said that his daughter was criminally assaulted by Bistu as result of which his life became miserable over and above his being a poor tribal man. His report says that the kiln owner returned his daughter after paying her the fair of return journey only. The intermediary had actually enticed a number of girls together with Somari such as Namsi (12 years), Randa (18 years), Parai (12 years), Chelg (10 years), Lukme(14 years) and Jambi (12 years), all minor girls.

According to another report the manager of Kiriburu Mines had taken away another tribal girl Ehando in 1980 in collusion with another tribal girl named Palo to Jaipur in Orissa. According to the statement furnished by Chando, she worked only for 30 days on the hillock and thereafter the mines were closed. At this, Chando started living with Palo at the residence of the aforesaid manager. Palo was already entrapped by the manager known as Choudhary and she was already aborted upon at Ranchi. Chando also said that Choudhary attempted to assault on her twice by entering her apartment but he fled away following a hue and cry raised thereby. She further said that Chaudhary did not allow either of them to go away from his clutches but ultimately after three weeks both of them were left by him at Chakardharpur. Chando was paid only a sum of Rs. 120/- for month's work.

According to the third report furnished by the Harijan Cell, Patna, a *sardar* named Pitambar Bodra of village Tesari in Chakardharpur had taken away Soma (13 years), Kairy (15 years), Tulsi (13 years) besides another married woman of village Uliguta in Chaibasa district but till now there is no trace of them. According to a report lodged by one Nandu Jamuda, his daughter Soma together with other girls was alleged to have been sold out to a contractor named Kawai Lal in Uttar Pradesh.

The Officer-in-charge of the Harijan Cell Police Station, Ranchi has started cases against the aforesaid culprits under the various sections of the Indian Penal Code.

These information appertaining to exploitation are under the purview of this research work as the Harijan Cell Police Station has got its jurisdiction over the entire Chotanagpur division. It is also very surprising that there is no assistant police officer other than the Officer-in-charge nor is any vehicle or any office elsewhere to deal with such cases of exploitations. (The Ranchi Express, dated 16. 4. 82).

So far as the physical exploitation of the *rejas* of Ranchi district is concerned, a survey report goes on as here under.

According to the Labour Commissioner of Tripura a good number of tribal *rejas* were taken away by intermediaries to brick-kilns at Agartala where they were deployed at various brick kilns here and there. On an information received by the Chief Secretary, Tripura, a number of raids were conducted at various brick kilns at Agartala and as many as more than 200 tribal girls ranging between the age of 10 and 18 were discovered. The inhuman treatment meted out there had actually broken them completely. The labour Commissioner Mr. R. B. Bhushan, however, managed them to send back to their village homes located in different blocks of the Ranchi district.

Among those girls Shanti, Basanti, Heera, Ragini and Meera informed that while passing through the Main Road at Ranchi on completion of their shopping business they were interrupted by a *sardar* near a hotel at Mohalla Hindpiri. The *sardar* offerred them the allurement of handsome amount of wages besides other amenities of modern life. Thus they were carried on trucks, bus and by trains to Tripura where dozens of tribal girls were being subjected to inhuman treatment. On hearing the woefull tale of those girls these newly recruited girls decided to come back but it was too late because the *sardar* had already left the place after realising their prices. Then they had no alternative than to succumb to the whims and desires of the kiln owners, *munshi* and others, besides putting in hard labour for fifteen hours daily. Thus, the price of their physical exploitation as well as manual labour was at the rate of only Rs. 15/- per week. The hutment in which they were stayed were fully guarded by the *Lathaits* lest they should fly away from there. According to a guess work as many as over 2000 minor or major girls are enticed away to brick kilns or other working centres every year. The beautiful or attractive girls among such enticed girls are generally sold out in the market of prostitution. By virtue of having been endowed with stout built and charming contours they are sold out in the market as hot cakes.

According to another report a similar tout dealing in the trade of flesh forcibly lifted one tribal girl Fulmani on February 20, 1980 while she was travelling in a crowded bus. But since Fulmani worked at the residence of Shri N. E. Horo, M. P., Ranchi, a hectic search was made to locate her. In course of the search Fulmani could be found out in a hutment made of bamboos and surrounded by barbed wires. That hutment was packed like *sardines* with hundred and fifty ill fated girls but all were, ultimately, freed (The Ranchi Express, dated 18. 4. 81).

Thus it can be adduced that all such victim girls are not fortunate enough to be releived off such miseries very often. But they have to curse their lots for ever as hardly do they come across benevolent, philanthrophists or social reformers to redress them of their miseries.. These are some of the instances based on different but authentic sources of information. But apart from them there are many more such instances which could not be brought to light and the poor victims are left to their own destiny to pass their helish life for ever.

However, there is no denying the fact that the tribal girls are always exploited by their co-workers may be *Sardars, munshis*, truck -drivers. *khālasis* and the like. Examples have come to our notice that very often the tribal girls develop some sort of affinity with their co-workers which in the long run lead to sexual exploitation. While examining this particular issue very critically it can be said that in such cases the affairs between the *rejas* and their co-workers may not be termed as sexual exploitation at all, because such acts are based on their mutual agreement and consents. But the acts are termed as exploitation indeed when they are left or deserted by their co-workers forever. Instances are also being noticed that in some cases their romantic affairs and in their marriage also, notwithstanding in their own caste or creed, they pass their life happily also. But such instances are rare among the rarest. In most of the cases the employers quench their lust for sex and desert the girls for ever leaving no alternative to them than to force them in the market of the trade of flesh forever.

We have already come across various instances of physical as well as sexual exploitation of the *rejas* and the more we try to enquire into such occurrences the more are the instances of exploitation among the tribal *rejas* engaged in different trades. For the *rejas* engaged on trucks for loading and unloading job, it came to light that one *reja* while returning to her village after day's work requested the driver to stop the truck near her village but the driver did not, instead sped it away.. The girl sensing the faul entention of the driver jumped down to her death and so did her other companions who miraculously escaped death but sustained injuries and were admitted to Khunti Sadar Hospital.

Psychological Exploitation

Psychological exploitation of the *rejas* emanate from all sorts of such exploitation which the tribal *rejas* face during the course of their day-to-day workings. The *rejas* are psychologically depressed and agonised due to the bad behaviour of employers, associates, inmates and other peoples. Having been poverty stricken, these *rejas* after leaving their hearths and homes set out in quest of their livelihood. But when engaged by some brick-kiln owner, managers, *sardars*, drivers etc. they are sujected to all sorts of maltreatments at the hands of sex-starved individuals. As a matter of fact society should be sympathetic towards this downtrodden section of the human society. But, on the contrary, they are exploited in various ways. Some of the *rejas* are sore over the preferential treatment of their masters which they resort to on the basis of beauty, charm and attraction possessed by some *rejas*. This preferential attitude of the masters or the proprietors force some of the *rejas* to a psychological suffering which in the long run is enough to diminish their capacity as well as efficiency to work.

Though the tribal *rejas* expect humanly treatment from their employers and associates but it has been observed that they are ill treated by them specially those who are working at outstation and are completely under their clutches. Such *rejas* have to work under constant mental pressure because a man of the employer keeps close watch on them so that they may not flee away from there. It is observed that in case of all the *rejas* whether working in the brick kiln, in construction works, on trucks, industries or engaged in miscellaneous types of work, they are kept under constant watch of a *munshi* or other such man of the employer who has been deputed there to take work from the *rejas*. Such *munshi*, *sardar* or midleman have full command over them and they use to take full work from them. They do not want to see any slackness in their work. *Rejas* are alwyas being rebuked by them and they remain in a state of tension because their employers or other associates do not have sympathetic attitude towards them. If they come late at their working sites then they are given threatening of dismissing from their job. Different types of threatenings are given to the *rejas* and *rejas* have to work accordingly. According to one *reja* whose husband also works as a coolie under a contractor, the employer of her husband and herself, behaved with them inhumanly so much so that the employer raped her by threatening to kill her husband so they have to work under such mental pressure. Their economic exploitation, social and physical exploitation etc. all lead towards their psychological exploitation because all sorts of exploitations create a sort of mental tenison and agony under which pressure the tribal *rejas* have to work to earn their livelihood.

Thus the stresses and strains caused due to all sorts of exploitations to the *rcjas* as a whole are more or less responsible for all sorts of evils pervailing in their life. The society ought to have shown mercy, sympathy towards such working female community of the society who have been trying to support themselves by dint of their hard labour. Under the circumstances this community of the *rejas* must be free, frank and fearless while discharging their duties so to enable them to bring about marked improvement in their day-to-day works. They must be psychologically independent to deliver the goods in right earnest.

By going into the details of various types of exploitations meted out to the tribal community particularly known as that of the *rejas*, we may conclude that the *rejas* are virtually very innocent as well as poor class of the scheduled tribe population. They do not prefer to live on the charity of the others. Instead they do not hesitate in putting their own efforts towards meeting their necessities of life. Thus, if the rejas are guided properly and at the same time encouraged in their profession they may prove a boon to the present day society. While working, these *rejas* unlike other labourers engaged here and there, do not shirk from discharging responsibilities assigned to them. Moreover they have to support males as well as female inmates of their families also with their meagre income so to say. But if this community is exploited either by fraudulent means or by way of deception the poor *rejas* will get entangled in various types of problems which ultimately debar them from delivering the goods to the much loss to the society and ultimately to the nation as a whole. They must not be, at any cost, exploited economically as we have seen earlier, for economy is the back bone of progress. In case of economic exploitation to the *rejas*, their backbones are broken into pieces shattering their life. The economic exploitation is not merely an exploitation which can be ignored at any step because this particular exploitation actually forces the *rejas* community to succumb to the lustful whims and desires of their amorous contractors, masters, proporietors.

What harm can these exploitations bring about in the life of the *rejas* is a vital subject of study by the anthropologist of all times to come so that some tangible efforts could be taken to do away with such deterrent features forever. We have already seen that all these exploitations are correlated with one another, and, hence all sections of the society must see to it and do something towards elimination of such evils of the present society in which the poor *rejas* have to struggle for their wherewithals.

Protective Regulations to Check Labour Exploitation :—

Though there are laws to enforce regular payment and prevention of unfair deduction of wages, provision of regular working hours, leave and holidays, proper environment, drinkinng-water and social security against old age, sickness, industrial hazards and death, there is no effective government machinery to monitor the implementation of these laws in the interest of tribal labourer in general and *rejas* in particular. The safeguards are provided through the Employees Provident Fund, Employees State Insurance and Family Pensions. Besides these, there are special provisions for women: Maternity benefit through paid leave and hospitalisation, prohibition of night work in certain kinds of hazardous jobs and weight-lifting, creches for children of working mother etc.

The Legislative provisions for protection and welfare of woman workers are largely inspired by the ILO's conventions on (i) Maternity Protection, 1919; (ii) Night- work, 1919; (iii) Underground Work, 1935, (iv) Equal Remuneration, 1951; and (v) Discrimination (Employment and Occupation), 1958. However, the actual wording of the enactments in India in which the protection is written draws heavily on the Indian experience. Maternity benefits are provided under the Employees State Insurance Act. 1943 and the Maternity Benifit Act, 1961.

In regard to daycare, although the Factories Act provides for the establishment of creches in factories employing women labour, there is a large scale circumvention in the provisions of the Act or the services rendered are far below the standard. Under the Contract-Labour (Regulation and Abolition) Act, 1970 there is provision for the maintenance of creches. It provides for location of creches within 50 metres of every establishment with 20 or more women employed as contract labour. The provisions also include a minimum standard of running of such creches and amenities to be provided. There are, however, loopholes in the law. The contractor can show, for instance, less than 20 women in the Muster Roll as there is hardly any supervision to ensure that the creches are functioning properly.

The Bihar Labour Inquiry Committee while condemning the practice of recruiting labour through contractors have said:

> "the contractors ordinarily lack a sense of moral obligation towards labour which the employers or managers are expected to have, and therefore, do not often hesitate to exploit the helpless position of labour in their charge."

There is the Inter State Workmen's Migration Act (1979) to stop exploitation and regulate the working conditions of migrant labourers. But its provisions are loose and inadequate. According to this Act, the state, from which the migrant labourer has come, has the right to raise the matter with the state in which the labourer is employed if his condition of work violate the Act. But it is the employing state which investigate the complaint and here lies the sang. Again, the Act nas no provision for the release of bonded labourers or for the criminal prosecution of those who keep labourers in a state of bondage. The Union Ministry of labour has done well by writing to the State Governments to implement this Act. The Act came into force in 1980 but most of the States have yet to promulgate rules envisaged under it. Even in the states like M. P. and Orissa that have framed the rules, the implementation machinery is weak and the rules have remained on paper only. Much of the migrant workforce is engaged in agriculture and construction work and is predominantly drawn from weaker and under privileged sections including tribal communities. In many States there is virtually no distinction between migrant and bonded labour, for inter-state workers are held in bondage by contractors. Migrant workers are preferred to local hands because they have a little bargaining capacity. More work can, therefore, be extracted from them.

Even so, the rules framed by the Madhya Pradesh Government are comprehensive in scope and could serve as a model for other States too. Under these rules, an employer will, at first, have to obtain a licence for employing migrant labour and pay them the minimum wages fixed for such jobs. Migrant workers have also been extended the facility of free legal aid to contest the cases concerning wages and compensation. The contractor is also bound to pay them return fare from the place of employment. If implemented effectively, these rules could constitute a new deal for migrant labour.

For successful implementation of the Inter State Migrant Workmen Act, several gazetted and non-gazetted posts have been created by the Bihar Government. Three posts of Deputy Development Commissioners have been created in the state and these officers will be posted at Chandigarh, Calcutta and Lucknow. These officers will look after the difficulties of the migrant workmen of Bihar working in the concerned states and will try to safeguard them from exploitation and torture by their employers.

The Government of Bihar have also organised two Rescue Squads to free the migrant workmen who are trapped either inside or outside the state. These Rescue Squads are also expected to ensure the return of the migrant workmen to their village homes. Besides, Deputy Collectors, there will also be provision for police officers in the squads. Concurrance was sought from the concerned States for the posting of Deputy Labour Commissioner outsite the State but so for no such concurrance except from the Government of Himachal Pradesh has been received. The services of two Deputy Collectors have beeen placed at the disposal of the labour Department by the Department of Personnel and Administrative Reforms for this work. But so far these two officers have not reported to the labour Department. The Home Commissioner as well as the Inspector General of Police, Bihar have been requested to make available the services of the Police Force. In this context this is also to be made known that the posts of female social welfare Inspectors for the north and the south Chotanagpur and the Santhal Parganas tribal areas have been created to put a stop to exploitation of such migrant workers. Action is on the way for the appointment of these 24 female social welfare Inspectors.

There also exists the Bihar State Unorganised Workers Group Insurance Scheme. Under this scheme the agricultural labourers, '*thelawalas*' and other employed in small work shops and establishements belonging to the unorganised sectors are covered under the scheme which has come into force on the lst of January, 1982 in the State of Bihar. The workers in the Age Group of 16-65 whose annual incomes do not exceed Rs. 6000/- and who belong to the class of agricultural labourers, thelawalas, pedlars, vendors, construction workers, transport workers, bidi makers, brick-kiln workers or employees in small shops and establishments of an unorganised sector, get in case of their death arising out of the accident or who lose their limbs in such accidents a cash compensation Rs. 2000/-. A sum of Rs. 100/- as cash payment is paid in case of loss of one limb. This scheme is to be implemented by New India Insurance Company Limited. Between January to March, 1982, i. e. for a period of three months this Insurance company has been paid in the form of premium a sum of Rs. 22,52,272/-. It has been decided by the Government that this scheme will be implemented upto December 1982 by this Insurance Company. (Sources—Welfare Department, Bihar).

But it is very sad to note that despite the existence of so many regulations pertaining to labour welfare, as referred to above, there is a staggering gap in regard to their effective implementation. It can be possible only if there exists a monitoring cell at the nodal level to monitor the effective implementation of the existing legal safeguards for the labour in general and the tribal *rejas* in particular.

Suggestions for Ameliorating the Socio-Economic Conditions of the Rejas

Besides the existence of the aforesaid labour legislations meant for protecting the interest of labour class, it is felt that the following suggestions which are based on the study of the problems of the tribal *rejas*, if adopted in practice, can also serve as guiding principles towards checking the exploitation of the tribal *rejas* at the hands of their unscrupulous and ruthless employers or contractors, whatsoever. The tribal *rejas* do not get any protection from women organisations, Trade Unions and Political parties as such they are urged upon to take up the matter in the name of the welfare of the tribal *rejas*.

The following suggestions if implemented in right earnest, may prove beneficial to the *reja*-community in getting rid of the exploitations from their employers, contractors and intermediaries—

1. The Ministry of Home Affairs be requested to issue necessary instructions to all the State Goverments to take immediate action against the tyranny and oppressive measures adopted by the contractors or employers towards the *rejas*. In this respect the problem of such exploited labourers who belong to a particular State but are exploited in some other State be investigated through the C. B. I.
2. Provision for a central fund be made so as to provide relief out of that to the tribal *rejas* who are exploited at the hands of their employers, contractors and intermediariaries, just on the lines of the provision made by the State Governments to provide compensations to Harijans and other exploited labourers.
3. The Ministry of Labour of the Government of India be requested to implement the terms and conditions

appertaining to the wages of those female-labourers who are taken out the State on the pretext of maidservants or ayahs and comprehensive legislations be enacted with the provisions to deal with the problom of sex exploitations meted out to them. The Labour Department of the Government of Bihar also should adopt similar measures towards the protection of the interest of the migrant tribal *rejas.*

4. The Social Welfare Department of the Government of India as well as the state Government be requested to prepare schemes so as to provide refuges to such female labourers who are set free from the clutches of contractors and intermediaries.
5. The Ministry of Home Affairs be requested for the issuance of proper directions to all the State Governments to trace out all such female labourers who have been enticed to other places. Just on the similar lines the State Government must issue instructions to the District Magistrates and the Superintendents of Police. In this respect it is also imperative to collect information through the officers placed at the District Administration to the effect as to who are those migrant female labourers who have not returned to their village-homes. Such information must be furnished further with the District Magistrates and the Superintendent of Police to the Tribal Welfare Commissioner and the Home and Labour departments who, on receipt of such information take suitable steps with the concerned State Governments.
6. Directions be issued to all the District Magistrates of the tribal belt to prepare a list of such villages wherever exists the problem of acute unemployment after and before the kharif-harvest and further they must prepare suitable schemes to provide succour to the labourers, implement hard as well as light manual schemes in case of failure of crops so that the labourers need not go away in search of work and employment. This must be adhered to in case of the female labourers. With such intention the State Governments may

request the centre to place necessary stock of grains, allotment of menures as well as cash amounts at the disposal of the State Governments.

7. Such welfare organisations, which look to the interest of labour community and try to protect them against exploitations, be recognised.
8 The Ministry of Home and Labour be requested to consider as to how the Government as well as semi-goverment organisations arrange importation of the female labourers so that they may not fall prey to deceit as well as frauds at the hands of contractors and intermediaries. With this very intention the formation of public-sectors corporation be considered in the States.
9. In the State of Bihar the tribal *rejas* working in road construction, brick-kilns, house building, etc. are exploited to a great extent in various ways, hence there is an imperative need to issue directions with the effect to free such labourers from all sorts of exploitations and oppressions. A meeting of a high level committee be convened to consider these problems of exp!oitations.
10. There is an urgent need for the establishment of such organisation which may be helpful in ameliorating the condition of the *rejas* at Block, Sub-division and District levels. Since there are many cases of exploitations, it is also essential to post one officer each at District and sub-divisional level who may be entrusted with the job of preventing exploitations to the *rejas*. The co-operation of Government, religious and other organisations be solicited for the purpose of providing safe-guards to the tribal *rejas*.
11. Camps or *shivirs* be put up at such places from where large influx of tribal *rejas* are imported to distant places so as to post them with all sorts of probable difficulties confronting the migrant labourers.
12. Steps may also be taken to educate such tribal *rejas* to seek legal as well as administrative aids in case of difficulties and exploitations.

13. At village level the information regarding migrant labourers be maintained by the authorities and the Block Development Officers be assigned with the responsibilities of collecting full information with regard to migrant labourers and keep the higher authorities informed of it. In this way the exploitations or misbehaviours towards the labourers will be minimised to a greater extent.
14. The tribal *rejas* must bc supplied with employment cards and attendance cards.
15. Measurement slip and wages slip should be introduced.
16. Payment of wages register and employment of workmen with full address to be maintained properly.
17. Minimum wages should be introduced.
18. 8 hours work with half an hour interval must be implemented.
19. Brick-industry owners must take licence from District Commissioner with full address and the Labour with identified photos.
20. Child labour act to be strictly enforced.
21. Government should appoint Tribal Welfare Advisory Council with the representatives from social workers, organisation and political parties working in tribal areas.
22. Creches and Maternity provisions to be introduced.
23. Supply of drinking water at working hours to be enforced.
24. Quarter with light, tubewell and latrine, bathroom should be provided.
25. Trade Union rights to organise themselves, freedom to participate in T. U. meetings after working hours must be enforced.
26. Inquiry committees with Parliamentary Member to be set up on working conditions of tribal *rejas* engaged in different labour centres.

27. Proper facility for improving primary education to tribal *rejas* must be made even by way of adult education or the like.

Thus after examining the above mentioned aspects we may arrive at a conclusion that if all the aforesaid facilities are provided to the *rejas* their sad plight may be minimized to a greater extent.

8

Summary and Conclusion

In the foregoing chapters a detailed study of the tribal *rejas* has been dealt with elaborately so as to have a complete and thorough idea about this teeming millions of Ranchi who have contributed much towards the progress of the nation in various ways.

From the primitive times, when men hunted animals, down to the present day when millions of men are employed in factories and other establishments, women are found to share the burdens of their respective families shoulder to shoulder with their partners in all the occupations. The early part of the present century reveals that only women folk belonging to the lower sections of the society sought employment at various labour centres. In fact they were pushed into service through sheer economic necessities and not lured by any other charm or attraction. No doubt a generation ago employment of women in any kind of occupation outside their own homes was looked on with disfavour or contempt but the situations are changing very fast, though there are still some forces—religious taboos and social customs—prevent the free flow of woman labourers to seek employment in large numbers. But at any rate, such restrictions also are fast weakening and the general attitude is becoming more and more plausible and helpful in widening the employment opportunities for woman labourers.

With the advent of industrialisation particularly in and around Ranchi a huge labour force was needed to cope up with the growing requirements at various labour-centres. Those engaged in industrial activities came out with a wide publicity to deploy a large number of labourers through their agents or sub-agents. With the result the tribal people got attracted with an intention to supplement their incomes by taking to the work of labourers in different areas of Ranchi. In the beginning it were men who joined first to be followed by women and thus the entire area started humming with the bustlings of tribal woman-labourers termed as *Reja* afterwards. These tribal *rejas* were deployed at various labour centres like brick-kilns, building constructions, industrial complexes, transportation of materials and the like, giving an emergence to a unique class of tribal woman-labourers popularly known as tribal *rejas*, a new concept of labour force altogether. This very labour force comprising the tribal *rejas* is, so to say, a new phenomenon in the tribal life of Ranchi in the wake of industrialisation as well as urbanisation.

The well known Oraon and Munda tribes of Ranchi are the chief contributors of the majority of the tribal *rejas* besides that of the Lohra tribe which has also the credit of contributing some *rejas*. These tribal *rejas* are seen busy from dawn to dusk at labour centres in different age-groups ranging from 10 to 60. Over and above, in the wake of dire necessities a large number of these tribal *rejas* migrate to distant places in quest of jobs with their own accord. They are, sometimes, enticed by the agents of employers or contractors with a view to serving their own ends by throwing employment opportunities to wandering tribal *rejas*.

Thus, the tribal *rejas* either join different labour centres with their own accord or they are employed through the agents or intermediaries of the employers. Roughly speaking the types of job undertaken by tribal *rejas* can be classified into five categories such as working at brick-kilns, construction work, engaged in transportation works and in industrial complexes as well as taking to miscellaneous works. In most cases the *rejas* engaged in different works are more or less specialised in their working patterns, hence they prefer to do the same types of job as far as practicable. In course of their jobs, they come in contact with a number of non-tribal and tribal populations or the like with whom they have to develop intimacy so as to win over their confidence in view of better prospects, amenities and facilities. These employers or contractors have already formulated a wage-structure which is more or less, common at all the labour-centres, but, of course, according to jobs. On one hand, the taibal *rejas* are busy earning for the betterment of their families, on the other, they have to maintain a particular type of standard which help them in continuing their jobs. Meaning thereby they try to look more tidy and smart as compared to others who have not taken to the profession of *rejas*. Similarly the *rejas* have to maintain a separate entity in their respective families as their status in the families are some what higher than those of non-earning members.

While throwing a glimpse to their pecuniary gains, by way of working as *rejas*, it has come to light that different wage structures have been formulated for *rejas* working at different labour centres. The *rejas* engaged at the sites of brick-kiln are said to be the lowest paid as compared to others though they have to put in much more strenuous labour in course of their duty. This happens because their labour is measured in terms of the total bricks carried by them on their heads. The other *rejas* are paid at the higher rates in comparison to those working in brick-kilns because they are paid at the rate of daily basis. On the contrary, if we look to their contributions towards supplementing the incomes of their families, the brick-kiln *rejas* actually contribute a major portion of their incomes whereas those engaged on trucks fail to contribute much, for their incomes are spent over their own expenditures viz. on dress and decorations as most of them are comparatively of younger age group and unmarried too. Thus it is but natural for them to be allured by outwardly attractions.

Although engaged in non-sedentary occupations these tribal *rejas* are not free from stresses and strains at various levels. Above all, they have to forbear inwardly as well as out-wardly conflicts in their families followed by at work sites and among their colleagues and companions. These stresses and strains, as we have already seen, can be attributed to many factors relating to jobs, employers, associates, etc., with whom they have got to adjust themselves despite their willingness or even non-willingness.

Thus, in course of passing through the state of conflicts and adjustments they have got to compromise with the circumstances for the purpose of bringing about betterment and uplift among themselves. There is no denying the fact that having been driven with poverty these tribal *rejas* take to various types of job which enable them to raise their resources which ultimately stand them in good stead. Marked changes are noticed in the life of the tribal *rejas* in respect of their living conditions, behaviour, attitudes, religious beliefs, political awakening, dress and decoration etc. These changes are the results of their constant contact with non-tribals which they establish in course of their new types of profession of *rejas*. As to their living condition the tribal *rejas* have started living in a better condition as compared to others. Their mud-built houses are kept clean and equipped with modern types of utensils in place of old aged pots. By and by they have become quite familiar with audio-visual aids, hence, at times, they entertain themselves by visiting cinema houses and listening to transistors during their leisures. Previously they were not inclined towards education to their children but now-a-days their attitudes in this respect have changed and they are now inclined towards its importance. This is indeed a redeeming feature in their changed careers though themselves are quite illiterate barring few of them only.

The illiteracy among the tribal *rejas* is very much responsible for their woeful conditions and plight which has become rather the order of the day. Although contributing their mite at various labour centres in and around Ranchi, these tribal *rejas* are still innocent and straight forward in their dealings which are easily exploited by those who are out to derive undue advantage from their simplicity. They are subjected to hard manual labours in exchange of a few chips only in exploitaion of their innocence, ignorance and poverty besides helplessness. Poverty as well as acute economic crisis are attributed for forcing this labour force to accept the work of *rejas* but even by doing a lot of labour, they are hardly rewarded amply and judiciously because they are still unaware of labour laws, legislations, trade unionism. For the sake of money these tribal labourers are enticed to far-flung areas and there they are subjected to all sorts of exploitations including rapes and tortures.

In this way, after going through the details of the activities, working conditions, ways of their life, conflicts including stresses and strains and types of exploitation meted out to them, we arrive to the following conclusions:-

1. Had there not been the growth of industries, there would have been hardly any employment opportunity to this huge labour force known as tribal *reja*.
2. Industrialisation acquired a vast tract of tribals land owing to which a huge influx of tribal population was deprived of agricultural yields which led them to set out to earn their livelihood elsewhere.
3. Poverty and economic needs necessitated the women folk to supplement the incomes of their families by taking to the work of *reja*.
4. The regular flow of income enabled the tribal *rejas* to fulfil their aspirations and ambitions to the extent they could acquire knowledge pertaining to modernism, of course, according to their capacity to spend. On the other hand, inability to fulfil their ambitions and desires gives rise to stresses and strains.
5. In order to fulfil their aspirations they, at times, easily fall victims to hoodlums, unsocial elements, cheats, frauds and the like who exploit them in various manners.
6. Illiteracy among the tribal *rejas* is the root cause of all sorts of evils and exploitations to them by their employers. contractors, intermediaries and so on.

7. On one hand, parents of *rejas* for the sake of money encourage them to take up the work, on the other, they cause stresses and strains by encroaching upon their wishes or independent thinkings.
8. By virtue of the regular contacts with the sophisticated class of population the tribal *rejas* have acculturised into altogether a separate class of workng people, as compared to the general tribal population.
9. Their socio-economic condition shows a marked improvement leading them towards progressiveness as they believe in balanced budgets and shun incurring loans.
10 Although exploited on various counts, the tribal *rejas* are economically better than many of those who have not taken to this profession, hence, day-by-day a number of female labourers are joining this profession ungrudgingly.

APPENDIX – A

Biographies

Appendix A—1

Name—Birsi Oraon
Age—65 years
Tribe—Oraon
Village—Burmu
Block—Mandar

(It is a biography of an old *reja* who used to distribute tiklis at a brick-kiln near village Ratu. There she was living with her second husband with whom she had picked up intimacy following the death of her legal husband. The second husband was also a supervisor at that brick-kiln).

I was born and brought up at village Burmu near Mandar in Ranchi district. From the very childhood I started working as a maid-servant and in course of it I had to serve at a number of houses in and around my village. When I reached the age of sixteen, I was married to a young man named Sukra. When I started living with Sukra, both of us left for Assam with a *sardar* to work as labourers in tea-estate. After a year or so we were blessed with a female child. Although earning our livelihood quite well we were lamenting for our village home because that place was not up to their liking. Thus, after staying there only for four years we all returned to our village-home and started working at brick-kilns. In the meantime my husband fell ill and later died of tuberculosis. After that both my daughter and myself were left alone at the merey of God. But in order to support ourselves, I restarted working as *rcja* at brick-kilns where I continued only for two years as I had to accompany a few colleagues of mine who were engaged on trucks for loading and unloading. While working on trucks I came in contact with a male *coolie* named Jattu Oraon of village Pandra. Jattu being a widower and having a female child with his former wife, developed much intimacy with me and thus both of us, eversince, lived together just like husband and wife. But fortunately or unfortunately we had no child afterwards except those two which we had from before. Jattu had some landed property which was mortgaged to the village *Sahukar* in lieu of a little amount which he had borrowed for the treatment of his first wife. Thus both of us while working together made up our minds to get the land released from the hands of the 'sahukars'. With this intention we were in search of some better prospects when we came across a *sardar* who presented before us all sorts of allurements for working at Alipore in Calcutta. For the onward journey the *sardar* advanced some money to all such labourers who had become ready to rush to Alipore. At Alipore all of us were entrusted with the job of tilling and reclaiming barren lands so as to convert them into cultivable lands. In this way with the help of different *Sardars* and agents we went to a number of places including Jalpaiguri, Siliguri, Bhutan and Burdwan. After staying at those places about twenty years we finally returned to Ranchi and started working again at brick-kilns. While working at remote places we used to come back to our village home for a while during which we got both the girls married to two young men of our own community in neighbouring villages.

Now we have been working at this brick-kiln on Devi Mandap road, Ratu for the last 10 years but my work has changed from an ordinary labourer to distributor of tokens whereas my husband's to a supervisor.

APPENDIX A—2

Name—Fulwa Oraon
Age—45 years
Village—Booty
Block—Kanke

(It is a biography of a tribal *reja* who went away with her emlpoyer and was later married to a non-tribal servant of her employer).

My name is Fulwa Oraon. Having born and brought up at village Booty, I was made to work as a maid servent at several houses. When I came of age I followed my mother who worked at brick-kiln in the village. My father was a drunkard hence he was never willing to do any work instead always kept on vexing my mother for money. My family comprised altogether ten members including my brothers and sisters. Thus both my mother and myself had to work for the support of our family. Meanwhile my employer got attracted towards me and he took me to his residence and appointed me as maid-servant giving me a higher salary. The employer thus further developed intimacy with me and started behaving with me just like a concubine of his though he was already married to two wives. Thus living together for sometime there ensued scuffle between his wives and him over me as such he took me to his village home in the district of Chapra where I was married to his non-tribal servant Siya Saran. Some how or other we managed to stay there for near about four to five years but the local people did not let us live there peacefully. During our stay at Chapra I learnt *Bhojpuri*, the native language of that area and started talking to other villagers in their own language. Nevertheless we were forced to leave that village and we had to come back to Ranchi. On return my husband took to the work of distilling country liquor assisted by me during my leisures. Generally I am busy working as *reja*, once again at different labour centres since fifteen years.

APPENDIX A–3

Name Budhni
Age—32 years
Tribe—Munda
Village—Palandu
Block—Khijri

My name is Budhni. I was born and brought up at village Jonha. My parents used to sell vegetables which they grew in their lands. We are three sisters and one brother, I am youngest of all. I being the youngest of sisters got fascinated towards my elder sisters for their working on trucks. At first when I expressed my views to accompany them they forbade me to do so because of my younger age. Thus I was left all alone at home to look after my only brother but the desire for working on trucks went on pestering me by and by and ultimately I too went on truck with my sisters when I was aged 15. After 3 years of working as *reja* I was married to a young man of village Palandu where I had to shift for ever. Here also I came in contact with those *rejas* who worked on trucks at different labour centres. When I expressed my desires to work on trucks for the sake of extra income, my husband at first objected to it as he was working as *mistry* in BISCOLAHF and later he himself managed to get me engaged as *reja* in that very establishment. Now both of us are busy earning our livelihood for the last ten years.

APPENDIX A—4

Name—Mangri Oraon
Age—50 years
Village—Khizirtola
Block—Kanke

My name is Mangri Oraon, a resident of village Khizirtola. Along with my parents I too used to work as labourer at different working centres. On coming of age I was married to a coolie with whom I had three daughters. I had occasions to travel with my husband and daughters to Orissa and Nagpur where we worked at different places in different capacities and passed many years. By the time all my daughters became adults hence for their marriages we had to come back where their marriages were performed. As a matter of fact I do not remember as to how many years we actually passed out of Ranchi but this much I can say that I remained out till my daughters became major. After their marriages my husband met with an accident and succumbed to injuries. Thus I was left alone and started working again as *reja* at different labour centres. My daughters though married, like to live with me and work as *rejas* preferably on trucks.

Since now I am not in a position to do strenuous jobs at brick-kilns, I work as maid-servant in urban locality but at times I join construction building works also for the sake of more money.

APPENDIX A—5

Name—Sahodari Munda
Age—22 years
Village—Bariatu
Block—Kanke

My name is Sahodari Munda. My parents are still young and active hence they are earning their livelihood regularly. My father works as plumber and my mother as mid-wife at a Government clinic. In the beginning I was sent to my village school where I learnt 3 Rs but soon afterwards I got attracted towards *rejas* of my village moving on trucks in colourful dresses chirping like birds. They often kept me persuading to follow them for the sake of more money and more fun. Thus the charms, one day, pushed me into the profession of *reja*. But my parents gave me a severe beating and kept me locked in a room for whole day and night. This behaviour of theirs aggravated me to a great extent as a sequel to which I managed to escape from my village and took to the profession of *reja* and went to Assam with other *rejas* with the help of *Sardarni*. But to my utter surprise there was only miseries and nothing else. The allurements given earlier turned out to be mirage and nothing else. Anyway I worked there for the whole season and came back to my village for ever. My parents however, excused me and got me engaged in a construction project.

Appendix-B

Case Studies

Appendix B–1

This case is narrated by Biran of Kishunpur village (Bariatu). In 1980 she had gone to work in the Talabir brick-kiln in Mogra in Hooghly district. Rupa and Parti also accompanied her in the same brick-kiln but they had to finally run away when they could not endure the torture of being raped repeatedly. Biran who worked with these rejas narrated the sordid story:

"Rupa was a pretty girl so when she went to work there she caught the eye of the contractor who raped her. She used to cry and tell us about this torture and about how unhappy she was. But she also knew that there was nothing that she could do to stop this. If she complained then she would not be given work and she would have to starve. But after sometimes she could not endure this any longer and ran away. She had to go to some other brick-kiln to earn some money before she could return home. No less brutal was the case with Parti also, who left the brick-kiln after being raped. Now they are not interested in going outside their village to work any where."

APPENDIX B–2

Laxmi Munda, a 20 years old girl, had gone to work in Nabagram in Burdwan district from her village Baragain in the year 1979, recollected how she was molested by some hoodlums.

We were sleeping in our huts when we heard some noise outside. We found that some local toughs had entered our kiln and were demanding liquour from our *Munshi*. He refused saying that he did not have any. The angry hoodlums then turned their attention to us. They came over to my hut and molested me."

Helpless, she had to submit

APPENDIX B—3

There is a brick-kiln situated at some distance of Bariatu Housing Colony, Ranchi. Though there is not much distance between the kiln and the colony, the situation of the kiln is such that there is no connection of the residents of the colony with the kiln. The owner of that kiln is also a resident of the colony. Some tribal rejas were brought from Khunti in 1981 for working in that kiln. They were provided their abodes near the kiln. Once at midnight the residents of the colony listened a great hue and cry coming from that side where the kiln is situated. By chance, the owner of that kiln was among them and he thought that this hue and cry might be coming from the kiln. He along with other members of his family and some other persons of the colony proceeded towards the kiln, with wooden mace and iron rods in their hands. When they reached near the kiln they found that some *goonda* elements of the nearby bastis had come there to molest the *rejas* living there. All the *goondas* were drunk but they could not get success because the owner of that kiln reached there in time and became successful in dispersing them. The *rejas* were not ready to continue the work there, therefore, the owner had to persuade the *rejas* to continue, and some more persons were alloted for their protection. The wife of the owner also went there and gave assurance of providing full protection to them, then only the *rejas* agreed to work there further.

APPENDIX B–4

Somari, though married to a man belonging to her own tribe, Oraon, was passing good days in the beginning. Later on she had an occasion to come back to her parents for a while where she took to the work of *reja* which she used to do prior to her marriage. She was working as *reja* in construction works. While working as *reja*, she was able to earn money with the help of which she had a satisfaction of leading an independent life. She was also able to fulfil her ambitious desires. Besides her own parents her husband too objected to her becoming a *reja* but she did not pay any heed to their objections and remained in the look out for getting rid of such strains for ever. One day she had a chance to come in contact with a military personnel towards whom she was infatuated as a result of which she eloped with him never to return.

APPENDIX B–5

Budhni, a 18 years old *reja* of Hurhari Basti, Ratu Road, went in search of job with her colleague, a coolie Jatru Oraon of the same basti in the year 1979. She had developed intimacy with Jatru while working in a construction project for nine months continuously. When that project was closed, both of them were free. Then Jatru gave her proposal to go to Dhanbad where his some relatives had already gone to work at brick-kilns. Thus obeying Jatru she accompanied him to Dhanbad for better prospects and more comforts. But there the situation was something otherwise. Jatru's relations were, on doubt, engaged in different labour centres and they were earning enough to maintain themselves. But when Budhni expressed her desire to go on work with them, they viewed it very seriously and did not allow her to go out for earning. On the contrary she was confined to do their domestic chores completely against her wishes and desires. Even Jatru who had enticed her acted against her wishes and sided his own relatives in not allowing her to work outside. Thus her hopes were shattered to her utter disgust. She had no alternative than to manage to escape away from there in the interest of her future career.

APPENDIX B–6

Tetri working at a brick-kiln near village Irwa hailed from Oraon community. She was working there as *reja* for more than three years. According to her employer shri R.N.Roy, Tetri was attractive to look at and quite efficient in the work assigned to her. While working there she used to contribute towards her family. But the inmates were never satisfied with the contribution she used to make. They often kept on scolding and rebuking her on even filmsy grounds which caused so much strains to her that she began to remain morosed. In the meantime she developed intimacy to a coworker with whom she eloped for ever perhaps to get rid of the stress and strains of her family or for better prospects.

APPENDIX B – 7

Shri Manohar Singh, a contractor for supplying *rejas* at brick-kiln sites out of Bihar while narrating about Etwaria, a *Sardarni* aged 40, said that Etwaria was previously working as *reja* at various labour centres under him. While working for years she had picked up all sorts of experiences. Thus, she thought of taking to the job of a *Sardarni* in view of more earnings. Because she had developed intimacy with shri Manonar Singh, she was pleased to take up the work according to her choice. Since then, doing the profession of *reja* she started acting like a *Sardarni* under the same contractor and recently (in 1982) she has collected a number of *rejas* from her village Gari and left for Punjab with them. In the capacity of a *Sardarni* she has already supplied *rejas* to work sites in Orissa as well as in Uttar Pradesh under the same contractor with whom she is living like a concubine.

APPENDIX B—8

An woeful tale of Sanichari of village Sidrol came to light in course of investigation. Sanichari was engaged on a truck as *reja* and was supporting her family including her husband and one male child. Her husband Mungra was doing nothing but he used to live on her earnings. Since he was idling away his time at home, he liked Sanichari also to remain always with him, hence, objections on her working on trucks. Moreover her relationship with the driver and the *khalasis* aroused suspicion to Mungra who was already suffering from inferiority complex because of his unemployment. Thus both of them were passing through stresses and strains of role-conflict which ultimately led Mungra to desert Sanichari for ever. Sanichari is still continuing her profession and leading her life with his son who is schooling in the village.

APPENDIX B–9

Meghia's plight is well known to the locality in which she is seen wandering in rags.

Once Meghia (35 years), a resident of village Angara, was taken to be a very efficient as well as dutiful *reja* by the contractors engaged in road construction projects. At home Meghia passing her days happily with her husband in the beginning who later on started misbehaving with her. Thus having been fade-up with her husband's behaviour she went back to live with her parents. Her parents also could not endure her for many days and started taunting her quite regularly. Though working as *reja* Meghia was able to support herself but the feeling of her being barren kept her pinching throughout. In course of time the misbehaviour of her husband, stresses and strains caused by her parents besides her innermost feeling for yearning a child forced her to become insane. Under this state of affairs, although still young, she is note in a position to attend to any work and now seen wandering in rags begging for the rest of her life.

Appendix C-I

Industrial Classification of Tribal Women at work and Non-works in Bihar (1971 Census)

Sl. No.	Name of Sch. Tribe	Total Population P	M	F	Total Workers	Culti-vators	Agrilabour-ers
1	2	3	4	5	6	7	8
	All Sch. Tribes	4725693	2350923	2374770	326915	133771	171204
1.	Asur–	7018	3597	3421	383	238	140
2.	Baiga–	1310	652	658	101	11	86
3.	Banjara–	119	68	51	15	1	8
4.	Bathudi–	879	492	387	145	–	145
5.	Bedia–	46761	23471	23290	2846	1237	1488
6.	Bhumij–	120144	59415	60729	10363	2466	7529
7.	Binjhia–	9115	4593	4522	307	168	123
8.	Birhor–	3447	1776	1671	424	18	151
9.	Birjia–	3360	1835	1525	241	26	174
10.	Chero–	38565	19892	18673	1733	361	1280
11.	Chik Baraik–	32291	15879	16412	1425	571	728
12.	Gond–	42928	21692	21236	3108	962	1812
13.	Gorait–	2874	1411	1463	270	54	188
14.	Ho–	479529	233358	246171	47372	21191	24618
15.	Karmali–	24116	12337	11779	1250	310	740
16.	Kharia–	122588	59138	63450	6480	2528	3574
17.	Kharwar–	138115	70466	77649	7142	1719	5202
18.	Khond–	485	243	242	83	–	28
19.	Kisan–	15966	7957	8009	424	174	235
20.	Kora–	19778	9511	10267	1578	188	1152
21.	Korwa–	18177	9386	8791	1972	181	1695
22.	Lohra–	110805	56611	54194	7100	1458	4772
23.	Mahli–	71389	36263	35126	6601	796	2305
24.	Mal Paharia–	48192	24103	24089	3452	1353	1847
25.	Munda–	686972	340282	346690	43397	24041	16443
26.	Oraon–	822841	406473	416368	49759	20927	24427
27.	Santal–	1762591	879527	883064	122939	50896	66605
28.	Parahiya–	14524	7667	6857	1292	96	1049
29.	Sauria Paharia–	58695	30693	28002	3192	1381	1695
30.	Savar–	3409	1900	1509	517	3	458
31.	Unspecified–	18710	10235	8475	1024	463	507

(Contd...)

Livestock Forestry Fishing Hunting & plantations Orchards and allied activities	Mining & Quarrying	Manufacturing process, Servicing & Repairs		Construction	Trade and Commerce	Transport, storage and communications	Other services	Non-workers
		Household Industry	Other and Household Industry					
9	10	11	12	13	14	15	16	17
2328	3751	8581	3472	—	—	—	2	3038
1	—	2	—	—	—	—	—	557
—	—	—	4	5	—	—	1	36
—	—	—	—	—	—	—	—	242
—	—	—	—	—	2	13	8	20444
9	62	3	24	4	26	37	75	50366
31	77	90	48	—	1	—	—	4215
2	2	—	11	—	—	—	—	—
44	1	177	32	—	—	—	1	1247
8	—	20	—	—	—	13	—	1284
9	3	4	65	—	3	—	8	16940
19	4	60	13	1	5	1	23	14987
2	92	151	60	—	11	—	18	18128
1	11	7	—	1	2	2	4	1193
188	415	113	354	36	27	132	298	198799
—	123	22	32	16	3	5	14	10529
38	26	71	30	3	26	4	180	56970
54	39	43	45	2	6	1	26	60507
—	54	—	—	—	—	1	—	159
2	—	1	—	—	—	—	12	7585
46	62	91	13	—	7	16	3	8689
31	7	24	4	12	1	10	7	6819
27	70	540	97	12	26	31	67	47094
13	90	3237	103	3	6	10	38	28525
83	4	51	17	—	37	6	34	20657
198	763	115	554	104	69	215	859	303293
306	584	113	1070	153	48	517	1614	366609
1175	1250	482	863	117	94	264	1220	760125
8	—	130	1	—	—	1	7	5565
31	2	13	9	—	42	3	16	24810
—	2	14	1	1	37	—	1	992
2	8	7	22	3	—	—	12	7451

Appendix C-II

Industrial Classification of Tribal Women at work and Non-work in Ranchi District, Bihar (1971 Census)

Sl. No.	Name of Sch. Tribe	Total population P	M	F	Total wor-kers	Culti-vators	Agri-labour-ers	Livestock Foresty, Fishing, Hunting, plantations, Orchards and Allied activi-ties.
1	2	3	4	5	6	7	8	9
	All Sch. Tribes	1451597	717472	734125	83338	45014	33332	321
1.	Asur—	6565	3345	3220	350	236	109	1
2.	Baiga—	326	137	189	—	—	—	—
3.	Banjara—	14	9	5	5	—	—	—
4.	Bedia—	22919	11843	11076	2053	832	1205	6
5.	Bhumij—	578	254	324	21	2	8	—
6.	Binjhia—	9054	4561	4493	292	167	109	2
7.	Birhor—	871	437	434	74	5	27	—
8.	Birjia—	1239	699	540	67	22	25	—
9.	Chero—	52	36	16	6	—	6	—
10.	Chik Baraik—	30658	15019	15639	1351	562	675	19
11.	Gond—	17258	8435	8823	1165	699	414	—
12.	Gorait—	2614	1261	1353	249	53	176	1
13.	Ho—	196	77	119	3	—	1	—
14.	Karmali—	3492	1733	1759	352	118	217	—
15.	Kharia—	111166	53597	57569	4845	2494	2121	25
16.	Kherwar—	8659	4328	4331	333	201	111	1
17.	Khond—	8	—	8	—	—	—	—
18.	Kisan—	6510	3244	3266	185	106	71	1
19.	Korwa—	2432	1112	1320	140	70	68	—
20.	Lohra—	80874	40922	39952	5150	1156	3392	14
21.	Mahli—	24963	12540	12423	1657	408	810	2
22.	Mal Paharia—	1	1	—	—	—	—	—
23.	Munda—	506348	250136	256212	31215	19893	10139	88
24.	Oraon—	610549	300246	310303	33372	17984	13227	161
25.	Parahiya—	451	249	202	25	1	16	—
26.	Santhal—	1128	579	549	428	5	405	—
27.	Sauria Paharia—	4	4	—	—	—	—	—
28.	Savar—	1	1	—	—	—	—	—
29.	Unspecified—	2667	2667	—	—	—	—	—

(*Contd...*)

Mining & Quarrying	Manufacturing process, Servicing & Repairs		Construction	Trade and Commerce	Transport, storage and communications	Other services	Non-workers
	Household Industry	Other and Household Industry					
10	11	12	13	14	15	16	17
181	1075	583	—	—	—	2	2870
—	2	—	5	—	—	—	189
—	—	—	5	—	—	—	—
—	2	—	—	1	—	7	9023
—	—	—	—	—	1	—	303
10	—	—	—	1	—	—	4201
2	—	11	—	—	—	1	360
—	41	—	—	—	—	—	473
—	20	—	—	—	—	—	10
—	—	—	1	4	—	23	14288
2	53	12	—	—	—	10	7658
3	7	—	1	2	2	4	1104
3	7	—	—	—	—	—	116
—	—	2	—	1	1	6	1407
1	3	5	2	8	1	149	52724
6	12	27	—	—	—	5	3998
3	10	2	—	—	—	—	8
—	—	—	—	—	—	6	3081
—	1	—	—	—	—	2	1180
—	—	—	8	23	17	53	34802
22	413	52	3	—	3	27	10766
4	383	17	—	—	—	—	—
—	—	—	—	—	—	—	—
39	50	180	14	57	120	635	224997
68	43	271	34	39	266	1279	276931
—	7	—	—	—	—	1	177
11	—	—	—	—	—	7	121
—	—	—	—	—	—	—	—
—	—	—	—	—	—	—	—
—	—	—	—	—	—	—	—

Appendix-D

Glossary

Terms Used	*English Equivalent*
Abhi	Now
Afim	Opium
Arkatia	Seller of human being in Munda language
Ashram	Shelter
Ayah	Nurse
Barish	Rains
Basti	Village
Bhang	Hamp
Bharat	India
Bindi	Vermillion applied in round shape on women's forehead.
Biri	An indiginous form of cigarette
Brahamcharini	Woman celibate
Chadar	Wrapper
Chappal	Slippers
Coolie	Male labourer
Dadoon	Advance paid to labourer

1	2
Dhibri	Tin-lamp
Dhoti	Male Gaement
Diya	Earthen lamp
Ghar	Home, House
Ghee	Clarified butter
Goonda	Hoodlums
Gur	Treacle
Haat	Market or Mart
Hanria	Country liquor made of rice
Inta	Brick
Jhopri	Hut
Kajal	black soot applied round eye lide, collyrium
Kameej	Shirt
Karahi	Pan or bowl shaped receptacles
Karta	Head of the family
Khaini	Dry tobacco
Khalasi	Assistant to Driver
Kuchha	Unbaked
Kurta	A loose male garment
Lathaits	Persons armed with sticks or lathis
Maa	Mother
Maar	Beat
Mela	Fair
Munshi	Manager
Nautanki	Theatre
Ojha	Exorcist
Paizama	Trousers
Pathera	Brick-moulder
Pathna	To mould the brick

1	2
Rab	A form of paste treacle
Sahu	Moneylender
Sardar	Chief Agent
Sardarni	Lady Chief Agent
Saree	A female garment
Sati	Lady who burns herself with her husband
Shivir	Tent
Thagar	The place where bricks are moulded
Tikli	Token
Tokri	Basket
Tripal	Tarpauline
Vaidya	Physician

Bibliography

Adyantha, N. K.	1955 :	*Women's Employment in India*, Ministry of Labour, Government of India, reprint from the International Review, July.
Altekar, A. S.	1956 :	*The Position of Women in Hindu* Civilisation, Benaras.
Anderson, Walfred A. and Frederick B. Parker	1964 :	*Society : Its Organisation and Operation*, D. van Nostrand Company, Canada.
Andreas, Carol	1971 :	*Sex and Caste in America*, Engliwood Cliff : Prentice Hall Inc.
Baig, Tara Ali	1976 :	*India's Women Power*. S. Chand and Co., New Delhi.
Belok, Dr. Michael V. (Ed,)		*Women : An International Perspective*, Anu Prakashan, Meerut.
Bhowmick, P. K.	1960 :	*Economic Life of the Lodhas*, The Eastern Anthropologist (Journal), Vol. XIII, No. 3, March-May.
Cormack, Margaret	1953 :	*The Hindu Women*, Bureau of Publications, Teachers College, Columbia University, Now York.-

Dahlstrom, Edmund 1967 : *Analysis of the Debate on Sex Roles*, in Edmund Dahlstrom (ed.) The Changing Roles of Men and Women, London; Gerald Duckworth and Co. Ltd.

Das, Veena. 1976 : *Indian Women: Work, Power and Status*, in B. R. Nanda (ed.). Indian Women; From Purdah to Modernity, Vikas Publishing House, New Delhi.

deSouza, Alfred (ed.) 1975 : *Women in Contemporary India: Traditional Images and Changing Roles*, Manohar Book Service, New Delhi.

Francis, E. Merill & H. Wentworth Eldrige 1952 : *Culture and Society* New York: Prentice-Hall.

Goswomi, M. C. & D. N. Majumdar 1965 : *A Study of Women's Position Among the Garo of Assam*, Man in India, Vol. 45, No. 1, January-March.

Gross, N. A. W. Mc Eachern and W.S. Mason 1957 : *Role Conflict and its Resolution*, New York, Biddle and Thomas.

Inamdar, N. R. (ed.) 1974 : *Community Development and Democratic Growth*, Popular Prakashan, Bombay.

Jain, Devaki (ed.) 1975 : *Indian Women*, Publication Division, Ministry of Information and Broadcasting, Govt. of India, New Delhi.

Kar, R.K. 1976 : *A Tribe in the Context of a Tea Industry in India: Some Preliminary Observation*, Anthropos. 71, 868-77.

Kar, R.K. and Geetanjali Baruah 1979 : *Tea Labour: Preliminary Appraisal of Common Identity in a Multiethnic Community in Assam*, Man in India, Vol. 59, No. 1, January-March.

Klein, Viola 1963-64 : *Industrialization and the Changing Role of Women*, Current Sociology, Vol. XII, No. 1.

Lal, A.K. 1979 : *Status of Women in Urban Setting: An Analysis of Role Differentiation in the family*, Man in India, Oct.-Dec. Vol. 59, No. 4.

L. Harold, Nix and *Frederick L. Bates* 1962 : *Occupational Role Stresses: A Structural Approach*, Rural Sociology Vol. 27, I. March.

Madan, Dr. Gurumukh Ram 1967 : *Indian Social Problems* (Social Disorganization and Reconstruction), Vol. II, Social Reconstruction, Allied Publishers Private Ltd., Bombay.

Mies, Maria 1980 : *Indian Women and Patriarchy*: Conflicts and Dilemas of Students and Working Women. Concept Publishing Company, New Delhi.

Nanda, B.R. (ed.) 1976 : *Indian Women: From Purdah to Modernity*, Vikas Publishing House, New Delhi.

Parsons, T. 1951 : "*The Social System*", New York, in Biddle and Thomas.

Piggott, Stuart 1950 : *Prehistoric India*, Penguin Books.

Rani, Kala 1976 : *Role Conflict in Working Women*, New Delhi.

Rayner, Louisa 1957 : *Women in a Village*, William Heinemann Ltd. , Melbourne.

Rothfeld, Otto *Women of India*, illustrated by M.V. Dhurandhar, Bombay D.B. Taraporevala Sons & Co.

Sachchidananda 1964 : *Culture Change in Tribal Bihar: Munda and Oraon*, Calcutta, Bookland (P) Ltd.

1978 : *Social Structure, Status and Mobility Patterns: The Case of Tribal Women*, Man in India, Vol. 58, No. 1, Jan-March

Sandhwar, A.N. 1978 : *The Korwa of Palamau: A Study of their Society & Economy*. Act a Ethnologica Et Linguistica, Wien (Vienna).

Sengupta, Shyamal-lkanti 1977 : *Applied Anthropology: Meaning and Necessity*, Firma KLM, Pvt. Ltd. Calcutta.

Sengupta, Padmini 1960 : *Women Workers of India*, Asia Publishing House, Bombay

Singh, V.B. and A.K. Saran (ed) 1960 : *Industrial Labour in India*, Asia Publishing House, Bombay.

Thomas, P. 1964 : *Indian Women through the Ages*, Asia Publishing House, Bombay.

Vidyarthi, L.P. 1959 ; *Anthropology ond Tribal Welfare in India* (ed). Council of Social and Cultural Research, Bihar.

1960 : *Indian Anthropology in Action (ed)*. Council of Social and Cultural Research, Bihar.

1968 : Applied Anthropology in *India* (ed). Kitab Mahal, Allahabad.

1968 : *Cultural Change in the Tribes of Modern India.* Journal of Social Research, 11 (1), 1-36.

1969 : *Cultural Configuration of Ranchi Survey of an Emerging Industrial City of Tribal India,* J. N. Basu & Co. Calcutta. Bookland (Pvt) Ltd.

1969 : *Aspects of Tribal Labour in Chotanagpur,* Tribe, VI, 3 : 1—9

1970 : *Socio Cultural Implications of Industrialisation in India: a case study of tribal Bihar,* Council of Social & Cultural Research, Ranchi.

1971 : *The Ranchi Tribals in Andaman and Nicobar Islands-* Journal of Social Research XIV, 2: 50–9.

1980 : *Cultural Factors in Development Process: Case Studies from Tribal Bihar,* Man in India, Dec. Vol. 60, No. 3–4.

Vidyarthi, L. P. & B. K. Rai 1977 : *The Tribal Culture of India,* New Delhi, The Concept Publishing House.

Vidyarthi, L. p. & Makhan Jha 1979 : *Growth and Development of Anthropology in Bihar,* Classical Publications, New Delhi.

Zweig, Ferdynand 1961 : *The Worker in an Affluent Society*-family life and Industry, Helnemann, London.

REPORTS

1953 : *Economic and Social Status af Women Workers of India*, Publication No. 15, Labour Bureau, Ministry of Labour, Government of India.

1969 : *Report of the National Commission on Labour*, Ministry of Labour and Employment and Rehabilitation, Government of India.

1974 : *The Fifth Five Year Plan*, New Delhi, Planing Commission.

1980 : *Report of the Working Group on Tribal Development During Sixth Plan* 1980–85, Ministry of Home Affairs, Government of India, New Delhi.

1975 : The Bihar Tribal Welfare Research Institute. Vol. XVII, No. 2.

Index

Tribal woman labourers engaged in various types of work in brick making complex

A *SARDARNI*, the tribal woman who acts as supplier of tribal woman labourers

Temporary shelter of the tribal woman labourers

Tribal woman labourer engaged in transportation work

Picture showing living conditions of the tribal woman migrant labourers

Tribal woman labourer engaged in brick-kiln

A tribal woman labourer engaged in construction work

Tribal woman labourer engaged in transportation work

FOLK STORIES IN LHOTA NAGA

Tex with interliner and running English Translation

By
J. P. MILLS

Edited with a glossary
By
SATKARI MUKHOPADHYAY

Published by

GYAN

Gyan Publishing House
5, Ansari Road
Daryaganj, New Delhi-110002
Phone: 011-47034999, 9811692060
E-mail: books@gyanbooks.com

Distribution Network
gyanbooks.com
India, USA, Canada, UK, Australia, France

© Author

All rights reserved. No part of this work may be reproduced, stored, adapted, or transmitted in any form or by any means, electronic, mechanical, photocopying, micro-filming recording or otherwise, or translated in any language, without the prior written permission of the copyright owner and the publisher. The book is sold subject to the condition that it shall not, by way of trade or otherwise, be lent, resold, hired out, or otherwise circulated without the prior publisher's written consent in any form of binding or cover other than that in which it is published.

ISBN: 978-81-212-0074-5 (HB)

Reprint in India, 2024
First Published, 2017

Printed at: Gyan Press, Delhi.

The views and opinions expressed in this book are author(s) own and the facts reported by them have been verified to the extent possible, and the publishers are not in any way liable for the same.

Folk Stories of Lhota Naga:
Text with Interliner and Running English Translation
Author: J. P. Mills, Satkari Mukhopadhyay

CONTENTS

INTRODUCTION

While working on the ethnography of the Lhota Nagas I realized how scanty had been the attention hithero paid to their language. The only existing grammar was that of Dr. Witter of the American Baptist Missionary Society, and this was not altogether satisfactory. The few little books of religious instruction were admittedly incomprehensible in places to the Lhotas for whom they were written. Clearly a fresh study of the language was called for, and I determined to attempt to combine with a record of their folklore a record of the language as actually spoken which might be of interest to philologists. and upon which a simple and consistently spelt written language might some day be founded.

I had on my staff a literate Lhota named Tsansao, whose assistance was absolutely invaluable and to whom my heartiest thanks are due. My method was entirely my own and for its defects I am solely responsible. It was as follows. Some Lhota, whose knowledge of folklore was known to be accurate and who spoke the Liye (Northern) dialect which Tsansao spoke, would offer to tell a story. We would listen to him. Then I would cause Tsansao to take it down word for word, a task I could not do myself. for no one but a Lhota could deal with the repetitions and omissions of one of his own tribe attempting to dictate for the first time in his life. The story was then read over carefully several times to the teller to make sure that his version had been accurately recorded. The next stage was to read it over to two or three old men and obtain their confirmation that the story had been told in a manner which accorded strictly with sound tradition. The folklore having been voted accurate we turned our attention to language and spelling. A simple phonetic system was used, without elaborate diacritical marks which would only be dropped in the hurry of everyday use if a written language grew up. I had each sentence pronounced very slowly and distinctly, and rewrote it with care. Then I made sure that I had cut it up into words properly—a very difficult task in a language where suffixes and compounds abound. I kept a small word list in which every word was entered, and against which every word was checked at each recurrence to ensure that the spelling was kept consistent. On a fair copy of each story an interlinear word for word translation was added, with each English word below its Lhota equivalent. Finally a running translation was made. The result is a small collection of specimens of modern Liye Lhota, which not only, I trust, show the structure of the language as actually spoken with its long and characteristic participial clauses, in a way no lists of artificial sentences could illustrate, but also reveal something of the mode of thought and traditions of those who use it.

1

THE WAX GIRL

Eran-na Nungkamchung-o vana-thang eloe
Ancestors Nungkamchung-at remaining-time woman
rchyua Yensali etsai Ezung-pfui vancho; hochi era loroe.
a Yensali called Ezung-woman was; she wax girl.
Hochi opoyang-na n-soa vantok to
Her parents not-marrying causing to remain indeed
tyutala. Tsontsotsü-na ntila n-wotok to
say. Tsontsotsü anywhere (will) not-allow to go thus
eloe-chi opoyang ezosi soa vancho.
woman's the (to) parents having said marrying remained.
Osi ntila n-wotok vantokcho. Onpoi
But anywhere not-allowing to go caused to remain. Couple's
ki-cho oyan li-lan nathango tssocho sakama
house-the village field-path near was because
oyamo-chiang-na li-lan sana yia-thang-ha na
villagers the field path all using coming-time-both and
li-lan sana woa-thang ha to Tsontsotsüang
field-path all using going-time too indeed (the) Tsontsotsüs
onpoi li mhonkana to tai tyuta sampicho. Ole
couple's fields very good thus only saying walked. Then
Yensali-na hochi zoiki orapvü-chi "E-ni ha
Yensali this hearing (to) husband-the "We-two also
ochö oli ze-lo wotaka" to ezosi ochö
tomorrow field see-to will go" thus having said next day
to oli ze-lo wotacho. Chisicho Tsontsotsü-na oli-na
indeed field see-to went. Then Tsontsotsü field to

owo eng-chi "Nno san-cho-lan
going (to) wife-the "You always using-going down-path

tonga chowo lung- pi-chi-na oli
going straight going down rock- flat top-that-from field

chani zesi chongi li-ki- na vana"
viewing having seen going up field-house- in remain"

to ezosi mbo-na li-tsa thrua oli-chi
thus having said he field-edge going round field-the

zeta chowosi chongi zele eng-
seeing having gone down coming up when saw wife

cho lung-pi-lo tyunkai sitakcho.
the rock-flat top-on having melted away perished.

Chisicho Tsontsotsü-na oyan-i oyi om-chi
Then Tsontsotsü village-to going (to) wife's father-the

"A-m, i-tsolo-cho lung-pi-lo
"My-wife's father, your-daughter-the rock-flat top-on

tyunkai sitaka" to ezole
having melted away has perished" thus when said

om-na "Nna mbo pipo-samlo-chiang tsam-n-
wife's father "You her ornaments-clothes-the touched-

tsamphila ?" to engale Tsontsotsü-na
not-touched ?" thus when asked Tsontsotsü

"N-tsamphika, a-m" to ezocho. Tole
"Not-have touched, my-wife's father" thus said. Then

om-na "Toka ochö ha eng-ya-thang owo
wife's father "Then tomorrow even sun-rising-time going

nshi-wo-ki ekhab-kasi zeta vanke"
nshi-leaves-with picking-having covered watching remain"

to ezocho. Ole Tsontsotsü-na nshi-wo-ki
thus said. Then Tsontsotsü *nshi*-leaves-with

ekhab-kasi zeta vanle chi-thang
picking-having-covered watching when remained that-time

otsak thrua oro soyingiki nchörang koto vancho
bees swarming come having begun before as was

san hoto kamiki ostan echekpya voncho orapvü-na
thus so (she) having become hair smoothing was husband

sosi yicho. Chitosicho eng-chi ntila n-
taking (her) went. After this wife-the anywhere not-

wotoko oki kham-cho-i tai vantokcho.
allowing to go home shade-the-in only made to remain.

Chisilocho oni-na otsoi epue nchyueni pokcho ; ole
After this they two children male two got ; then

eramo-chicho Champomung tsa na okhawo-chicho
elder-the Champomung called and younger-the

Shishanga tsa to tssocho. Tsontsotsü-na champo-i tai
Shishanga called thus became. Tsontsotsü-by *morung*-in only

munga shishang-cho tssoko-na eramo-chi
sitting *shishang* ceremony-the being-because elder-the

Champomung tsa na okhawo-chi Shishanga
Champomung called and younger-the Shishanga

tsa to tssocho. Hochi tssoko-na nhungacha
called thus became. This being-because till now

Champomung tsoronichen-cho Champomungdri echan
Champomung's descendants-the Champomungdri are called

na Shishanga tsoronichen-cho Shishangdri to echanala.
and Shishanga's descendants-the Shishangdri thus are called.

Motsü-shi nhunga tsoren tiing aria tsso.
Story-this now generations seven so much happened.

In the days when our ancestors lived at Nungkamchung[1] there was a girl of the Ezung clan whose name was Yensali. And she was a wax girl. Her parents did not wish to marry her to anyone, but Tsontsotsü promised never to let her go out in the sun anywhere, so her parents gave her to him in marriage. And he was careful to keep his promise. Now he built his house near the path which the villagers used going to and from their fields, and as the villagers went to and from their fields they kept saying, as they passed the house, how good Tsontsotsü's fields were. Because she always heard this

1 The oldest Lhota village. from which all other Lhota villages are believed to have sprung For some uuknown reason it has dwindled greatly of recent years and became extinct while I was in the Naga Hills.

said Yensali said to her husband "We will go together and see the fields to-morrow." So the next day they went, and when they reached the field Tsontsotsü said to his wife "You go down the track and look at the fleld from that big rock there. Then go up to the field-house and wait there." And she went down along the edge of the field and got up onto the big roek to look. But wheh she got into the rock she melted right away. Then Tsontsotsü went up to the village and said to his father-in-law "Your daughter has melted away on the big rock." Then his father-in-law asked him whether he had touched her clothes and ornaments, and when Tsontsotsü said he had not, he said "Go down early to-morrow morning and sprinkled *nshi* leaves on the place." So Tsontsotsü went and sprinkle *nshi* leaves over his wife's remains and a swarm of bees appeared and turned into his wife as she was before. And she brushed her hair back with her hand and went home with her husband.

After this he never let her go anywhere, but always made her stay in the shade of the house. And in due time two sons were born to them. The elder was called Champomung and the younger was called Shishanga. They were so called because Tsontsotsü spent all his time in the *morung* (*champo*) and because he did the Shishang ceremony. That is why to this day the descendants of Champomung are called Champomungdri and the descendants of Shishanga are called Shishangdri. This is a story of what happened about seven generations ago.

2

THE STORY OF HUMCHIBILIO

Onche-ni eramo-chi-na okhawo-chi nti
(Of) brothers-two elder-the younger-the anything

nti-na n-chocho. Eramo-chicho omholi mhom mhom
anything-by not-did excel. Elder-the fields well well

chon-na m-mhom chonche na eloe ha mhon mhon
cultivates-if not-well cultivating and girl too good good

tai soa va-na m-mhom kam to tssocho.
only marrying kept-if not-good turning into thus became.

Osi nchokacho onche-ni owo oli chhani
But one day (the) brothers-two going fields from fari

zetasi okhawo-chi 'li mhom-ochi eramo-chi
having examined younger's-the field good-the (to) elder-the

pi eramo-chi 'li m-mhom-ochi okhawo-chi pi
giving elder's-the field not-good-the (to) younger-the giving

to oni tongtacho. Ole eramo-chicho oli mhom-
thus they-two exchanged. Then (to) elder-the field good-

ochi piala m-mhom kam na okhawo-chicho oli
the giving not-good turning into and (to) younger-the field

m-mhom-chi mhona kam to tssocho. Chitosicho
not good-the good turning into thus became. After this

eramo-chi-na ongo eng mhomo-chi soa
elder-the younger brother's wife good-the marrying

vam kilato nchama ongo
would keep intending thinking (his) younger brother

etchüthechi-lo ora-i hono-hambong hantasi wotacho.
deceive-to jungle-in fowl-cock taking (they) went off.

Osi ota-na ongo-chi etchüthechi-lo
But elder brother-the younger brother-the deceive-to

owo "A-ngo, nno meta-shi tsi-n-tsi
going "My-younger brother, you place-this know-not-know

tsi-n-tsi ?" to sopiya ezole ongo-na
know-not-know ?" thus taking when said (the) younger brother

"A-ta, shicho a-po e-ni
"My-elder brother, this my-father we-two

tsang-wo-pen, shicho chungra tong-pen,
(wood) to cut-going-place, this bird trap setting-place,

shicho tsirhi tong-pen, shicho yanyo-pen
this rat trap setting-place, this searching-place

na shicho tyoka-pen to ezokhancho. Tole
and this fishing-place thus kept on saying. Then

ota-na ongo-chi tampoe
(the) elder brother younger brother-the (to) another place

soa owo lungrhen-pang-i "A-ngo, shicho
taking going cliff-top-at "My-younger brother, this

tsi-n-tsi ?" to ezole ongo-na
know-not-know ?" thus when said (the) younger brother

"A-ta, shicho n-tsi" to ezocho.
"My-elder brother, this (I) not-do know" thus said.

Chisicho ota-na "A-ngo, shi-lo
Then (the) elder brother "My-younger brother, this-at

yiptaka" to ezoa chi-lo-na tsantyani
(we) will sleep" thus saying that-at-in (a) meal

tsotasi sheyu-tong echoi chi-lo
having eaten (a) plantain-tree having cut and trimmed it-on

ossü epfukai va na hono-hambong-chi ha
cloth having wrapped putting and fowl-cock-the too

oni khamki va tosi ota-cho
they-two at the head of placing having put elder brother-the

sheyu-chiwo yip na ongo-cho
plaintain tree-by the side of sleeping and younger brother-the

mbo chiwo-i yiptok to tssocho. Tole
him by the side of-at making to sleep thus became. Then

ota-na ongo yipthetoksi
(the) elder brother (the) younger brother having let get well asleep

mphoa tsancho. Chicho hono-chi-na
concealing (the fact) escaped. Then fowl-the

"kukuriaku, i-ta tsantaka,
"cock-a-doodle-do, your-elder brother has escaped,

kukuriaku, i-ta-na i-mphoa
cock-a-doodle-do, your-elder brother (from) you-concealing

yitaka" to khule ongo-na panthiki
has gone" thus when called (the) younger brother getting up

ota tsaya sheyu-lo ossü
(his) elder brother thinking it was plantain tree-on cloth

epfukai evao-chi "A-ta, hono khuala ;
wrapping put-the "My-elder brother, (the) fowl is calling ;

wonchiala ; panthia" to ezoa chepile
it is getting light ; get up" thus saying when pushed

lungrhen-chi eria choicho. Ole mbo-na "A-ta
cliff-the rolling fell down. Then he "My-elder brother

eriala, a-ta eriala" to tyua phana
is rolling, my-elder brother is rolling" thus saying chasing

cho-wo zele sheyu-chi sakama
down-going when saw plantain tree-the because (it) was

echoroi sisi ota
cutting into small pieces having thrown away (his) elder brother

tsa "E-ni nlhancha-na tsangon-hambong sailika ;
calling "Our-two spittle-with sunbird-cock is caught ;

e-ni chitaka a-nhyaka" to thanga phanala n-phayacho.
we-two will share me-await" thus calling chases not-did catch.

Osi ota-na chi zoiki mbo 'sü
But (the) elder brother that hearing his track

n-drruchetoko kilato mbo sü-chiang na mbo
not-would allow to follow intending his tracks-the and his

ncha mpato yontsi-na lenroi vaisi
spittle too spear butt-with scratching over having kept

"Hepina yiaka ; roke" to ezoa yicho.
"This way (I) am going ; come" thus saying went.

Ongo-chi mbo n-phayao milani-ti oyi
Younger brother-the him not-catching evening-at coming

zowoti lamalo ethi licho chi-lo chungo tsanka-i yipcho.
zowoti fruit many growing was it-in climbing top-at slept.

Tole zowoti-chiang chi-zamo-tai mhenkhani-chiang
Then *zowoti* fruit-the that-night-only ripened-the

hloi tsoa vancho. Ole mharr-na sepu rhamiki
picking eating remained. Then (a) tiger sambhur having caught

nhyanchap-na onhyan tsso seno-na echan
cobra-from carrying band becoming barking deer-from back

ela na nipong-na kurri ela to tssosi
pad and wild boar-from head pad thus having become

tsopelak tsanglapkakana süsi nlapiya
long bladed spear very bright having carried flourishing

"Tsong-rong, tsong-rong" to khua oyi zowoti-tong-
"Ho-ho, ho-ho" thus calling coming *zowoti*-tree-

chi chanale "Ekam-ramdhram tssoa" to tyua
the when reached "Live-scent becomes" thus saying

zekachicho. Ole kyon-chi-na "A-motzü, a-
looked up. Then man-the "My-grandfather, my-

motzü, oyam-na i-tsangthi-shi hlokato
grandfather, some one else your-fruit-this in case should pick

a-na i-nhyakia vanaka" to ezocho. Chitosi
I you-awaiting have remained" thus said. Then

kyon-chi-na zowoti-chiang hlo-hloi tsotoksi
man-the *zowoti* fruit-the pick-picking having given to eat

nnyo-i ntsangatai tssoale "A-motzü, nhungo
top-at one only when became "My-gr ndfather, now

a-na n-yonchanka i-tsopelak a-pikachia
I not-can reach your-long bladed spear (to) me-hand up

nnyo-i-chi elang-chochi i-tsotokoka" to ezoa
top-at-the cut off-the you-will give to eat" thus saying

mbo pikachitokcho. "Osi nko setya opang
him made to hand up. "But legs spreading apart mouth

khu na omyek chok tosi vanke, a-na zowoti
open and eyes shut having put remain, I *zowoti* fruit

hloi i-pang-i shamthechika" to ezocho. Ole
picking your-mouth-in will throw down" thus said. Then

mharr-chi-na kyon-chi-na ezoa to lui vancho. Ole
tiger-the man-the saying thus doing remained. Then

mbo-na shamchochia chenle n-drako
he throwing down (i.e. the spear) striking not-hitting

nko-i lentheicho. Mharr-chi-na "Acho, nno nto
feet-at struck the earth. Tiger-the "Hallo, you what

luiala ?" to ezole kyon-chi-na "A-motzü,
are doing ?" thus when said man-the "My-grandfather,

a-motzü, nungri kama i-tsopelak-chi
my-grandfather, boy because (I) am your-long bladed spear-the

m-penkoko nsechicho." Nhunga apikachilana
not-being able to hold it fell." Now (to) me-hand it up again

osi nthang lui vana to mhona lui vana"
but just now doing remaining thus well doing remain"

to ezocho. Mharr-chi-na kyon-chi-na ezoa to lui
thus said. Tiger-the man-the saying thus doing

vanle shamchochia opang-i-na
remaining (the man) throwing mouth-in-from

songdra chentsangcho. Tole kyon-chi-na
spearing through pierced. Then man-the

mharr-chi tchhitchhianato zowo-yo-chiang
tiger-the was dead or not (to test) *zowoti*-leaves-the

ntonchochia vanle ntchhio
picking and throwing down while was remaining not-being dead

enno-chi elhampia vancho. Osi okaiti zowo-yo ntsanga
ears-the moving remained. But at last *zowoti*-leaf one

tai enhyui-chi ntonchochile enno-chi
only remaining-the when picked and threw down ears-the

n-lhampio tchhicho. Ole kyon-chi-na choi mharr-chi
not-moving was dead. Then man-the descending tiger-the

woni hansi mharr-chi-na nyana to
going having carried tiger-the-because of chanting thus

nyana oyi tchhüka ntsanga chancho. Ole
chanting coming (village-) spring a reached. Then

tchhüka-chi-lo loroe orotsakatara vancho. Mbo-na loroe-
spring-the-at girls washing remained. He girls-

chiang-knoto nchyua mhom hüngi hochi lamma
the-among one beautiful seeing that one desiring

tsopelak-chi tchhüka nkho-lo "tong-tonga"
long bladed spear-the spring fence-at "ping-ping"

lenkasi mbo cha-chü-küpi mphoi vancho.
having thrown himself worm-cast-behind hiding remained.

Ole loroe-chiang-na ekhentsangra chungi oyamo ezocho.
Then girls-the fearing going up villagers told.

Oyam-chiang-na choro "Shio ocho-na ato?" to
Villagers-the coming down "This who (did) thus?" thus

tyuta tsangpitala n-tsangchecho. Ole mbo-na "Hi-hi,
saying pulling not-pulled out. Then he "Ha, ha,

chi-tia m-phechikotkaka. Nte-na shi-lo chorotsakao
that-even not-can pull out. You this-at bathing

loroe mhom-ochi a-pio a-na phe to pheche nten
girl beautiful-the me-giving I pull thus pulling out you

pio" to ezocho. Oyam-chiang-na "Shia ocho-la?"
will give" thus said. Villagers-the "This who-is?"

to tyua lomo-ro mpia laplap shoisia yanala
thus saying grass-little even all scraping over search

n-yanchecho. Ole loroe mbo elamm-ochi ekyung-chi
not-did find. Then girl he desired-the (of) chief-the

tsoi sakama chi-na "Toka ocho sana phechekok-na
daguhter being he "Then whoever it be can pull out-if

a-tsoi-chi i-pika ; oyi phecheta" to
my-daughter-the you-will give ; coming pull out" thus

ezole mbo-na cha-chü-küpi-na chui
when said he worm-cast-behind-from coming out

phechecho. Chisicho mbo-na loroe-chi soa vankato
pulled out. After that he girl-the marrying to remain

wole loroe-chi opo-na mbo loran-chicho pipo
when went girl's-the father his servant girl-the ornaments

elam to pipotoksi samsam lui
many indeed having made to put on beautiful making

vantok na otsolo-chicho chamchak-ssü-ro-na
causing to remain and daughter-the rags-clothes-small-with

lui maku-ki ntyazhua vantokcho. Toala
making husks-with sprinkling caused to remain. Yet (of)

epue-chi elam to chethang-mothang-cho sakama
man-the much indeed wiliness-cunning-the because was

otsolo chi soa vancho. Ole mbo-na eng-chi
(real) daughter-the marrying remained. Then he wife-the

yengki-lo thei hansi oyi
carrying basket-in putting having carried coming

n-hankokale lanrhu-lo ntongi vasi
not-being able to carry cross roads-at upright having left

potsocheni tsa-lo yicho. Chisicho Humchibilio otyon
relations call-to went. Then Humchibilio ugly

m-mhom-ochi-na otchhü-lo cho-wosi hochi hüngki
not-beautiful-the water-to down-having gone this seeing

yengki-chi elhichi zesi loroe-chi süchei
basket-the opening having seen girl-the dragging out

nshioroi tchhüka tchhü-cho shamochchi
tearing in pieces spring (in) water-the throwing down

sisi mbo yengki-chi tsanthei vancho. Osi
throwing away her basket-the entering remained. But

mbo potsocheni-chiang soa yi hanai elhechei
his relations-the bringing coming carrying opening

zetasi chiang-na "Heto soa yicho
having looked they "This marrying have come

e-tsato?" to mbo emaicho. Mbo ha "A-na
us-do you call?" thus him mocked. He too "I

soa vam-ochi shi mak-la" to nchama
marrying will remain-the this not-is" thus thinking

elam to yikra vancho. Chisilocho Humchibilio-na
much indeed shame remained. After-that Humchibilio

nshioroi esi-ochi-na ewo kami
tearing in pieces threw away-the-from bamboo shoot becoming

samsam shongi lile epue-chi-na hüngi "Shicho
beautiful growing when was man-the seeing "This

nkolo etsong-i essa" to tyua phangi raki
former wife-to like" thus saying breaking off peeling

hanai chamkachele orapvü-na vana-na
bringing putting on to boil (her) husband remaining-if

"lak-lak" to elak na Humchibilio tai
"bubble-bubble" thus bubbled and Humchibilio only

tssoa-na "Humchibilio-na a-nshiorocho, lak-lak
being-if "Humchibilio me-tore in pieces, bubble-bubble

lak-lak" to tai elakcho. Chicho Humchibilio-na
bubble-bubble" thus only bubbled. Then Humchibilio

orapvü-chi "Epue, chan-shi-na heto
(to her) husband-the "Husband, vegetable-this thus

khua elakaka enga" to ezole orapvü-na
calling out bubbled; listen" thus when said (the) husband

enga vanle otso-tso chi to khua
listening when remained true-truly that indeed calling out

elaka sakama khantsang-i penchochi sicho.
bubbling because was back of house-at picking up threw away.

Chitosicho hochi-na nhunga knogken kami nnyo-ro-
After that she now orange tree turning into top-tree-

i-na ntsanga tai ethiki Humchibilio-na woa-na
at-from one only growing Humchibilio going-if

nnyo-i chungi na orapvü-na woa-na konga choi
top-at ascending and husband going-if bending descending

to tai tssocho. Chi ha "Shicho nkolo etsong-i
thus only become. (Of) this also "This former wife-to

essa" to tyua hloiki yenki thei vacho.
like" thus saying picking (in) basket putting kept.

Hochi-na kyon kamiki ompoi-na omholi-lo
This-from human being turning into man and wife fields-to

wotaka-na "Tyengramo-na ekhomka, trangrang" to
went-when "Wifeless man will abuse, tinkle-tinkle" thus

tai tyua yengki-na tsokchok tsokchok to tssocho.
only saying basket-from jump jumping thus became.

Osi hochi-na Humchibilio pelang-i-cho tyoka
But she Humchibilio's bed-on-the easing herself

nnyungkai kurr shaka shakai vai na orapvü
urinating ashes picking up putting and husband's

pelang-i-cho l·plap pfui vai na oki ha laplap
bed-on-the much wiping keeping and house too much

khethangkheri na tsantyani vai to tssocho.
sweeping and cooking keeping thus became.

Orapvü-na oyi "Ocho-na heto lui e-vaia.to ?
Husband coming "Who thus doing (for) us-kept indeed?

E-na n-tso-yu-lia chi pika" to
We not-eat-drinking-even (to) that (man) will give" thus

yankho-eli enga-na chiang na "E-ki tia
khel-men asking-if they "(In) our-house even

n-tssochoa-na ocho-na chi to nte luiala ?"
not became-if who this indeed (for) you is doing ?"

to tai ezoracho. Ole nchokacho orapvü-na
thus only kept saying. Then one day (the) husband

woa etchüsi yingto oyi cheta vanle
gone deceiving quietly coming watching while remaining

nchürang tyua to tyua eloe-chi-na yengki-na
before saying indeed saying woman-the basket-from

tsokchokcho. Tole orapvü-na "E, nno koi-na
jumped. Then (the) husband "Ho, you where-from

yichola ?" to ezoa rhamacho. Tole eloe-chi-na
have come ?" thus saying seized. Then woman-the

nchürang Humchibilio na nshi oro-chiang na ewo
before Humchibilio tore in pieces-the and bamboo shoot

kamo-chiang kongken kamo-chiang topu ezoracho.
turned into-the orange-tree turned into-the all told.

Ole epue-chi-na Humchibilio-chi langta kilato lepok
Then husband-the Humchibilio-that to kill intending *dao*

thyaki vasi nhyaka vanle Humchibilio-na
sharpening keeping waiting while remaining Humchibilio

oli-lo wosi otsang-ha na yekrho-ha to
field-to having gone wood-load and wild taro-load thus

hansi oyi honkhui-na "Epu, chu-ro, oha-shi
carrying coming outside-from "Husband, out-come, load-this

a-chamchoya" to ezothechile orapvü-na chu-wo
me-lift off" thus while saying (the) husband out-going

echunga-na epanthangcho. Chi-thang Humchibilio-na
once-by killed. (At) that-time Humchibilio

"yekrho" to tyucho. Hochi-na nhungaliya yekrho
"wild taro" thus said. This-from till now wild taro

lepok-na rharoi ekhu-na enthakala to tyutala.
dao-with cutting up cook-if it hurts thus (they) say.

Chitosi ompoi vantalanchokatola
After this husband and wife would have remained

eloe-chi Humchibilio 'rru-chi-na hepi
(but) woman the Humchibilio's bones-the-with hither

hepi wo-na tsok-tsoki nti-ntila n-wocheo
hither going-if pierce-piercing any-any way not-going

pomtsangi tchhicho to taì rutala kyon-na.
swelling died thus only tell men.

Once upon a time there lived two brothers, of whom the younger was always luckier in everything than the elder. However, carefully the elder cultivated his land the crops were always bad, or if he married a pretty wife she always grew ugly. One day these two went down and looked at their fields to see how they were doing, and exchanged their land, the younger giving his elder brother the fields he had prepared so well, and the elder giving his younger brother his bad fields. But the fine fields which were given to the elder brother grew poor crops, while the poor fields which the younger brother received did splendidly. Then the elder brother desired to take his younger brother's wife, who was very beautiful ; so meaning to lay a trap for him he went with him into the jungle, taking a cock with him. As he led the way in the jungle the elder brother kept asking "Do you know this place or not?" and the younger brother would answer "This is where father and I gather firewood" or "This is where I set traps for birds" or "This is where I set traps for squirrels" or "This is where I look for game" or "This is where I fish." At last they arrived at the edge of a cliff and the elder brother asked "Brother, do you know this place," and the younger brother replied "I do not know this place." Then the elder brother said "We will sleep the night here," and when they had had a meal he cut a length from the stem of a plantain tree and wrapped it in a cloth. Then putting the cock at their heads the elder brother lay down by the plantain stem and made his younger brother sleep behind him. At night when the younger brother was fast asleep the elder brother stole quietly away. But the cock called out "Cock-a-doodle-do, your brother has run away; cock-a-doodle-do, your brother has given you the slip and gone." Then the younger brother woke up and thinking the plantain tree wrapped in a cloth was his brother said "Brother, it is cockcrow. It will soon be light" and gave the plantain tree a push, so that it went rolling down the cliff. "My brother has rolled down, my brother has rolled down" he cried, and climbed down after it. Then whan he saw that it was the plantain tree he hacked it into little pieces and threw them away. and called to his brother and said "A *tsangon* bird is caught in our spittle. We will share it. Wait for me," and went after his brother, but could not find him. His elder brother, when he heard his younger brother calling, scratched over his footprints and spittle with his spear but so that his tracks would be lost, and with a shout "I am going this way. Come along" made off.

The younger brother tried in vain to catch up with his elder brother and in the evening came to a tree loaded with big red *zowoti* fruit. Up this he climbed and slept in the branches. That night the *zowoti* fruit ripened and in the morning he picked and ate some of it. Now there came to that place a tiger carrying on his back a sambhur he had killed. His carrying-band was a cobra, and he had a barking deer for a pad in the small of his back and a wild boar as a pad behind his head. In his hand was a very bright long-bladed spear which he twirled and flourished, chanting "Ho, ho, ho" as he bent under his load. When he came to the *zowoti* tree he said "I smell something alive" and looked up into the branches. Then the man said "I am keeping watch over this fruit of yours, grandfather tiger, in case some stranger should come and pick it." Then he kept picking the fruit and handing it to the tiger to eat, till there was only one fruit left at the very top of the tree. Then the man said "There is a fruit at the very top of the tree which I cannot reach. Give me your long-bladed spear, father tiger, and I will cut it off for you. You stand down below with your legs wide apart and your mouth open and your eyes shut and I will pick the fruit and throw it right into your mouth." Then the tiger handed up his spear and stood as the man told him. And the man hurled down the spear and struck the earth at the tiger's feet without touching him. "Hullo," said tha tiger, "What are you up to ?" "I am only a boy, father tiger," he replied. 'I could not hold your spear properly and it fell out of my hands. Hand me up your spear again and be careful to stay as you were before." Then the tiger did as he was told and the man speared him right through the mouth. Then he kept picking and throwing down leaves on the tiger to see if it was dead or not, but it was not dead, for its ears twitched when a leaf hit it. At last there was only one leaf, and when he picked this and threw it down onto the tiger its ears did not twitch for it was dead.

Then the man came down from the tree and picked up the body of the tiger, and, chanting as the tiger had chanted, went on his way till he came to a village spring. Now there were some maidens bathing at the spring, and one of them was very beautiful, whom when he saw he greatly desired to take to wife. So he threw the long-bladed spear, and, 'tong' it stuck in the wooden fence below the spring, but he lay hidden behind a worm-cast. But the maidens were frightened and ran up to the village and told the men what had happened. And the men came down and wondering who had done this thing tugged at the spear but could not pull it out. Then the wanderer from his hiding place laughed at them and said, "Cannot you even pull the spear out ? I will pull it out 'top' for you if you will give me the beautiful maiden who was bathing here to be my wife." Then the men of the village said, "Who was that ?" and even searched among the fallen leaves looking for him, but could not find him. Now the maiden whom the wanderer desired was the chief's daughter, and her father called out "Whoever you may be if you can pull out this spear I will give you my daughter to wife. Come and pull it out."

Hearing these words the wanderer came from behind the worm-cast and pulled out the spear.

Now when the wanderer was going to take his bride the maiden's father dressed up his slave girl in fine clothes and beautiful ornaments and put rags on his own daughter and threw rice husks over her. But the wanderer was too clever to be deceived in this way and took with him as his bride the real daughter.

Putting his bride into a carrying basket he set off to carry her to his village. but when he came to where the paths met below his village he found the load too heavy. and leaning the basket up against the bank he went up to the village to cell his relations to help.

Now an ugly woman called Humchibilio on her way to the spring to fetch water saw the basket and opening it peeped inside. And finding the maiden in it she dragged her out and tore her to pieces with her hands. Then throwing the remains away below the spring she got into the basket herself and waited. When the birdegroom's relations had carried up the basket for him they opened it and looked inside and said "Is this the kind of bride you call us to carry up." and mocked him. And he. knowing that this was not the bride he had brought, was full of shame.

After a time from the pieces Humchibilio had thrown away there grew up a very beautiful bamboo shoot. When the bridegroom saw it he said "That is like my lost bride." Then he broke it off and peeled off the outer skin and brought it home and put it in the pot to boil. When he was present it only boiled "bubble, bubble. bubble," but when Humchibilio was watching it alone a voice came from the bamboo as it boiled "Humchibilio tore me in pieces. Bubble, bubble, bubble." Then Humchibilio said to her husband "Husband, listen to the noise this bamboo makes as it boils." Then he listened and heard a voice come from it as she had said, and took it off the fire and threw it out behind the house.

After a time this too grew into an orange tree with a single orange at the top. When Humchibilio went near the orange was high up at the top of the tree, but when her husband went near it bent down towards the earth. Then her husband said, "That is like my lost bride" and picked it and put it in a carrying basket.

Then the orange turned into a maiden. When the husband and wife had gone to the fields she said "My beloved will be angry if I do not clean the house. He has no proper wife," and with a tinkle of ornaments she jumped out of the basket and set to work. She defiled Humchibilio's bed with filth and took ashes and poured them on it, but her husband's bed she dusted carefully. Then she swept out the house thoroughly and prepared a meal. When the husband and wife came in they said "Who has got all this ready for us ? Even if we go without food ourselves we must give him something." So they went and asked their neighbours. But their neighbours only answered, "We cannot get through our own work. Who would do so much work for you ?" Then one day the husband pretended to go out to work, but came back quietly and kept watch. And when the maiden jumped out of the basket, her husband exclaimed, "Eh, where have you come from ?" and caught hold of her. Then the maiden told her husband the whole story of how Humchibilio had torn her in pieces and how she had become first a bamboo shoot and then an orange. Having heard the tale her husband sharpened his *dao* and waited for Humchibilo, intending to kill her. After a little while Humchibilio came up from the field with a load of wood and wild taro, and called from outside to her husband within the house, "Husband, come out and lift down my load for me." At these words her husband came out and killed her with one blow, and as she fell she gasped "Wild taro." That is why nowadays if you eat wild taro which has been sliced with a *dao* you get a sore throat.

After this the bride was wedded to her husband, but whenever she went out she pricked herself on Humchibilio's bones till at last she could not leave the house and her wounds swelled up and she died.

This is the end of the story.

3

THE STORY OF LANKONGRHONI

Eran-ren-i eloe nchyua Lankongrhoni etsai
Old men-time-at woman a Lankongrhoni called

vancho. Mbo otsoi ha epue nchyua otyon elam to
was. Her child too male a very much indeed

mhona vancho. Hochi 'myang Arilao to tsacho.
handsome was. His name Arilao indeed called.

Ole oyan loroe topu-na chi tai reta lammsi
Then village girls all him only desiring wanting

tampoi-chiang n-lammcho. Chisicho oyamo topu-na mbo
others-the not-wanted. Then villagers all him

mezeni sio tyaktacho. Osi oyamo topu-na "Tyozhu-lo
to kill taking plotted. And villagers all "Fishing-to

ocho-na n-roa-na wok-tsü tsoi" to thangtacho.
who not-come-if pig-big (we) will eat" thus announced.

Chitosi nchok eni-tham-o oyamo-na tyozhu-lo wotacho. Ole
Then days two-three-in villagers fishing-to went. Then

opvü-na otsotyingo-chi "A-ngo, tyozhu-lo ti-woa" to
mother (to) son-the "My-boy, fishing-to do not-go" thus

ezoala Arilao-na "A-pvü, nno eni wok-tsü-chi
says Arilao "My-mother, you of us two pig-big-the

n-zanchoani?" to opvü ezoa
not-care about or what?" thus (to) mother having said

tyozhu-lo wocho. Oten-na zukhu-i-na owo vekhu
fishing-to went. They river-at-to going pig trough

shaniki vasi "Ocho etamo sana yipi zeta"
making keeping "Who nice looking is lying down see"

to tyuta oyamo topu-na yipi zetasila "Nni-a
thus saying villagers all lying down seeing "You-indeed

n-tam nni-a n-tam" to tai
not-nice looking, you-indeed not-nice looking" thus only

ezotaracho. Osi okaiti "Nhungo Arilao
kept saying. But last "Now Arilao

yipitoka" to tyuta Arilao
(we) will make to lie down" thus saying Arilao

yipitoksi "Arilao etamo, Arilao
having made to lie down "Arilao nice looking, Arilao

erhyuala, Arilao erhyuala," to tyuta
are pounding up, Arilao are pounding up," thus saying

ono-lo Arilao-chi erhyunhyacho. Ole Arilao
fish poison-in Arilao-that pounded up. Then Arilao's

okamo-cho "Nchingo a-kamo tchhio kama" to
friend-the "To-day my-friend has died because" thus

nchama nungra tchhü-cho-wo-i-na cho-wo esütchhü
thinking sad stream-down-going-at-to down going tears

zana vancho. Ole okamo Arilao nyimtyep-chi
shedding was. Then (of) friend Arilao's nail-the

pfua choi mbo pfukacho. Chicho mbo-na
floating descending him floated against. Then he

"A-kamo-cho heto kamtakaka" to tyua okamo
"My-friend-that thus has become" thus saying friend's

nyimtyep-chi khikai tseni rikab-o
nail-the picking up wrapping up (i.e. in a leaf) belt-in

nchai hancho. Oyamo-na ongo elam to tchhi
tucking carried. Villagers fish many indeed dying

rhamtala Arilao okamo-cho ongo-tia n-rhamo nungra tai
catching Arilao's friend-the fish-any not-catching sad only

vancho. Osi oyamo-chiang yirasanati mbo silamo
remained. And villagers-the when going home he last

yicho. Ole Lankongrhoni-na otsotyungo lanyi-lo
went. Then Lankongrhoni son meet-to

rosi oyamo-chiang "Na, i-cheni,
having come (of) villagers-the "You, your-companion

i-kamo, i-ngo, i-ta-cho
your-friend, your-younger brother, your-elder brother-the
kato ?" to oyamo-ching topu engaracho, Tole
where ?" thus (of) villagers-the all kept asking. Then
oyamo-chiang-na topu-na "A-cheni, a-kamo,
villagers-the all "My-companion, my-friend,
a-ngo, a-ta-cho silamo loroe oten
my-younger brother, my-elder brother-the last girls they
ematha tsaka ; nhunga yika" to ezora
laughing will come ; now will come" thus keeping saying
yiracho. Osi okaiti Arilao okamo-chi silamo nangra
kept going on. But at last Arilao's friend-the last sad
esütchü zana yia vanle Lankongrhoni-na "A-ngo,
tears shedding going when was Lankongrhoni "My-boy,
rna, i-kamo-cho kato ?" to engale hochi-na
you, your-friend-that where ?" thus when asked he
"A-pvü, nna nungra kama ; i-n-zo" to
"My-mother, you sad will become ; you-not-will tell" thus
ezocho. Chisicho Lankongrhoni-na, "A-ngo, a-na
said. Then Lankongrhoni "My-boy, I
n-nungrala a-zoa" to ezole hochi-na "A-pvü,
not-sorrowing me-tell" thus when said he "My-mother,
a-kamo heto kamchoche" to ezoa mbo-na okamo
my-friend thus has become" thus saying he friend's
nyimtyep rikab-o nchai hamo-chi echücho. Ole
nail belt-in tucking carried-the showed. Then
Lankongrhoni-na chi-thang-cho nungra yingtovansi
Lankongrhoni that-time-the sad remaining quiet
ochö-rachötoti "Ochö oyamo nungri topu
next day-the day after "To-morrow villagers children all
soa ro ; a-ki-[i] mungtokra n-na a-woko
bringing come ; my-house-[at] making to collect I my-pig
tsopo-chi noni tsoa mungtokoka" to thanga
big-the killing eating will make to collect" thus giving notice
wocho. Tole ochoto-cho oyamo-chiang-na nungri-chiang
went. Then next day-the villagers-the children-the

topu soa wo Lankongrhoni 'ki-[i]
all taking going Lankongrhoni's house-[at]
mungtoksi oli-lo woracho. Chisilocho
having made to collect fields-to went off. Then
Lankongrhoni-na oyamo nungri-chiang mbo woko-chi noni
Lankongrhoni villagers children-the her pig-the killing
tsoa mungtokcho. Osi mbo-na nungri-chiang topu
eating made to collect. But she children-the all
takhui khalınchi vantoksi mbo honkhui chui
inside shut up having made to stay she outside coming out
"Nungriten, oki-[i] epo kolo-kolo poa?"
"Children, house-[in] holes where-where have become?"
to ezo-na nungri-chiang-na "A-tsü
thus saying-from children-the "My-grandmother
a-tyoh chilo ha poa" na "hochi ha
my-grandmother here too have become" and "this too
poa" to ezoa oki-[i] epo-chiang ethakhana
has become" thus saying house-[in] holes-the closing
wotokcho. Okaitis mbo-na "Nungriten, nhungo epo
made to go on At last she "Children now holes
ba-m-ba?" to ezothechile nungri-chiang-na topu-na.
are-not-are?" thus when kept saying childern-the all.
"A-tsü, a-tyoh, nhungo epo m-mba".
"My-grandmother, my-grandmother, now holes not-are"
to ezochokchicho. Ole mbo-na "Nungriten, toka nhungo
thus said from inside. Then she "Children, then now
mukuku-lo omi yukaka; omi a-pichokchia" to
pipe-in fire will put; fire me-give from inside" thus
ezole nungri-chiang-na omi mbo pichokchicho.
when said children-the fire her gave from inside.
Chisilocho mbo-na omi-chi-ki oki-chi rongkachi
Then she fire-the-with house-the having set alight
nungri-chiang topu rongtsangkhani sitokcho. Osi
children-the all having burnt up made to perish. But
mbo potsowoe-na oyeng sangchochicho-chi mpanga
she sky folk-the thread having let down-the climbing

potsowo-i chungi sicho.
sky-to ascending went.

Toala oyamo-chiang-na n-tsio vancho. Ole
Yet villagers-the not-knowing remained. Then

kashak-chi-na owo oli-[i] aku oyamo-chiang mhatongina
crow-the going fields-[in] all villagers-the in front of

konrossü eramsi "Arilao opvü-na oyan
little girl's skirt having put on "Arilao's mother village

nungri sha-sha" to tai khua tsokpya
children destroyed-destroyed" thus only calling out hopping

wocho. Chisicho oyamo-chiang-na "Nchingo ntoko to
went. Then villagers-the "Today what indeed

etsso kashak-na heto khua echüa to ntia
happening crow thus calling out behaves indeed something

kiya ntsso" to tyuta topu-na oyan-i
for nothing not-happens" thus saying all village-to

yitacho. Tole chiang-na ote 'tsoi
went. Then they their children

rongtsangkhamo-chiang zetasi onte
burnt up-the seeing those two

onte-chi "I-tssoko-na,
those two-the (i.e. to each other) "Your-happening-from.

i-tssoko-na" to ezota
your-happening-from" (i.e. "it is your fault") thus saying

laplap langtatarai tchhikhancho. Osi
all having cut each other to pieces died. But

ndrindran ontyai chicho hochiang zesi
orphan brother and sister there they having seen

khyua hono-hanki-[i] tsankai mphoi vancho
fearing fowl-house-[into] getting up hiding remained.

Chitosicho oyamo-chiang laplap tchhikhansi ochiang ote
Afterwards villagers-the all being dead they them

n-vanta kama
not-to marry because (i.e. since there was no one for them to marry)

ontyai vantasi poni tssoa yicho.
brother and sister marrying mating becoming went.

Chisicho oni-na otsoi cho-yingdro
Afterwards they two-from children leg-fingers (i.e. toes)

khe-yingdro i-na mpato poki limha-lo kyon hetata
hand-fingers-in-from also being born world-in men so many

kama to mpato kyon-na rutala.
becoming thus also men say.

In the days of our ancestors there lived a woman called Lankongrhoni. She had a son who was very handsome. His name was Arilao. All the girls admired only him and wished to marry him. They cared nothing for the other men. So all the men of the village planned to kill him treacherously. They agreed that on any day when they should all go down to the river to poison fish whoever failed to come was to be fined a big pig. Two or three days later they went down. Then Arilao's mother said to him, "Son, do not go." But he said, "Do you want us to lose our big pig, mother ?" and went. And the men felled a tree on the river bank and hewed a trough out of it said, "Let every man lie in the trough in turn and see if he looks a fine man. So they each lay down in turn, but as each man lay in the trough the others kept repeating, "You don't look nice, you don't look nice." At last they said, "Let Arilao lie down," and made him get into the trough, and calling out, "Arilao looks nice; we are pounding up Arilao, we are pounding up Arilao," they pounded him up with the fish poison.[1] Now Arilao had a friend, and he was very sad because Arilao had been killed that day, and waited weeping further down stream. Soon the finger-nail of his friend Arilao came floating down and lodged against him. Then he said, "It this all there is left of my friend ?" and with these words lifted the nail off the water, and wrapping it in a leaf slipped it into his belt. The villagers made a fine haul of fish, but Arilao's friend was so sad that he did not

1 The ordinary Naga method of fishing is by poisoning the water with certain berries or creepers pounded up.

trouble to catch a single one. When the villagers trooped off up towards the village he hung back to the last.

Now Lankongrhoni came to meet her son on the way and asked each of her fellow-villagers. "Where is your companion ?" or "Where is your friend ?" or "Where is your younger brother ?" or "Where is your elder brother ?" And each man replied, "He is coming behind, laughing and talking with the girls. He is just coming." At last came Arilao's friend, weeping and very sad. When Lankongrhon asked him where his friend was he said, "The news would make you sad, mother. I will not tell you." But she repied, "I shall not give way to grief, my son. Tell me." Then he said, "Mother, this is all that is left of my friend," and gave her his friend's nail which he had carried up in his belt. Then Lankongrhoni was very sad, but she hid her grief, and a few days later gave notice to the village saying, "To-morrow bring all the children to my house. I am going to kill my big pig and give them a feast there." So the next day the villagers brought all their children to Lankongrhoni's house and left them there and went down to their fields. Then Lankongrhoni killed her big pig and feasted the village children on it. Afterwards she made the children remain shut up in her house while she went outside and said, "Children, tell me where there are holes in my house," and they replied, "There is a hole here, granny," or "There is a hole there, granny," and she stopped up the holes as the children told her of them. At last she called from outside and said, "Are there any more holes, children ?" And they replied, "There are no more holes, granny." Then she said, "I want to light my pipe now. Give me a brand." So they gave her a brand and she set fire to the house and burnt all the childern to ashes. But she hereself climbed away up a thread thrown down from the sky and disappeared.[1]

Now the villagers knew nothing of what had happened.

1 The version of the story given here is that current among the Northern Lhotas. In the Southern Lhota account Lankongrhoni escapes into a porcupine's hole, from which she is afterwards dug out and killed.

But a crow went from field to field and hopped about in front of the workers dressed in a skirt like a little girl, and said, "Arilao's mother has utterly destroyed the children of the village." Then the villagers said, "What does it mean to-day, a crow behaving like that? Surely something has happend," and so saying they all went off home. And when they saw that all their children had been burnt up, each said to his neighbour, "This is your fault, this is your fault," and they fell upon each other and killed each other so that they all died. But two orphans, a brother and a sister were frightened when they saw this and climbed up into a fowl-house, and hid. Afterwards, all the villagers being dead, there were none for them to marry so they became husband and wife and from these two, even from their fingers and toes, were born all the men there are in the world. This is one of the stories which men tell.

4

THE STORY OF THE KITHANG CLAN

Yanzo to etsai Kikung nchyua-na mbo phurro
Yanzo indeed called Kikung a his dogs

toku sosi 'so phano wocho. Ole phurro-chiang-na
nine taking game to chase went. Then dogs-the

otoug ntsanga tsang-kuk mbata licho chilo tai
tree a wood-hole remaining was there only

chapva thryuta mungcho. Chisicho
running backwards and forwards barking remained. Then

Yanzo-na "ʌ-phurro-na thamacho heto n-thryu" to
Yanzo "My-dogs for nothing thus not-do bark" thus

tyua otong-chi tani zele ora-kyon nchyua
saying tree-the cutting when looked jungle-man a

tanchecho ; hochi mbo-na soa yi ekhamsi
cut out ; him he taking going having brought up

Kithamo tsacho. Chisicho Kithamo-na otsoi nchyua
Kithamo called. After this Kithamo-from son a

vanle Mering tsacho. Hochi eloe nchyua Khamdrio
when was Mering called. (To) him girl a Khamdrio

to etsai vancho soa vantokcho. Hochi tsan-cho
indeed called was married made to be. Her hair-the

esi ntia-si raho. Osi
long outstretched arms-long one outstretched arm. But

mbo-na nchoka kurr nzhüle otsan ntsanga otchhü-i
she one-day head when washing hair a water-in

elhungthecho ; hochi pukiro-na nzücho. Pukiro-chi-na
fell ; this (a) little fish swallowed. Little fish-the

zukhu tsunga choile Asam nchyua-na rhamacho.
stream along when went down Assamese a caught.

Ngo-rham-chi-na pukiro-chi thanle otsan-chi hüngi
Fish-catcher-the little fish-the when split hair-the having seen

emhoktsanga khi hansi ekyung-chi echücho. Chisicho
amazed taking carrying (to) king-the showed. Then

ekyung-chi-na tsan-pfui sosi yita to ezoa emenopang
king-the hair-owner bringing come thus saying councillor

etssoi nchyua na mbo woro to Mering 'van-i
being a and his servants indeed Mering's village to

wotokcho. Toala Mering-na zikhra-ki epi vacho
sent. But Mering stinging leaves-with fenced kept

sakama ekyung woro-chiang-na hochi yaki n-wochecho.
because (the) king's servants-the this piercing not-went.

Tole emenopang etssoi-chi-na ekyung woro-chiang
Then councillor being-the king's (to) servant-the

"Wo-a teni hanta oyi ekyung echuka" to
"Leaf-one picking carrying coming (to the) king will show" thus

ezoa chiang teni hantoksi oyi ekyung-chi
saying them picking making to carry coming (to) king-the

"Heto-na pikhu epi lia kama kotoli yaka
"Thus-with fortification fenced is because in any way piercing

n-wo" to ezocho. Ole ekyung-chi saü-küpi-na
(we) not-went" thus said. Then king's-the clothes-inside-on

mma-no taki zetokle noa kama
stomach-on stinging when caused to see pain because of

ekyung-chi-na emenopang etssoi-chi "Mering-cho
king-the (to) councillor being-the "Mering-that

nto-nto-na khyua sana enga" to ezoa engatokcho.
what-what-by frightened is ask" thus saying made to ask.

Ole Mering-na "Limha-lo-cho ntia a-n-khyu;
Then Mering "World-in-the anything me-not-frightens;

osi sotsü tokü manku-i khongkho kokai sosi
but (of) elephants nine back-on cotton piling up bringing

chong-ro-na chicho a-khyu" to ezolancho. Chisicho
up-come-if that me-frightens" thus replied. Then

ekyung-chi-na sotsü toku-chi zikhra epi epfu
king-the elephants nine-the stinging leaves fence lines

toku-chi ro-lo chong-rotokcho. Chisicho Mering-na otso
nine-the come-to up-made to come. Then Mering spear

rinyu-na vansi sotsü-chiang-na chong-ro
heating red hot-by being elephants-the up-coming

zikhra epi-chi chanale chencho. Tole
stinging leaves fance-the when reached threw his spear. Then

khongkho-chi rongi sotsü-chi rong chanale
cotton-the catching alight elephant-the fire when reached

chi-na thampo-chiang 'yoi tsana thrile
it others-the among running away when going in

chiang ha pongkarai rong na sotsü-chiang-na
they too one after the other caught alight and elephants-the

tsana-thang kyon ha elam to samtsangkhancho.
(at) running away-time men too many indeed trampled to death.

Chisicho ekyung-chi-na "N-khontala, shishotaka" to
Then king-the "Not-quarrel, trade" thus

ezoa" to tyua Asam nchyua "Senthan
say" thus saying (to) Assamese a "(Of) cornelian beads

mori ntsanga hansi chongoke, osi shio to tyua lia
pot a taking go up, but buying indeed saying is

ti-shitok-na yenpya wosi zikhra 'yai
do not-allow to buy-from hawking going stinging leaves among

nrokthechi sisi choike" to ezoa chongo
scattering having thrown come down" thus saying going up

chito liutokcho. Tole Mering-na mbo zikhara
thus made him do. Then Mering his stinging leaves

pikhu-chi laplap tsoni sia senthan
cence-the all cutting down throwing away cornelian beads

chiang yantokcho. Chisicho ekyung-chi-na
the allowed (men) to seek. Then king-the

mbo kyon-ki phurro sonhyasi Mering phano chong-
his men-with dogs having taken Mering to chase up-

rotokchol. Ole Mering-na Yanzo 'yan-i tsana oyi
made to go. Then Mering Yanzo's village-to fleeing going

Yanzo tsankacho. Tole Yanzo-na mbo 'ki
(with) Yanzo took refuge. At that time Yanzo his house

etsso lishu kholok tssoi vao-chi küpi
building thatching grass heap being kept-the underneath

mphotokcho ; osi chi 'poni tyokaivacho. Chisicho
made to hide ; but it on the top of eased himself. Later

Asam-chiang-na phurro sosi lishu kholok
Assamese-the dogs having brought thatching grass heap

tssoi vao-chi shyupya yanle chi-thang
being kept-the scratching aside when searching (at) that-time

"Nte Asam phurro-cho ntsaila to-na a-na
"Your Assamese dogs-those are knowing thus-from I

tyoivale chi yantalakato ?" to ezocho. Chisicho
defəecating that are they looking for ?" thus said. Then

Asam-chiang-na yikara phurro-chiang esükha sosi
Assamese-the in shame dogs-the whipping off taking

yiracho. Chitosi Mering to na Yanzo to
went-away. After this Mering indeed and Yanzo indeed

oni chibu-a khamo kothanga eloe n-soa vantao
they two clan-one becoming ever wife not-taking would be

echhama yonchak etsi erhansotacho. Chisi Mering-na
swearing iron staff broke. Later Mering-from

otsoi nchyua vancho, chi 'myang Rapvu tsacho ; hochi-na
son a was, his name Rapvu called ; he

Nungkamchung-o vancho. Ole mbo-na Kikung nchyua
Nungkamchung-at lived. Then he Kikung a

eng-thangi oshom tssole chi-na otsoi epue
woman-with committing adultery being her-from child male

nchyua poki hochi 'myang Lobemo tsacho. Lobemo
a begetting his name Lobemo called. Lobemo's

rui nhungacha Tsingaki-lo vana, osi Rapvu eng
descendants still Tsingaki-at live, but Rapvu's wife's

nthang-chi 'tsoi-chiango Kithang chibu echancho.
real the children-the Kithang clan formed.

One dey a man of the Kikung clan named Yanzo took his nine dogs with him and went to hunt deer. But they would do nothing but jump and give tongue round a tree with a hole in it. Then Yanzo, knowing that his dogs would not give tongue for nothing, cut down the tree to see what was inside it, and found in it a jungle man.[1] This man he took home and brought up and called Kithamo. Kithamo had a son callad Meriog, for whom Yanzo arranged a wife called Khamdrio. Now Khamdrio had wonderful long hair once and a half as long as a man could span with outstretched arms. One day when she was washing her head at the river one of her hairs fell in and was swallowed by a little fish, which went down the stream and was caught by an Assamese. The fisherman was amazed when he split open the fish and saw the hair, and took and showed it to the king. Then the king gave order that the woman to whom the hair belonged was to be brought to him, and sent one of his councillors with his soldiers to Mering's village. But Mering had fenced his village with a hedge of stinging leaves, which the king's soldiers could not penetrate. Then the councillor ordered his soldiers to pick one of the leaves and take it back with them. And he came to the king and said, "The village is fenced with a hedge of this, so that we could by no means force it." And the king took and put the leaf on his stomach under his clothes to see how it would sting, and he understood how terrible, the pain was. Then he sent the councillor to inquire of Mering whether there was anything of which he was afraid. And Mering made answer, "There is nothing in the whole world of which I am afraid You can only make me afraid by sending up to my village nine elephants with cotton piled on their backs.

1 Most Naga tribes have stories of the adoption of jungle men. They are probably based on the absorption of Negrito aborigines.

That will make me afraid." So the king sent up nine elephants to break down the nine hedges of stinging leaves. Then Mering heated his spear red hot, and waiting till the elephants had reached the fence, threw it at the first one. The cotton on its back caught alight, and when the flames reached its body it ran in among the other elephants and set them alight one after the other. Then the elephants fled and trampled many of the men to death. Then the king announced that he would cease to fight with Mering and would trade with him instead. And he called an Assamese and said to him, "Take a pot of cornelian beads with you and go up to Mering's village. If anyone wishes to buy from you, do not sell, but go on hawking your wares right through the village, and as you go scatter beads in the hedge of stinging leaves. Having done this come down to me again." And he went and did as he was bade, and the men of Mering's village cut down and destroyed all their hedge in their search for the beads which had been scattered there. Then the king sent men into the hills with dogs to hunt down Mering, and Mering fled to Yanzo's village to take refuge with him. It so happened that Yanzo was building his house. He therefore made Mering hide under a heap of thatching grass which was lying ready to hand, and then went and eased himself on the top of the pile. When the Assamese came up with their dogs they began to toss the thatching grass to this side and that in their search for Mering. Then Yanzo said to them, "Your dogs are very clever. Perhaps they are looking for this filth here." At these words all the Assamese were filled with shame and whipped off their dogs and departed. Because of this Mering and Yanzo broke an iron staff and swore on it that they would become one clan and would never intermarry. Afterwards a son was born to Mering whose name was Rapvu. He lived at Nungkamchung, where a bastard son was born to him of a woman of the Kikung clan. This son's name was Lobemo and his descendents still live at Tsingkaki. But the legitimate children of Rapvu are the ancestors of the Kithang clan.

5

THE STORY OF LICHAO'S DAUGHTER

Echunga kyon nchyua-na nipong-na mbo 'li elam
Once upon a time man a wild pig his fields much

to tsoicho-na mbo-na sotyemo wocho. Tole mbo-na
indeed ate-because he to hunt went. Then he

nipong ntsanga chenchi rua rua wole
wild pig a having speared following following when went

Lichao 'ki ruchokchicho ; hochi nipong tyemstü
Lichao's house followed up to ; he (of) wild pig (was) guardian

'motzü. Osi loroe nchyu' eni-na mbo-na chenchi-ochi
grand father. But girls one two he speared-the

ochak pia vancho. Hochiang-na "Ntolo rochola?" to
food gave remained. They "Why have (you) come?" thus

mbo engacho. Ole mbo-na nipong chenchi langta
him asked. Then he wild pig having speared to kill

kilato osü rua wochi tyuo khyua n-zocho ;
intending track following came to say fearing did not-say ;

hochi-tssoko-na mbo-na "Nte-ki-[i] loroe mhon nchyu' eni
this being-from he "Your-house [at] girls fine one two

vana to tyuta 'zocho-na nchyua a-na soa
are thus speaking (men) said-because one I marrying

vanka to ze-lo rocho" to ezocho. Tole oten-na
w'll remain indeed see-to came" thus said. Then they

"Tsangon-poeti ro" to ezole mbo-na yicho. Chitosi
"Day-another come" thus when said he went. Afterwards

mbo-na wolanle Lichao-na mbo ndri loroe-chi olantaro
he when went again Lichao his slave girl-the something

mhon mhon pipotok na ossü
fine fine having made her put on ornaments and clothes

mhon mhon mpenssütoksi vantok na
fine fine having made to put on caused to remain and

mbo otsolo-chi shilap shilap mmena mmena lui
his daughter-the untidy untidy dirty dirty making

mpongki-[i] vantokcho. Toala
outer room of the house-[in] caused to remain. Nevertheless

epue-chi n-tchüthechicheo tssocho. Mbo-na Lichao
man-the not-to be deceived was. He Lichao's

'tsoi nthong-chi lamm-i-ki hochi soa
daughter real-the preference-with-by that one marrying

vam kilato tssocho. Osi Lichao-cho mharrekam
would be intending was. But Lichao-that were-tiger

kyon 'so etsoi sakama mbo chenchisi
men's flesh eater being him having made to work

hochi n-ngaiche-na rham kilato nchama
him not-fulfilling-if would seize intending thinking

chenchicho. Osi loroe-chi-na mbo soa vam
made to work. But girl-the her marry would remain

etsso epue-chi "A-po-na i-chenchi-na a-zoke a-na
(to) man male-the "My father you-sets tasks-if me-tell I

i-zoka" to ovung-na ezoi vacho. Ole
you-will inform" thus first-from having said kept. Then

nchokacho Lichao-na otsolo soa vam tsso-ochi
one day Lichao daughter marry would be man-the

"Owo kotyoh koremyoi oyo epo ti-mbatok-na
"Going thorns brambles leaves torn not-allow to be-if

chok na i-tsak-ko ha tara-tia
picking and your-body-on too a little-only

ti-rhashak-to-na choki hana yia
prevent-scratch-even-if having picked bringing come

to-na a-tsolo i-soa
thus-by (i.e. then) my-daughter you-marrying

vantokoka" to ezocho. Tole loroe-chi-na
will allow to remain" thus said. Then girl-the

orapvü-chi "I-tsak-ko okhu mba na
(to) husband-the "Your-body-on scratch is and

oyo-chiang epo mbo to tssoa yichocho a-po-na
leaves-the torn are thus being coming my-father

i-rhamka" to ezole orapvü-chi-na owo mbo
you-will seize" thus when said husband-the going his

tsak-o ha okhu okhu m-mba na oyo-chiang
body-on too scratch scratch not-is and leaves-the

ha epo m-mba to-na terra shichei hanai
too torn not-are thus-from small having rolled up having broght

Lichao picho. Osi Lichao-na "Oyo shi-tai-
(to) Lichao gave. But Lichao "Leaves these-only-

na-cho e-n-tsochuola to ezoa lamphei
from-the we-not-eat enough" thus saying having opened

zele mbo honkhu-chi sazhucao.
when saw his outside of house-the was covered.

Chitosi ha Lichao-na "Nhungo woke i-poti-na
Afterwards too Lichao "Now (a) pig you-alone

rhamai changa to-na a-tsolo i-soa
having caught tie up thus-from my-daughter you-marrying

vantokoka" to ezoa orr m-pom pile
will allow to remain" thus saying cane un-split when gave

woko-chi nipong sakama kotolui rhamao
pig-the wild pig because was how possibly would catch

to nchama vanle eng-n "N-na woko-chi
indeed thinking while remaining (his) wife "You pig-the

rham-shukchocho a-po i-rhamka ; mhona lui
(if) catch fail my-father you-will seize ; good having made

rhamake" to ezoa mhona rhamatoksi
catch" thus saying well having made to catch

eng-na orr m-pom-chi echekrhui

(his) wife cane un-split-the having hit on the ground

pile orapvü-na kheta-na woko-chi

when gave (the) husband (one) hand with pig-the

rhamai nanyasi khet-na

having seized having held against himself (the other) hand-with

orr-chi ntyiorhui changcho. Tole Lichao-na

cane-the having split pieces off tied up. Then Lichao

otsolo-chi soa vantokcho.

daughter-the marrying (him) allowed to remain.

Chitosi eloe-chi-na orapvü 'ki yisi

After this girl-the (her) husband's house (to) having gone

nsangkangu kyon 'so-chi n-tsotyatale elam to

a little later men's flesh-the not-getting to eat very indeed

kurria ethu n-chhüo olampemo yicho.

becoming weak strength not-having idle became.

Ole orapvü-na "Nno nto-tsso-na heto

Then (her) husband "You what-being-because of thus

i-kurria ethu n-chhüa to ?" to

you-becoming weak strength not-have thus ?" thus

ezole eng-chi-na "Nkolo a-po ete-tso-

when said wife-the "Formerly my-father our-food-

pen-yu-pen n-tsoyao chi-na a-kurria

gave-drink-gave not getting to eat this-from I-becoming weak

ethu n-chhüala" to orapvü ezocho.

strength not-do have" thus (to her) husband said.

Chisicho orapvü-na "I-po nteno nkoto

Then (her) husband "Your-father you what kind of

tsotala ?" to ezolo eng-na "A-poang 'ki woa

do eat ?" thus when said (his) wife "My-parents' house going

to-na oso nkapi i-hantokoka

thus-from meat having wrapped up (they) you-will cause to carry;

lamphei ti-ze-na hana-ya" to ezoa

having opened do not-look-by bring-come" thus saying

wotokle eng-chi opoang-na kyon 'so
when made to go wife's-the parents men's flesh

nkapi pio-chi lamphei n-ze-na
having wrapped up gave-the having opened not-seeing-by

hanai pia tsotokle chi-topo eloe-chi
bringing giving when made to eat this-through girl-the

peleta nchürang essa ethu chhüa yicho. Chitosi
strong before like strength having became. After this

nchokania tai tssoa nhunga eloe-chi-na kyon
a few days later only being again girl-the men's

'so n-tsotyatale nhunga elam to kurria
flesh not getting to eat again very indeed becoming weak

ethu n-chhüo olampem kamcho. Osi
strength not-having idle became. But

orapvü-chi ezolancho "Opoang
(to her) husband-the (she) said again "(To) parents'

ki owo oso khi hanai pi" to
house going meat fetching bringing give" thus

ezocho. Olo orapvü-na eng-chi opoang ki owo
said. Then (the) husband wife's-the parents' house going

oso khilani hanai ntokoto 'so
meat fetching again bringing what kind of meat

tso-na eng kurria ethu n-chhüo
eating-from (his) wife becoming weak strength not-having

olampem kam-ochi mhona sana to 'so-nkap-chi
idle became-the well is indeed meat-parcel-the

lamphei zeo kilato nchamcho. Toala
having opened to see intending thought. But

Lichao-na kyon-'so-nkap-chi olan-i
Lichao men's-flesh-parcel-the road-on

n-lamphetoko kilato woro-ro pana
not-would allow to open intending (a) bird-little with (him)

wotokcho. Ole kyon-chi-na Lichao-na otsolo
made to go. Then man-the Lichao daughter's

echi 'so-nkap hantoko-chi olan-i-na
share meat-bundle made to carry-the path-on-from

lamphei zeo kilato tsampi-na woro-ro-chi-na
having opened to see intending touched-if bird-little-the

"N-na hochi lamphechocho a-na a-motzü ezo,
"You that if open I my-grandfather will tell,

n-na hochi lamphechocho a-na a-motzü ezo"
you that if open I my-grandfather will tell"

to tai ezosi mbo-na 'so-nkap-chi lamphei
thus only having said he meat-parcel-the having opened

n-zechecho. Tokatola mbo-na 'so-nkap-chi
not did look. Then he meat parcel-the

hanai eng pisi oki-na opo-na
bringing (to his) wife having given home-from (her) father

ntokoto 'so hantokcho sana to mphoa
what sort of meet made him bring is indeed hiding

yingto cheta vancho. Ole opo-na kyon
quietly watching remained. Then (her) father men's

yingdro tai nkaprhui hantok-ochi
fingers only having wrapped up made to carry-the

otsolo-na lamphei omi-na pham-phami
(his) daughter having undone fire-with roast-roasting

tsoa vancho, orapvü-na hochi hüng-ki lamm
eating remained, (her) husband this seeing-by liking

n-tsso eng-chi ezocho, "I-poango nto
not-being (to) wife-the said, "Your parents what

'so i-hantokchola, na nto 'so tai
meat for you-cause to be brought, and what meat only

tsotatoala to ezole eng-na "Mo, i-n-zo ;
do you eat ?" thus when said (his) wife "No, you-not-I tell ;

n-na lamm tsso ma-kama na i-khyu
you liking being not being-because and you-fearing

tsso-kama" to ezole orapvü-na
being-because" thus when said (her) husband

"A-n-khyula ; a-zoa" to ezocho. Tole eng-na "Toka
"I-not-am afraid ; me-tell" thus said. Then (his) wife "Then

a-na mharr kama a-na opang khusi
I tiger shall turn into I mouth having opened wide

erhua pongpi-na n-na okhyu-ki a-venyake, osi
roaring wander-if you basket-with me-cover up, but

chi-thang a-n-venya-na i-lia i-rhamka" to
that-time me-not-cover up-if you-even I-shall seize" thus

ezosi mharr kama opang khusi
having said tiger turning into mouth having opened wide

erhua pongpile orapvü-na okhyu-chi-na
roaring when wandered (her) husband basket-the-with

venle venshuki-ki eng-chi-na
when covering failing to cover-through (his) wife-the

rhami mbo tsocho. Shi motsü-shi tai.
having seized him ate. This story-the only.

Once upon a time wild pigs damaged a man's crops very badly, so he went down to hunt them, and wounded one with his spear. This he tracked and tracked till he came to the house of Lichao, the old man guardian of wild pigs. There he found two maidens feeding the pig he had wounded. They asked him what he had come for, but he was afraid to tell the truth and say that he was tracking a wild pig that he had wounded, so he replied, "Hearing that there were two beautiful maidens at your house I came to see, hoping that I might take one as my wife." Then they told him to come another day, so he departed.

When the man came a little later Lichao made his slave-girl put on beautiful ornaments and fine clothes, but his real daughter he made to sit all in rags and dirty in the outside room. But the man was not to be deceived. He loved Lichao's daughter and would only take her. Now Lichao used to turn into a tiger and eat human flesh. Therefore, he set his son-in-law hard tasks, meaning to devour him if he did not fulfil them. But when she knew this the maiden said to him, "Whatever task my father gives you to perform, tell me and I will reveal to you his purpose." So one day Lichao said to the man, "Go and pick the leaves of *kotyoh* thorns and *koremyoi* thorns, and bring them without a single leaf being torn and without a single scratch on your body. If you do this I will let you depart with my daughter." Then the girl said to her husband, "If you come home with the slightest scratch on your body, or with a single leaf torn, my father will devour you." So her husband went and picked the leaves without a single one being torn and without scratching his body in the least, and rolled them into a very tight bundle and brought and gave them to Lichao. Then Lichao said, "Only that amount will not be enough for us," but when he opened the bundle to look, the leaves covered all the ground in front of his house.

A few days later Lichao said, "If you can catch and tie up one of my pigs alone I will let you take my daughter and go," and with these words gave him a length of unsplit cane. Then the man fell to thinking how he could catch one of the pigs, for they were wild pigs; and his wife said to him, "If you cannot catch a pig my father will devour you." At last he caught a pig, and his wife beat the cane on the ground to fray it and gave it to him. Thus holding the pig with one hand he pulled of strips of cane with the other and bound the pig fast. Then Lichao let him take his daughter and go.

So the girl came to her husband's house. But there she could get no human flesh to eat, and soon become so weak and thin that she could not work. One day her husband said to her, "Why are you so weak and thin?" To which his wife replied, "I am thin and weak because I cannot get the food which my parents used to gave me." Then when her husband asked what her parents used to give her to eat she replied, "I will send you to fetch a parcel of meat wrapped in leaves from my parents' house. But bring it straight here. Do not open it and look to see what is inside." So he went, and his wife's parents gave him some pieces of human flesh wrapped up in leaves. This he brought straight home to his wife without opening the leaves to look to see what was inside, and when she ate it, it made her as plump and strong as ever. But in a day or two, because she could get no more human flesh to eat, she again became so thin and weak that she could not work. Then she spoke to her husband again and told him to go and fetch some more meat from her parents' house. Now her husband was determined to open the bundle and see what kind of meat it was that made his wife get well again when she was so thin and weak that she could not work. But Lichao sent a little bird to go back with him so that he should not open the parcel of human flesh on the way. When the man fingered the parcel which Lichao had given him, having it in his heart to open it, the little bird said to him. "If you open it I shall tell my grandfather; if you open it I shall tell my grandfather." So he did not open it to look inside. But when he had given the parcel of meat to his wife he went and hid and watched quietly to see what kind of meat her father had given him to bring. Now it was nothing but human fingers tied up in leaves that her father had given him to bring. And his wife undid the leaves and roasted the fingers lightly in the fire and ate them one after another. Now when he saw this her husband was much troubled and said, "What meat have your parents sent you? What meat is that you are eating?" But she said, "Nay, I will not tell you. You will only be troubled at heart and filled with fear." But he said, "I shall not be afraid. Tell me." Then his wife said, "I shall turn into a tiger. When I go about the house showing my fangs and roaring you must slip a basket over me. If you cannot slip a basket over me I shall devour even you." With these words she turned into a tiger, and her husband tried to cover her with a basket but could not, so she caught and ate him. That is the end of the story.

6

THE STORY OF RAMPHAN

Longcham-o vana-thang mharr elam to
Longcham-at staying-time (a) tiger much indeed

ntacho. Engana eloe yinga otsak toku rhamkhancho.
attacked. One day women party all nine seized.

Ngarohang nchyua rhamnhyacho. Hochi Ramphan eng.
Pregnant one seized. This Ramphan's wife.

Tole oyamo kyon topu-na "Oyan-shi-lo n-van"
Then villagers men all "Village-this-in not-stay"

to tai tyutacho. Ramphan-na "Oyam-oten, a-na
thus only said. Ramphan "Villagers-all, I

owo zeka" to tyua yantheng honsi owo
going will see" thus saying long *dao* carrying going

yingdro aku-lo ticha zenthei omang toku-chi-
finger each-on thin bamboo fixing corpses nine-the-

lung-i-na mharr-chi yipa nhyakcho. Chisilocho
among-in-at tiger-the lying down awaited. Later

mharr-chi-na oyi omang toku-chi "Shicho 'li-lo
tiger-the coming corpse nine-the "This one field-to

woi rhamcho, shicho 'tsang-o woi rhamcho,
going (I) seized, this one wood-for going (I) seized,

shicho tchhü-lo woi rhamcho, shicho 'yo chong
this one water-to going (I) seized, this one leaves plucking

rhamcho, shicho 'hanteng rhamcho, na
(I) seized, this one relish (while fetching) (I) seized, and

shicho 'tyokha-i rhamcho" to tyua 'so-khyu
this one fishing-at seized" thus saying meat-piece

'so-khyu-na nkakchosila va-va to tssoa
meat piece from taking a bite leaving leving thus being

oyi Ramphan chanale "Shicho 'so-tacho"
coming Ramphan when reached "This one meat-extra"

to tyua echami thampoi vasi mharr-chi
thus saying seizing laying aside having left tiger-the

yipcho. Tole Ramphan-na yingdro aku-lo ticha
lay down. Then Ramphan finger each-on thin bamboo

zenthe-ochi mharr-chi yip-yipa-na to ticha-chiang
fixed-the tiger-the asleep-asleep-if indeed thin bamboos-the

emerap-na nharr-chi-na n-yipo enno-chi elhampya
snapping-if tiger-the not-asleep ears-the twitching

van van to tssocho. Okaiti Ramphan-na
remaining remaining indeed was. At last Ramphan

ticha toku emerapsi ntsanga tai tssoale
thin bamboos nine having snapped one only when was

"A-na shi emerapsi mharr-chi n-yip-na tai
"I this having snapped tiger-the not-asleep-if only

ka" to tyua ticha ntsang-chi emeraple
is" thus saying thin bamboo one-the when snapped

mharr-chi enno n-inampyo yipisicho. Tolo Ramphan-na
tiger-the ears not-twitching was asleep. Then Ramphan

mbo yantheng-chi-ki hana 'wo mharr-chi
his long *dao*-the-with taking going tiger-the

woni hansi tungti-lo-cho hoki
having beheaded carrying (the head) peak-on-the war cry

ten. Ekok-i-cho eng rham-ochi nchamchei nungra
shouted. Valley-in-the wife seized-the remembering sad

to tssoa "A-na yanri tyoa
indeed becoming "I village-enemy having defeated

tsaka, oyam-oten oyan ti-tyontana a-nhyakle"
am coming, villagers-all village not-deserting me-wait for"

to thanga yile mbo-na oyan chanacho
thus shouting when coming he village (when) reached

oyan-chi tyona yitakcho. Oyamo-chiang-na
village-the (they) deserting had gone. Villagers-the

ekoni-na mbo thangchicho "O en-a wokopu manku-i
afar-from (to) him shouted "O we sow's back-on

tsokzhu ntyakai sua yika ; chi rrüa yike"
husks sprinkling taking will go ; that tracking come"

to ezochia yiracho. Tole Ramphan-na hochi rrüa
thus saying went on. Then Ramphan that tracking

yile olan-i eloe ranoi nchyua phayacho.
when going path-on woman leprous a caught up.

Hochi 'myang Mangtsilo to tsacho. Mbo-na
Her name Mangtsilo thus was called. She

Ramphan-chi "A-motzü, ntoku to ets-osa-na
(to) Ramphan-that "My-grandfather, what indeed being-from

ndrrütsu-shi-na "Ndrrü hau ndrrü hau hau,
snake-this "Snake plant ho sanke plant ho ho,

Mangtsilo" to khua oyi a-cho-lo apyukaicho ?
Mangtsilo" thus calling coming my-leg-on crawled ?

Hochi ntoko to etssoa to, a-motzü ?"
This what indeed happened indeed, my-grandfather ?"

to mbo engacho. Tole Ramphan-na "Toka hochi
thus him asked. Then Ramphan "Then this

nnoki thei zeta" to ezoa hochi nnoki
crushing putting see" thus having said that crushing

thei zetokle eloe orano-chi pocho.
putting when made to see woman leprous-the was cured.

Chisicho eloe-chi Ramphan-na soa vancho.
After that woman-the Ramphan marrying remained.

Enga mbo-na eng-chi mbo honkhui ossü
One day he wife-the his (house) outside cloth

taka vantoksi mbo ndri-chiang phiro
weaving having caused to remain his slaves-the tops

emunga emunga owo Mangtsilo 'tyai-chiang noa
spinning spinning going Mangtsilo's brothers-the enticing

noa oyi mbo honkhui-na phiro-chi eng
enticing coming his (house) outside-from tops-the wife

nthangi tai emungchitokcho. Ole ote nchyua-na
near only made to spin. Then (of) them one

Mangtsilo-chi mhona chetheiki oyi opo ha
Mangtsilo-that well recognising going (to) father and

oyo oni "Ochicho a-ta-na atato vana"
mother both "That (woman) our-sister-to like is"

to ezocho. Tole opo ha oyo oni-na-chi
thus said. Then father and mother both-( )-those

n-nungtso "I-ta-cho nkolo-na orru-long
not-believing "Your-elder sister-the before-from bones-and all

mpato nrhonroi sitakna kolo i-ta
too rotting having been lost where your-elder sister

vana to?" to tai ezona mbo-na "A ta-na
is indeed?" thus only saying he "Our-elder sister to

atato ochi vana" to tai ezomungcho. Chisicho
like that is" thus only kept saying. Then

opo ha oyo oni-na owo zele otsotso
father and mother both going when saw truly

Mangtsilo sakama Ramphen-thangi oman
Mangtsilo since was Ramphan-from marriage price

choncho. Osi Ramphan-na "A-mo
demanded. But Ramphan "My-father in law

khulichotan a-pia; to-na oman nte-
marriage meat me-give; thus-from marriage price (to) you-

pika" to omo ezocho. Chisicho
will give" thus (to his) father in law said. Then

omo-na. "A-rro, toka nto lua
(the) father in law. "My-son in law, then what (shall I) do

to; yengkok ntsanga na otsap ntsanga to
indeed; spoon a and bamboo spoon a thus

tai lui a-pia" to ezole mbo-na
only making me-give" thus when said he (i.e. Ramphan)

yengkok ntsanga na otsap ntsanga to tai lui
spoon a and bamboo spoon a thus only making

omo picho. Hochi-tssoko-na Ramphan
(to his) father in law gave. This-being-from Ramphan

onpoi-na otsoi epue nchyua eloe nchyua to
couple children boy one girl one thus

tai pokcho.
only got.

Ramphan-na mharr womo yantheng-chi nhungacha
Ramphan tiger beheaded long *dao*-the to this day

Akuk-i lia.
Akuk-at is.

When the Lhotas were living at Longcham[1] a tiger caused them grievous loss. One day it killed all of a party of nine women. Among them was Ramphan's wife, who was about to-become a mother. At this disaster all clamoured to abandon the village, but Ramphan said he would go and face the tiger. First he put on each of his fingers a section of thin bamboo. Then he took his long *dao*[2] and lay down among the corpses of the nine women and waited for the tiger. Soon the tiger came and went to each corpse and ate a little of the flesh and laid it on one side, saying as he did so, "This one I killed on her way to the fields," or "This one I killed when she went to cut wood," or "This one I killed on her way to fetch water," or "This one I killed when she went to pick jungle leaves." or "This one I killed when she went to get vegetables," or "This one I killed when she was going down to fish." At last he came to Ramphan and said, "This

1 long abandoned site on Wokha Hill, the first settlement of the Lhotas after they split off from the Rengmas.

2 A long *dao* of obsolete pattern of which a few are still preserved at heirlooms. One which is owned by the leading family of Akuk village is reputed to be the actual one mentioned in this story. It is rarely shown to strangers,

one I do not remember," and picked him up and laid him aside, and then settled himself down to sleep. Then one by one Ramphan began to snap the pieces of bamboo on his fingers to see if the tiger was asleep or not. But at each snap the tiger pricked up his ears. At last when he had snapped nine of the pieces of bamboo and there was only one left, Ramphan thought to himself, "If the tiger is not asleep when I snap this I am done for." But when he snapped the last remaining piece of bamboo the tiger did not prick up its ears, for it was fast asleep. Then Ramphan rose up and cut off the tiger's head with his long *dao*, and climbed with it up to the top of a high spur and shouted the shout of a warrior who has taken a head. But he was sad when he thought of his wife lying dead in the valley below. And he called to his village men and said, "I have slain our enemy. Do not desert your village Wait for me." But when he reached home he found that the villagers had already abandoned the place. From far away they shouted back to him, "We have sprinkled the back of one of our sows with rice husks, which fall as she walks. Follow the track of that and come." Now as Ramphan followed the trail of rice husks he caught up on the path a woman who was a leper. And the woman, whose name was Mangtsilo, said to Ramphan, "What does this mean, father ? A poisonous snake here said, 'Snake-plant, snake-plant, Mangtsilo,' and glided over my leg What does it mean ?" Then Ramphan told her to crush up some leaves of the snake-plant and lay them on her leg. And she did as he told her and leprosy was cured. Then Romphan took her as his wife.

One day when Mangtsilo was weaving outside her house, Ramphen's slaves began to spin their tops near by. They made Mangtsilo's brothers join in, and drew them on and on till they came close to her house. Then one of the brothers recognized his sister Mangtsilo, and went and told his parents that he had seen a woman exactly like his sister. But his parents said, "Your sister was lost long ago. Her very bones have rotted away by now. How could you have seen her ?" But he said again and again that he had seen a woman exactly like hts sister, so that at last his parents went to see and found that it was indeed Mangtsilo. Then they demanded her marriage price from Ramphan, but Ramphan said, "First give me the marriage feast and then I will give you the marriage price." So her father said, "What can I do ? Make and give me only a bamboo spoon and a bamboo rice-stirrer." So Ramphan made and gave him only a bamboo spoon and a rice-stirrer. That is why Ramphan and Mangtsilo only had one son and ane daughter born to them.

7

THE TWO FRIENDS

On-cheni eramo-chicho yantsai osi nungowo-chicho
Two-brothers elder-the poor but younger-the

elam to licho. Nungowo-chi-na ota-cho
much indeed was rich. Younger-the elder brother-the

nzam n-zehungo okamo-chi tai elam to nzana
comfort not-seeing (his) friend-the only much indeed loving

oni tai tyengtacho. Osi mbo-na nchokacho
they two only were friendly. But he one day

okamo-ehi "A-kam, nchingk e-ni sheriti
(to) friend-the "My-friend, to-day we-two red berries

hloi tso-lo wotaka" to exoa oni
having picked eat-to will go" thus having spoken they two

wotacho. Chisicho mbo-na otong-i chungo
went. Then he tree-in having climbed

sheriti-chi hloi tsoale na otsak
red berries-the having picked when eating and body

nzale to tssoi "A-kam, a-khangala"
when smearing thus having become "My-friend, I am falling"

to ezoa vanchole, okamo-na choi
thus having spoken failing (the) friend having descended

mbo zesi "A-kam, e-ni chibo-poe
him having seen "My friend, we-two (of) clan-different

kama a-na-cho, koto i-n-zeka. A-na
because I, in any way you-will not-look after. I

oyi i-ta ezoa rotokuka," to
going your-elder brother telling will make to come," thus

ezosi mbo n-zeo sisi yicho, Osi
having said him not looking after having left went. But

ota oyi ezoicho ; ole ota-na owo
elder brother going told ; then (the) elder brother going

zesi "A-ngo, lamm n-ramo n-no
having seen "My-younger brother, love not-remembering you

okame-cho a-nzam a-n zchungo i-kamo-
(when) alive my-comfort me-not-looking after your friend-

sho-mo nto tai nzanta tyentaracho," to ezoa
that-only you only loving were affectionate," thus having said

owo sükale chi-thang ongo-na
going while lifting up (at) that-time (the) younger brother

"A-ta, ntia ntssoka" to
"My-elder brother, what will become (i.e. is the matter)" thus

tyua panthiki ota-chi pulansi yicho.
saying having got up elder brother-the having picked up went.

Chitosicho okamo oni n-tyentao ota
After that friends they two not-being friendly brothers

oni tai elam to nzanta tyengtacho. Hochi-tssoko-
they two only much indeed loving were friends. This being-

na nhungaliya kyov-na ekamo popo potsocheni nzanta
from till now men alive own relations loving

tyengta rata vancho n-chan to tyutala.
friendly cared not-like thus say.

There were once two brothers. The elder was poor, but the younger was very rich. The younger brother ignored the elder and kept all his care and affection for his friend. One day the younger brother said to his friend, "My friend, to day we will go and pick and eat red berries." So saying they went. The younger brother climbed the tree, and while he was picking and eating the berries smeared himself all over with the red juice. Then he called out, "Friend, friend,

I am falling" and tumbled out of the tree. His friend climbed down and looked at him as he lay on the ground and said, "You are no relation of mine. I shall not look after you. I will go and tell your brother and get him to come." With these words he went away without attending to him at all. But his brother came and saw him, and looking at him said, "My brother, forgetful one, when you were alive you scorned and neglected me and kept all your love and affection for your friends." With these words he picked him up to carry him, but the younger brother said, "Brother, there is nothing the matter with me," and got up and himself carried his elder brother home. Thereafter the friends were friends no more, but the two brothers loved one another. That is why men say that there is nothing in life equal to the love of one's own relations.

8

THE GIRL WHO MARRIED A TIGER

Eloe ngarohang nchyua-na phendran-i
Woman pregnant a last year's field-to

phendkhyu-lo wole shomo hungi
look for self sown vegetables-to when went (a) gourd seeing

hloa vancho. Tole mharr ntsanga-na oyi mbo
picked remained. Then tiger a coming her

hüngcho. Mharr-chi-na "A-shomo-la ; nno nto luo shi
saw. Tiger-the "My-gourd-is ; you what hoing this

hloala ? I-rhamka" to ezoa rhamacho.
are picking ? (I) You-will-seize" thus saying seized.

Chisicho eloe-chi-na "A-na ngaro hamo-shi
Then woman-the "I child carrying in womb-this

vantoksi i-soa vantokuka.
having given birth to you marrying will cause to remain.

A·ti·rhama" to ezoa mharr-chi-ki mbo
Me-do-not-seize" thus saying tiger-the-with her

vachitokcho, Chisicho eloe-chi-na ngaro-chi
made to leave go. Afterwards woman-the-from child-the

vancho. Hochi zoi mharr-chi-na eloe-chi
was born. This hearing tiger-the (to) woman-the

"Ngaro-chi van-n-vanha ?" to tai engamungcho.
"Child-the (is) born-not-born ?" thus only kept asking.

Eloe-chi-na mharr-chi "Ngaro-chi vantaka" to ezocho.
Woman-the (to) tiger-the "Child-the is born" thus said.

Tole mharr-chi-na "Tona nhungo otsang otchhu-lo
Then tiger-the "Then now wood water-to

wowokoka na yanvanpikoka ?" to
is able to go and is ready to be given in marriage ?" thus

engacho. Tole eloe-chi-na "Nhungacho otsang otchhu-lo
asked. Then woman the "Yet wood water-to

n-wokoka" to tai ezoa van-vansi
not-is able to go" thus only saying remaining-remaining

okaiti osi-na tyutai vachokama to nchama
at last before-from saying leaving indeed remembering

"Nhungo otsang otchhü-lo wokoktaka,
"Now wood water-to can go,

yanpikoktaka" to ezocho. Chisicho eloe-chi-na
can be given in marriage" thus said. Then woman-the

otsolo-chi yanpia-thang mpensi yitoko kilato
daughter-the marrying-time wearing to cause to go intending

ossü taka-thang "A-tsoi-cho mharr 'pang-i
cloth weaving time "My-child-that tiger's mouth-into

thriosaka" to nchama nungra-tsanga esütchu-na
has entered" thus thinking sad-miserable tears-with

ossü-chi zanzhya taka vancho. Opo-na ha hochi
cloth-the sprinkling weaving remained. Father too this

to nchama etsolo yanpia-thang hansi yitoko
indeed thinking daughter marrying-time carrying to cause to go

kilato esütchhü zana phari taka vancho.
indeed tears shedding carrying basket weaving remained.

Hochi hungi otsolo-chi-na "A-pvü nno nto-tsso-na
This seeing daughter-the "My-mother you what-being-because

esütchhü zanato ? to engale opvü-na
tears are shedding ? thus when aksed (the) mother

"A-ka tsirochonglong-na omhyek-i a-rakthechicho"
"My-child shuttle-with eye-in me-poked"

to mbo ezocho. Opo ha "A-po, nno
thus her told. Father too "My-father, you

nto-tsso-na esütchhü zanato" to engale
what-being-because tears are shedding" thus when asked

opo-na ha "A-ka omu-na omhyek-i
(the) father too "My-child bamboo strip-with eye-in

a-rakthechicho" to mbo ezocho. Chisicho opo ha
me-poked" thus her told. Afterwards father and

opvü oni-na mharr-thangi yanpia yitokcho.
mother both tiger-to marrying caused to go.

Nzua-ria vansi onpci-na otsoi eloe-roro
Year-about having remained (the) couple child girl-little

nchyua pokcho. Osi ngaro-chi-na oyo-na soa-na
a got. But child-the mother-with stayed-if

n-tya na opo-na soa-na tya to tai
not-crying and father-with stayed-if crying thus only

tsshocho. Tole eng-na mharr-chi "Nno nto-tsso-na
was. Then wife (to) tiger-the "You what-being from

a-ka tata tyatoka to" to ezole
my-child so much make to cry indeed" thus when said

mharr-chi-na "A-mehm-na tsoki tyaka" to
tiger-the "My-beard-with pricking cries" thus

eng-chi ezocho. Osi nchokacho eng-na chetha
(to) wife-the said. But one day wife seretly watching

vanle mharr-chi-na ngaro-chi nchüna kurri-lo
when remaining tiger-the child-the hearth stones head-on

thiphyi thiphyi echen zantoksila nnyak nnyak to
drip drip blood letting drop licking licking thus

tssoa vancho. Hochi eng-na hüngi mharr-chi sisi
being remained. This wife seeing tiger-the leaving

kilato "A-ka opo, a-na otsang-o woka ;
intending "My-child's father, I wood-for am going ;

a-ka sosi vanana" to ezole mharr-chi-na
my-child holding stay" thus when said tiger-the

"A-na role" to ezocho ; na toka "A-na
"I am coming" thus said ; and then "I

otchhü-lo woka, oli-[i] woka, na ora-i
water-to am going, field-[to] am going, and jungle-to

woka ; a-ka sosi vanana" to ezolanle
am going ; my-child holding stay" thus whenever said

mharr-chi-na chi ha "A-na role" to tai
tiger-the (to) that too "I am coming" thus only

ezoa mbo phanpimuhgcho. Osi nchokacho eng-na
saying her always accompanied. But one day wife

"A-ka opo, a-na pussü-shi tchhükha-i-na
"My-child's father, I carrying cloth-this spring-at-to

chowo etsika. A-ka soalo" to ezoa
going down will wash. My-child hold" thus saying

sotoksi tchhükha-i-na chowo orhak ntsanga
having made to hold spring-at-to going down louse a

na tezhu ntsanga to pussü-chi "tyak-tyak" khua
and flea a thus carrying cloth-the "plop-plop" saying

etsia vantockcho. Mbo opoyang 'ki-[i] tsana
washing caused to remain. Her parents' house-[to] escaping

yicho. Tole mharr-chi-na orhak to na tezhu-to-chi
went. Then tiger-the louse indeed and flea-indeed-the

eng tsaya "A-ka opvü a-ka
(his) wife (was) thinking "My-child's mother, my-chiid

tyaka, chungi zua" to ezosi
will cry, coming up give it to suck" thus saying

n-chungiale chowo zecho. Eng-chi n-vancho.
when not-came up going down looked. Wife-the not-remained.

Orhak to na tezhu to sakama "Nte
Louse indeed and flea indeed because were "You

hetonacho a-chithechiake" to tyua orhak-chicho
so much me-would deceive" thus saying louse-the

ehitsangi sicho, osi tezhn-chicho tsoka
crushing with his nail threw away, but flea-the jumping

yicho. Tole mharr-chi-na "A-ng hepi yiyi ?"
departed. Then tiger-the "My-wife this way went ?"

to olantaro enga enga phana wole topu-na
thus all asking asking pursuing when went all

"N-hung n-hung" to tai ezorasi okaiti
"Not-seen not-seen" thus only kept saying at last

sangalia engale chi-na "Nhungati shilo
the *sangalia* creeper when asked it "Just now hither

yiana" to ezoiki phana owe emangoti
came" thus having said (the tiger) pursuing going at dusk

opoyang ki nthango-na phayacho. Tole
(her) parents' house near-at caught up. Then

eloe-chi-na yungai opoyang ki-pang-na oyochi
woman-the running parents' house-door-at having arrived

"A-yo, chüro oki a-chonchia" to
"My-mother, coming out house (for) me-open" thus

ezothechile oyo-na "Ocho sana ? 'Yo otsoi
when kept saying mother-the "Who is that ? My child

n-vankama ; etsoi-cho nkolo-na montakama" to
not-is ; child-the before-from disappeared" thus

ezosi chüwo n-chonchicho. Tole otsolo-na
having said going out not-opened. Then daughter

"A-yo n-na nkolo nungo-thang woko-tsak
"My-mother you long ago (I) little-time pig-food

yengkok-na a-kho chilala" to ezoa phurro-pe-
spoon-with my-head hit" thus saying dog-entrance-

khu-i-na peta thria vanle chi-thang
hole-in-at squeezing in entering when was that-time

mharr-chi-na och-woi na oyo-na chüro kurri-woi to
tiger-the leg-half and mother coming out head-half indeed

rhamasi tsangta-tsangtasi mharr-chicho ocho-woi na
having seized pull-pulling tiger-the leg-half and

oyo-cho kurri-woi to oni rangsotacho. Tole
mother-the head-half indeed they two pulled apart. Then

mharr-chicho mbo 'ki-[i] hanai vasi chakcha
tiger-the his house-[to] carrying keeping whisk

pensi peno-tia n-wotoko phana vansi
holding fly-a single not-letting come driving away remaining

shothecho. "O a-ka opvü, ekamocho chan
buried. "O my-child's mother, when alive relish

tssoliya oso-ngo tai i-tsotokcho;
for meat-and such like only you-caused to eat;

changram changricho i-n-tsotoka" to tyua
leaves vegetables you-not-caused to eat" thus saying

tya vanle eng oyona
weeping when remaining woman (i.e. the mother) coming

mharr-chi "Nno nto-tsso-na tya vanala?
(to) tiger-the "You what-being-from weeping remain?

'Yo e-ni rangsotao-chi heto ekhui tsoakama,
We we-two pulled apart-the thus cooking eat,

he" to ezoa oni rangsotao kurri-woi
now" thus having said they two pulled apart head-half

'so-chi echakaro ekhui hanao mharr-chi picho.
meat-the a little cooking bringing (to) tiger-the gave.

Tole mharr-chi-na "Eyo aka opvü 'so kama
Then tiger-the "Our child's mother's flesh because is

n-tso" to tyua van-vansi okaiti khi tsocho
not-eat" thus saying remain-remaining at last taking ate.

Chitosicho mharr-chi-na "Kyon 'so-cho mhona yia"
After that tiger-the "Man's flesh-the good is"

to tyua mbo-na shothe-vao-chi mpato shochei
thus saying he buried-kept-the also digging up

tsosi kyon mpato rhami tsoa yicho. Hochi
having eaten men also seizing eating went. This

tssoko-na nbungaliya kothang-kothangnacho mharr-na
having been-from till now sometimes-sometimes tigers

kyon rhamala.
men seize.

A woman one day went down to her field to fetch some vegetables. She saw a fine gourd there and was just going to pick it when a tiger saw her and said, "That is my gourd. Why were you going to pick it? I shall kill you." With these words he caught her. But the woman, who was about to become a mother, said, "Do not kill me. and I will give you my baby when it is born." So the tiger let her go. In due time a daughter was born to the woman. When the tiger heard of this he kept asking the woman if her child was born yet, till at last she told the tiger that it had been born. Soon the tiger asked her if her daughter was strong enough to fetch firewood and water yet and whether she was old enough to be married. But the woman kept putting him off by saying that her daughter was not yet old enough to carry wood and water and was too young to marry; till at last she saw that she must keep her old bargain and admitted that the girl was old enough to work as his wife. As she sat weaving a cloth for her daughter to wear on her wedding day she was overcome with grief when she thought how her child would surely be killed and eaten by the tiger, and her tears fell fast on the cloth she was making. Her husband too was sad as he worked at a basket he was making for his daughter to carry when she went to her husband's house and his tears fell fast on the basket. When the girl saw this she said, "Why are you crying, mother?" and her mother answered, "I poked myself in the eye with my bobbin." To her father too the girl said, "Why are you crying, father?" And her father replied "I poked myself in the eye with a slip of bamboo." Then when the day came her parents gave her in marriage to the tiger.

About a year later a little daughter was born to the tiger and his wife. When her mother carried her she never cried but when her father carried her she cried all the time. So his wife said to the tiger, "Why do you make our daughter cry so much?" The tiger replied "It is because my beard pricks her." But one day the woman hid herself and watched and saw the tiger knock his little daughter's head "tap, tap" against a hearth stone and lick up the blood which dripped down. When she saw this the woman determined to leave the tiger and said to her husband "I am going to fetch some wood. Hold the baby till I come back," But the tiger said "I am coming too." And whenever she asked him to look after the baby while she went to get water, or went to the field or into the jungle, the tiger always replied "I am coming too," and never let her out of his sight. At last one day she asked him to look after the child while she went down to the spring to wash its carrying cloth.[1] So he took the child and she went down to the spring and set a louse and a flea to wash the cloth. "chuck chuck, chuck-chuck," while she ran off and made for her parents' house. The tiger, thinking the noise made by the louse and the flea was his wife washing the cloth, kept calling out, "The baby is crying. Come up and nurse it." But when she did not come up he went down to look for himself, and found his wife gone and the louse and the flea there instead. Then he said, "You would play tricks on me, would you ?" and crushed the l use with his thumb-nail, but the flea jumped and got away.

Then the tiger set out to search for his wife and asked everyone he met whether they had seen her pass. All replied that they had not seen her, till at last he came to the *sangalia* creeper, who said she had just gone by that way. Then he chased and chased her till he came up with her at dusk at the door of her parents' house. The woman cried out, "Mother, come out of the inner room and open the door for me." But her mother replied, "Who is that ? I have no daughter. My daughter disappeared long ago" and would not come out and open the door. Then the woman said again, "I am your own daeghter, mother, whom years ago, when I was little, you hit on the head with the pigs' food ladle. Do you not know me now ?" With these words she began to squeeze through the little opening by the door left for the dogs, but the tiger seized her legs while her mother seized her head and shoulders. And they pulled and pulled till she was torn in two and the tiger was left with her lower half and her mother with the upper half. Then the tiger took his half to his house and kept watch over it with a whisk so that not a single fly should settle on it and buried it. And he wept, saying "O my wife, when

1 The implication is that she would take the opportunity of bathing. It would not be proper for her husband to follow her.

you were alive I loved you so much that I was careful always to give you good meat to eat as relish with your rice. You never had to eat leaves and such-like poor fare.' But her mother said, "Why do you weep so? We have torn her in half. Now we will cook and eat her." And she cooked a ltttle of the flesh from the upper half of the girl and offered it to the tiger, who refused it, saying, "How can I eat the flesh of the mother of my daughter?" But at last he ate it. Then he said, "Human flesh is good," and went and dug up the portion he had burried and ate that too. That is how the tiger came to eat human flesh, and that is why to this day tigers sometimes kill and devour men.

9

THE WOMAN WHO MARRIED A CATERPILLAR

Eloe nchyua-na epue nchyua-thangi yampile
Woman a man a-with marrying

epue-chi-na zamo-thang-cho kyon na engo-cho
man-the (in) night-time-the human being and (in) day-the

momo kam to eloe-chi-na n-tsia
hairy caterpillar turning-into indeed woman-the not-knowing

vancho. Osi nchokacho eloe-chi-na "Aiyo ochö
remained But one day woman-the "I to-morrow

oyo choko woka" to tyusi yiple
leaves to pluck shall go" thus having said going to sleep

eng-ya-thang-cho orapvü-na vunga owo
(at) sun-rising-time (the) husband first going

momo kami cherhalomo-yo
hairy caterpillar having become vegetables-leaves

nkapchochi-rhui vasi nhyaka vancho. Ole
nipping off-leaving having put waiting remained. Then

eloe-chi-na owo cherhalomo-yo-chiang hungi, "E,
woman-the going vegetables-leves-the having seen, "Oh,

momo-na nkapchochicho, heto khi hankila"
(a) hairy caterpillar has nipped off, this taking am carrying"

to tyua khi hansi yicho. Osi mbo-na
thus saying taking having carried went. But she

zamo-thang yipa-thang orapvü-chi "Aiyo nchingo
(at) night-time sleeping-time (to) husband-the "I to-day

cherhalomo-yo momo-na nkapchochi-rhui
vegetables-leaves (a) hairy caterpillar having nipped off-left

licho khi hansi yicho," to ezole,
were taking having carried went," thus saying,

chi-thang orayvü-na "Hochi ana-la" to ezocho.
(at) that-time (the) husband "That I-am" thus said.

Hochi-tssoko-na eloe-chi-na lamm n-tsso
This-being-from woman-the heart not-becoming (settled)

yipa-thang orapvü-chi engyhia engyhia chowo
(at) sleeping-time husband-the pushing pushing downward

omi engyhitechi rongtsangtokcho.
(into the) fire having pushed off caused to be burnt.

Chisilocho eloe-chi-na tso-yu-na etso-yu
After that woman-the eating-drinking-from food-drink

aku momo tsanchi tso-nhya-yu-nhya
every hairy caterpillar hair eat-swallow-drink-swallow

tso-nhya-yu-nhya to tssoa ekhutsangi
eat-swallow-drink-swallowing thus becoming coughing

tchhicho: Hochi-na nhungaliya ekhutsangka
died This-because of till now if you cough

"Momo-chi omi-na ti-rong," to
"Hairy caterpillar-the fire-with do not-burn," thus

tyutala.
(men) say.

A man and his wife lived together. Now at night the husband was a man, but in the day he turned into a hairy caterpillar. His wife did not know this. One night before she went to sleep she said, "To-morrow I am going to gather some leaves for vegetables." Early in the morning her husband left the house first and turned into a caterpilla and nipped off the leaves and waited at the place. Then the woman came and at the sight of the leaves exclaimed, "Strange, a caterpillar has nipped off the leaves. I will take them and go." So saything she took the leaves and went. But that night when they were in bed she said to her husband, "To-day I found that a caterpillar had nipped off the leaves I went to gather." Then her husband said, "It was I". At these words she was greatly troubled, and when he was asleep she gently pushed and pushed her husband till he fell off the bed into the fire and was burnt. After that the woman swallowed caterpillar hairs with her food, whenever she ate, and coughed and coughed till she died.[1] Therefore nowadays if anyone coughs much people say, "You should not burn a caterpillar.'

1 The hairs of this caterpillar contain an irritant poison.

10

THE OLD WOMAN AND THE *MORUNG*

Eran-na tyutala Nungkamchung-o vana-thang emi
Old men say Nungkamchung-at living-time old woman

nchyua-na woko tsopo ekamchecho. Enga züro
a pig big kept. One day (the) forty

champo-i-na emi woko-chi otsok-men epvucho.
morung-men old woman's pig-the rice-price took on credit.

Chisilocho emi-chi-na nchokapen "A-woko otsok-man
After that old woman-the every day "My-pig rice-price

epvu-chi a-pia," to züro champo-i
taken on credit-the me-give," thus (to) forty *morung*-men

ezole oten-na m-picho. Ole emi-chi-na yonchak
when said they not-gave. Then old woman-the iron

etsi-lo tiloran eshoi
staff-into sand and powder (i.e. magic powder) pouring

süsi owo champo thrrupya "A-woko
having taken going *morung* walking round "My-pig

otsok-man epvu-chi a-pia a-pia" to ezoa
rice-price taken on credit-the me-give me give" thus saying

lenpya wocho. Chisilocho esangaro tai tssoa
tapping went. Then a little later only being

mpongki yipo-chi tai
(in) wind-house (i.e. front room of *morung*) sleeping-the only

tsoka chusi emi-chi-na yonchak
jumping up having come out old woman-the iron

etsi-lo tiloran eshoi lenpya wo-chi
staff-into magic powder having poured tapping gone-the
ntante menchoi kyon topu menzhuisicho. Osi oyan-na
so far earth opening men all were engulfed. But villagers
rhonche kilato oyan sani rhontala nchyua-tia
dig out intending villagers all digging one-even
n-rhoncheo leshu-chak ntsanga tai rhonchecho.
not-digging out thatch-wisp one only dug out.

Old men say that when the Lhotas lived at Nungkamchung a widow had a big pig. One day the boys of the *morung*[1] took the pig, promising to pay for it with rice. But they did not pay, though every day the widow came and said, "Give me the price of my pig which you bought for rice." At last she took her iron staff and poured magic powder into it and walked round the *morung* saying. "Give me the price of my pig which you bought with rice. Give it, Give it," tapping the ground with her staff as she went. Suddenly the ground opened wherever she had tappend it with her staff containing magic powder and all the inmates of the *morung* were swallowed up, only those in the front room of the *morung* having time to jump to their feet and escape. Then the village all set to work to dig them out, but could not dig out a single man, only a wisp of thatch.

1 *Morung* is the Anglo-Assamese term for the bachelor's house which each section of a Lhota village contains. It serves as a club and sleeping place for the boys and unmarried men and in the old days was used as guard house. This institution is found in nearly all Naga tribes.

11

CHUNGAO AND THE WATER SPIRIT

Ntonsito pochung tiroko aria yitaka Morakcho-i
About generations six so much gone by Morakcho-at

Chungao etsa-i nchyua-na Tchhüpfuo[1]-thangi okamo
Chungao name-by a (man) Water Spirit-with friend

tssocho. Mbo-na zhu-khu-i-na ngokung na ongo ekhu-
became. He pool-hole-in-from dried fish and fish cooked-

cho to tai "Tchhüpfuo-na picho" to tyua hansi
the thus only "Water Spirit gave" thus saying having carried

yi mungcho. Mbo-na ngokung na ongo ekhu-chiang
came collected. He dried fish and fish cooked-the

Tchhüpfuo-thangi-na hansi yicho to ezo-na
Water Spirit-with-from having brought came thus saying-by

mbo oshom-chiang-na mbo yi-chi ko-thang ha
his friends the his words-the any-time indeed

n-nangtsocho. Chitosi mbo-na mbo yi-chi chiangki
not-believed. Then he his words-the them

nangtsotoko kilato etyou tssocho. Mbo-na
would make to believe intending anxious become. He

oyamo kyon topu sosi tyozhu-lo Tchhüpfuo
villagers men all having taken fish-to (the) Water Spririt's

evamo ezhutsak-chi-lo wocho. Osi oten-na hochi-lo ono
lair pool-that-to went. But they that place-at poison

thethale ongo ha elam to hungcho. Chi-thang
when they put fish indeed much indeed caught. That-time

1 Literally "Water Master," a being like a man with hair of enormous length.

mbo-na oyamo-chiang "Omi mhona tssota" to
he (to) villagers-the "Fire good let there be" thus
ezole oten-na omi tssocho. Ole mbo-na mi-cham
when he said them-from fire was. Then he fire-brand
khi pensi ezhu-chung-i thro-wocho. Esangaro tai
taking holding pool-bottom-to down-went. A little later only
tssoa mbo-na ngokung-chang-cho ha na ongo
becoming he dried fish-bundle-the both and fish
ekhu-cho ha to hansi chu-yicho. Chitosicho oten
cooked-the also thus carrying out-came. Then they
topu-na mbo-na nto tyucho sana hochi otsotso
all he what said was that true
Tchhüpfuo vampen-i-na hansi chu-yicho to
(the) Water Spirit's lair-at-from bringing out-came thus
nchamracho. Hochi-tssoko-na mbo myang-chi
believed. This-happening-from his name-the
"Tchhüpfuo okamo" to tsatacho. Osi mbo lap-chi
"Water Spirit's friend" thus was called. And his grave-the
ha nhungacha Morakcho-lo liya.
too till now Morakcho-at is.

All this happened about six generations ago. A man of Morakcho called Chungao was a friend of the Water Spirit, He used to bring up from the river dried fish and cooked fish which he said the Water Spirit had given him. But his friends never believed him when he told them that the Water Spirit had given him these things, through he tried hard to persuade them that it was true. One day he took the whole village down to fish and they came to the very place in the river where the Water Spirit lived. There they put poison in the water and got a fine catch of fish. Then Chungao said to his companions "Light a big fire" ; so they lit a big fire. From it he took a brand and plunged into the pool. Soon he came up with a bundle of dried fish and cooked fish. Then they all believed that he had spoken truly when he had said that the Water Spirit gave him these things and they nick-named him "Water "pirit's Friend." His grave is to be seen at Morakcho to this day.

12

THE FISHERMAN AND THE WATER SPIRIT

Kyon nchyua-na osa sa-munga-lo tai
Man a fish trap fish trap-setting place-at only

nchunko tongcho. Osi nchokacho mbo-na sa-ranki-na
always set up. But one day he fish-trap-shed-in

yipayisi panthile mbo nthango
having gone to sleep when he awoke him near

Tchhüpfuo zai vancho. Kyon-chi-na
(the) Water-Spirit standing was. Man-the

"O Tchhüpfuo, ntia a-ti-zaptoke"
"O Water Spirit, anything me-to not-allow to come to harm"

to ezocho. Tole Tchhüpfuo-chi-na kyon-chi mpho-chi
thus said. Then Water Spirit-the (of) man-the sole-the

khokai zele cho-mpho-chi sena ntsanga
having lifted up when he saw foot-sole-the white clean

kama-shicho nchunko otchhü-i samphio sa-tong
being-the always water-by wandering fish trap-setter

saka to nchama "Nno nchunko shi-lo osa
was thus understanding "You always this-at fish traps

tongke, olia kyon ethan-cho ti-rotoke" to
go on setting, but man new any do not-allow to come" thus

ezocho. Chi-sicho nchoka kyon ethan nchyua-na wocho.
said. This-after one day man new a went.

Tole Tchhüpfüo-na mbo ntoki cho-mpho-chi
Then (the) Water Spirit him having met foot-sole-the

khokai zele n-sen n-ntsangcho.
having lifted up when he saw not-white not-clean was.

Nto-tssole ? Mbo ko-thanga otchhü-i
What-becoming (i.e. why) ? He (at) any-time water-by

n-samphio-chi-na. Osi Tchhüpfuo-na kyon ethan
not-wandering-the-from. But (the) Water Spirit man new

ro-na lamm n-tssoko to nchama vancho.
coming-from heart not-becoming indeed feeling was.

Hochi-tssoko-na mbo-na oki yile chi-zamo-na
This becoming-from he home when he went that-night-at

tchhisicho to tyutala.
died thus (men) say.

There was once upon a time a man who always set his fish-trap in the same place. One night he awoke from sleep in his hut by the water and saw a Water Spirit standing near him, and cried out, "Please do not hurt me, O Water Spirit." Then the Water Spirit lifted up the man's foot and saw that the sole was white and clean and understood that he was a fisherman who spent his life wandering by streams. So he said to the man "You are an old fisherman. Go on setting your traps. But do not let any new-comer set traps." A little later a new man came and met the Water Spirit, who lifted up his feet and looked at the soles and saw that they were brown and dirty, for he was a man who had never spent his days wandering by the streams. Then the Water Spirit was angry because a new man had come. So that the man died when he reached his home that night. That is the story.

13

THE MAN WHO VISITED THE WATER SPIRIT

Oyan tyozhu-lo wotale nchyua-na
(The) village (men) fish-to when went one (man)

ezhu-i ongo yana throwole ezhu-nhung-i livero sena
pool-in fish seeking when dived pool-bottom-at dry sand white

kyon kurri etham-na nchü chami licho yanchecho. Osi
men's heads three-with hearth made was found. But

chilo Tchhüpfuo ha vancho. Ole chilo Tchhüpfuo-chi-na
there Water Spirit also was. Then there Water Spirit-the

kyon-chi "A-kam, nhungo ti-thororoke," to
(to) man-the "My-friend, now do not-come in," thus

ezoa ngokung changi pia
having said dried fish having wrapped up having given

chutokcho. Chisicho kyon-chi-na Tchhüpfuo-na
allowed to emerge. Then man-the (the) Water Spirit

ngokung changi pio-chi hana chui
dried fish having wrapped up gave-the carrying having emerged

oyamo kyon-chiang "Aiyo ezhu-i throwole a-kamo
(to) villagers men-the "I pool-in having dived my-friend

Tchhüpfuo 'ki yanchecho. Chicho livero sena
(the) Water Spirit's house found. There dry sand white

kyon kurri etham-na nchü chami lia, osi nhungo
men's heads three-with hearth prepared is, but now

ti-throro to a-zocho" to tyuo oyamo-chiang
not-to come in thus me-told" thus having said (to) villagers-the

ngokung-chi, p'cho. Osi mbo-na elani ngokung khi-lo
dried fish-the gave. But he again dried fish get-to

throwolanJe chitosicho n-chuosicho.
when dived in after that did not-emerge.

A man who had gone down with the rest of his village to poison a stream dived into a pool to look for fish. At the bottom he came to a stretch of dry sand and saw the Water Spirit sitting near a hearth made of three human skulls, The Water Spirit said to the man. "My friend, do not come in now" and tied up a present of dried fish and sent him away. Then the man came to the top with the dried fish which the Water Spirit had given him and said to his fellow villagers, "When I dived into the pool I came to the house of my friend the Water Spirit. There is a stretch of dry sand and a hearth of three men's skulls. But he told me not enter then." With these words he gave the dried fish to his fellow villagers and dived in again to get some more dried fish. But he never came up again.

14

THE WATER SPIRIT AND THE BOY

Nchoka nungri nchyua-na Pofu-i ongo yana
One day boy a Diyung-to fish seeking

cho-wocho. Osi milani-cho elani oki [i] n-yicho ;
down-went. But (in) evening-the again home-[to] did not come;

ole opoyang-na ekhentsangcho. Ochöato opo-na.
then parents were anxious. Next day (his) father

oyamo sonyhasi owo yanala n-yanchecho.
villagers having taken with going seeking did not-find.

Chitosi opo-na otsotyungo 'mang-tia n-hüngo lamm
Then (the) father son's corpse-even not-seeing heart

ntsso mbo-ti Pofu-tsa
not-becoming (at) ease) he-alone (along the) Diyung-bank

thrrua yana cho-wocho. Ole mbo-na otsan ntsanga
walking seeking down-went. Then he hair one

loko-i licho hüngcho. Mbo-na hochi otsotyungo 'tsan
ground-on was saw. He this (his) son's hair

tsaya tyokacho. Mbo-na otsan-chi ocham
supposing (to be) picked up. He (of) hair-the end

esana-tai-na khikale elam to sapocho. Hochi
one-only-by when he picked up very indeed was long. This

mbo-na mbo yingdro-lo eyikacho. Mbo-na eyia
he his finger-on wound round. He proceeding

eyia wole otsan-chi esi tchhü-kok tiza tssocho.
proceeding when went hair-the long river-bends eight became.

Otsan-chi Tchhüpfuo kurri-na n-sangchok-chi
Hair-the (the) Water-Spirit's head-from not-bound up-the

vacho sakama owo Tchhüpfuo chancho. Tole
was being going (the) Water Spirit reached. Then

Tchhüpfuo-chi-na kyon-chi "A-vachia" to ezole
Water Spirit-the (to) man-the "Me-release" thus when said

kyon-chi-na "A-tsoi-chi n-na sosi thrichokama
man-the "My-son-that you having seized plunging in

n-na soa-chu-ro a-m-piocho i-n-
you seizing-emerging-coming me-not-giving you-not-

vachi" to ezoa rhamacho. Tole
will release thus having said held (him). Then

Tchhüpfuo-na kyon-chi "I-tsotyungo a-na
(the) Water Spirit (to) man-the "Your-son I

soa-chu-ro hilo vantokuka ; a-vachia;
seizing-emerging-coming here will cause to remain; me-release;

osi chi n-na a-n-nangtsa-na kyon-na nto mua
but this you me-not-believe-if men what forbidden

echham to sana hochi a-chhamtoka," to
oath whatever is that me-you may make swear" thus

ezocho. Ole kyon-chi-na vachicho. Tchhüpfuo-chi-na
said. Then man-the (him) released. Water Spirit-the

mbo ngokung ngoyi na ngo-hamponi vao-chiang
his dried fish fresh fish and fish-relish kept-the

o-kamo pisi ezocho, "A-na ochöa
(to his) friend having given said, "I tomorrow

i-tsotyungo soa-chu-ro hilo vantokuka
your-son seizing-emerging-comig here will make to remain

n-na li-lo-wo-i ewolo oro hilo vana
you field-to-going-men when they go coming here is

hüngka" to ezocho. Osi kyon-chi-na Tchhüpfuo-chi-na
will see" thus said. But men-the Water Sprit-the

ezo-chi enga ochöa-to li-lo-wo-i ewolo
said-the obeying next day fields-to-going-men when they went

chilo wole otsotso otsotyungo chui vancho.
there when went truly (his) son having emerged remained.

Osi otsotyungo-na opo-chi ezocho, "A-po,
But (the) son (to) father-the said, "My-father,

otchhü-i ongo tsapo hüngthechicho ; hochi rhama-lo
water-in fish big (I) saw ; that seize-to

throwole hochi-na ezhu-chung-i fung-khu ntsanga-lo
when I dived in it pool-bottom-at stone-hole a in

otchhü n-chüo chi a-süsi thricho. Chi
water not-being there me-having dragged kept. There

kyon kurri-na nchü chami tyingsorok-na licho ; hochi
men's heads-from hearth made dry pleace-in was ; that

Tchhöpfuo vanpen." Toala nungri-chi
(the) Water Spirit's lair," Nevertheless (to) boy the

ntia n-tsso n-zaptoko Tchhüpfu-
anything not-happening not-allowing to be harmed Water Spirit-

chi-na solana chu-ro nungri-chi opo oni
the bringing out emerging-coming boy's the father they two

tyutao chilo vantokcho, Ole opo-na ochöa
saying there caused to remain. Then (the) father next day

to yana wole Tchhüpfuo oni tyutao chilo
indeed seeking when went Water Spirit they two saying there

chui vancho hüngi oki sosi yicho
having emerged remained having seen home having got went

to nhungaliya rutamungala.
thus till now (men) tell the tale.

One day a boy went down to the Diyung to fish. When he did not return home in the evening his parents became very anxious, and in the morning his father took some men down to search for him ; but he was nowhere to be found. Then his father was sad at heart and went wandering alone along the Doyang, determined to find at least the dead body of his son. As he went he saw a hair on the ground, and picked it up, thinking it belonged to his son. But it was so long that he only picked up one end of it, and walked on winding it round and round his finger. He went on and on until he had passed eight bends of the river, so long was the hair. At last he came to a Water Spirit, for the hair was one of the Water Spirit's which he had forgotten to wind round his head. Then Water Spirit cried out, "Let me go," but the man replied, "You have seized my son and taken him to your home in the water. I will not let you go till you bring him out and give him back to me." Then the Water Spirit said, "Let me go and I will bring your son and leave him here. If you do not believe me you may make me swear the most solemn oath known to men." At this the man let him go, and the Spirit gave him a gift of friendship, dried fish and fresh fish and fish paste, and said, "In the morning I will bring your son out of the water and leave him here. Come at the time when men go to their fields and you will find him."

Obedient to the words of the Spirit the man came in the morning at the time when men go to their fields, and there sure enough was his son on the bank. The tale he told his father was this: "I saw a big fish in the water, and dived in and caught hold of it. It dragged me into a hole under the rocks in the pool, where there was no water. There on the dry sand was a hearth made of three human skulls. It was the lair of the Water Spirit." The Water Spirit had not hurt the boy, but had brought him out and left him on the bank as he had promised to his father. So the father found his son safe by the side of the water and they both went back home. The tale is remembered to this day.

15

HOW THE VILLAGERS TRIED TO KILL APFUHO

Oyan-na Apfuho etchüthechi-lo wüzü-i sosi wotacho.
Villagers Apfuho deceive-to pond-to taking went.

Osi oyamo langchang-na wüzü-i-na owo kozuta
But villagers a pond-at-from going swing

kozutasi Apfuho silamo kozutoksi oyamo-chiang-na
swinging Apfuho last making to swing villagers-the

Apfuho-chi wüzü-chongi elhungthei tchhitoko
Apfuho-that pond-into falling to cause to die

kilato n-zeo yiracho. Ole Apfuho wüzü-
intending not-looking went away. Then Apfuho pond-

chi-[i] elhungtheo tai tssoa kozua vanle
the-[into] falling only becoming swinging while remaining

chi-thang epue nchyua na eloe nchyua to pipo
that-time man a and woman a indeed ornaments

elam to pipo na tsiro ntsanga sheni
many indeed wearing and *mithan* a tied with rope

süta tosi sochota yia
bringing indeed having taken each other (i.e. eloping) coming

vancho hüngcho. Tole Apfuho-na "Ochiang sana toka ?
were saw. Then Apfuho "Who are you ?

Hepicho elam to zürozüiya mhonaka. Aiyo heto
Here much indeed breeze is good. I thus

kozuaka ; ni-ni-ha pipo-chiang pongi na
have swung ; you-two-also ornaments-the taking off and

tsiro-chi sheni va tosi oyak-i
mithan-the tying up keeping indeed forked stick-with

a-yichesi oro kozu-pi zeta" to ezocho.
me-pulling in coming swing-giving see" thus said.

Chisicho chi-to-ni-na Apfuho 'yi enga
Then they-indeed-two Apfuho's words hearing

pipo-chiang pongi va na tsiro sheni
ornaments-the talking off keeping and *mithan* tying up

va tosi owo Apfuho-chi oyak-i yichesi
keeping indeed going Apfuho-that forked stick-with pulling in

oni-na kozutacho. Osi oni-na "Yiche" to ezoala
they two swung. But they two "Pull in" thus saying

Apfuho-na n-yicheo wüzü-i elhungthei tchhitokcho
Apfuho not-pulling in pond-into falling caused to die.

Chitosi Apfuho-na chi-to-ni pipo-chi
Then Apfuho (of) them-indeed-two ornaments-the

pipo na tsiro-chi sü tosi oyan-i
putting on and *mithan*-the taking indeed village-to

yicho. Ole oyamo kyon-na emhokta "Apfuho,
went. Then (the) villagers men surprised "Apfuho,

nno kulo-na pipo hetata na tsiro to
you where-from ornaments so many and *mithan* indeed

yanchei hansi yichoato ?" to engacho. Tole
having got bringing have come ?" thus asked, Then

Apfuho oyamo-chiang "Wüzü-chongi-cho pipo ha
Apfuho (to) villagers-the Pond-in the ornaments both

elam to li na tsiro ha elam to van ;
many indeed are and *mithan* also many indeed are ;

toala a-na shi-tai khi hansi yi-na nte
nevertheless I this-only taking carrying came if you

kni-hng-na nte ha owo wüzü-chongi throwotakato"
take-wish-if you also going pond-into plunge down"

to ezocho. Chisilocho oyamo kyon toyu-na
thus said. After this villagers people all

Apfuho-chi "Apfuho, toka a-na a-sosi
(to) Apfuho-that "Apfuho, then I (want some) me-taking

woa, a-na a-sosi woa" to ezoracho. Ole
go, I (want some) me-taking go" thus kept saying. Then

ocho-racho to
to-morrow-the day after to-morrow (i.e. a few days later) indeed

Apfuho-na oyamo-chiang topu wüzü-chi-[i] sokhansi
Apfuho villagers-the all pond-the-[to] taking

owo otsak aku wüzü-chongi echam echami
going all every pond-into picking up picking up

shamthechisi enato thri-na chiango "Chicho pipo
throwing in slowly sank-if (of) them "That one ornaments

na tsiro mhonkhango-cho n-yanche" to ezo : na
and *mithan* very good-the not-gets" thus said ; and

elam to ethon pia ehraktsanga thri-na chiangcho
much indeed struggle giving spluttering sinking if (of) them

"Hochi-na pipo na tsiro mhon-tso-chi
"That one ornaments and *mithan* good-truly-the

yanchekache" to tyua kyon-chiang topu wüzü-chi-i
has got" thus saying people-the all pond-the-into

shamthechikhani tchhiratokcho. Osi eson
having thrown caused to die utterly. But old (woman)

mhyekchung nchyuacho tchhü-tsai epopya
blind a water-by the side of groping

etyanpya vanle Apfuho-na hochi mha-tungi
feeling her way when was Apfuho her face-in front of

owo yonkitam ntsanga vaicho. Ole hochi-na
going old *dao* a put. Then she

hochi etyancheki "Ei, a-na samona kama
this touching "Oh, I even being able

ekamo elam to
live mean (i.e. in possession of all their senses) much indeed

yancheraosala" to tyucho. Chi-thang Apfuho-ha
are surely getting" thus said. That-time Apfuho

chi-mpato owo "Ei, eson ha heto thro-woa
her-up to going "Oh, old (woman) also thus in-go

kama tchhü-tsai nto luato ?" to
if able water-by the side of what are doing ?" thus

ezoa rhamai wüzü-chongi shamthechi chi ha
saying seizing pond-into throwing her too

tchhitokcho.
caused to die.

The villagers, meaning to put an end to Apfuho,[1] took him with them down to a big pond. Then when they got to the water they all began swinging out over the pool on a creeper swing. They made Apfuho use the swing last and went away and left him, thinking he would fall off into the middle of the pond and be drowned. Apfuho kept swinging and swinging and could hardly hold on any longer, when he espied a man and a woman wearing fine ornaments and leading a *mithan*[2] by a rope. He saw that they were an eloping couple and called out to them, "Who are you ? There is a beautiful breeze here which makes swinging very pleasant. Take off your ornaments and put them on the ground and tie up the *mithan*. Then pull me in with a hooked stick and come and have a good swinging." They, on hearing Apfuho's words took their ornaments off and put them down and pulled Apfuho in with a forked stick ; and both began to swing.

But when they asked Apfuho to pull them in, instead of doing so he let them fall into the water and drown. Then Apfuho put on their ornaments and took their *mithan* and went up to the village. And the villagers were astonished and said, "Where have you come from with those ornaments and that *mithan*, Apfuho ?" And he said to them, "In the middle of the pond there are many ornaments and many *mithan* too. I only brought away these. If you too want to get some you should go and dive into the pond " Then all the villagers said to him in chorus, "Take me, Apfuho ;

1 A mythical mischievous character, who is the subject of many tales. He corresponds to Tki in Sema tales.

2 The domestic bison (*bos frontalis*).

take me, Apfuho." So a few days later Apfuho led the villagers in a body down to the water. There he picked them up one by one and threw them in. Of the men who sank quietly he said, "The ornaments and *mithan* he gets won't be very good." But when people struggled hard, with the water pouring from their mouth and nose, he said, "The ornaments and *mithan* he gets will be splendid." So he let all the people of the village whom he had thrown into the water drown.

Now a blind old woman was stumbling along, feeling her way by the water's edge. Apfuho put an old worn *dao* in front of her, and when she found it as she groped she said, "Well, if a person like me can find this, people with no infirmities will get a lot." Then Apfuho went up to her and said, "Now, old woman, you go in too. What are you doing on the edge?" and with these words he caught her and threw her into the middle of the pond so that she was drowned.

16

HOW APFUHO TRICKED THE VILLAGERS

Oyan-na Apfuho etchüthechi omi-ki
(The) villagers Apfuho deceiving fire-with

rongtsangtoko kilato oli ri-chi nchok
would make to burn intending fields burning-the day

Apfuho 'yak chungo wotokcho. Tole Apfuho-na
Apfuho forked tree climbing made to go. Then Apfuho

owo oyak-chi chungo echangpisila
going forked tree-the climbing having pruned a little

"Ayo, a-lepok-ro-chi esoktaka"
"Dear me, my-*dao*-little-the has come out of its handle"

to tyua choi loko-chi
thus having said having descended ground-the

chi-chi to tssocho. Heto oyan-na oli
digging-digging thus became. Thus villagers fields

richiale mbo-na oyak-i-na choi loko
while burning he tree-in-from having descended ground

chi-ochi-lo thri 'lung tyak-ki hlaplanchi
dug the-in having entered stone flat-with having closed

vancho. Chisicho omi-chi paktokale
remained. Afterwards fire-the when (they) allowed to abate

mbo-na vunga chui seno omi-na
he first having emerged (a) barking deer fire-by

rongtsangi licho tyoi hansi oyì
burnt was finding having carried having gone

lanrhu-lo oso-cho ora-i mphoi vasi
cross roads-at meat-the jungle-in having hidden having kept

errü-chi-ki mbo mman-i shakai
entrails-the-with his stomach-on having spread

hansi nthikoro yipa vancho.
having carried on his back lying down remained.

Taratssosi oyan-na oyi zesi lom-na
A little later (the) villagers having come having seen some

"Apfuho nzanti" to tyu, lom-na "Apfuho ha nchingo
"Apfuho (I) pity" thus saying some "Apfuho too today

mbo mhona-chi" to tyuta yirachok. Chisicho
his good-the" thus saying passed on. Afterwards

Apfuho-na panthi mbo-na oso ora-i
Apfuho having got up be meat jungle-in

mphoi vao-chi khi hanai, "Apfuho nzanti"
having hidden kept-the taking carrying, "Apfuho (I) pity"

to tyu-chiango ozu pi na "Apfuho-ha nchingo
thus (to) saying-the meat giving and "Apfuho-too to-day

mbo mhona-chi" to tyu-chiango orru pi to
his good-the" thus (to) saying-the bone giving thus

tssocho. Chitosi oyan-na oso-chi tsokhantakle
because. Later (the) villagers meat-the when had eaten up

"Oso nte-pio-chi a-pia ; chi n-li-na otsok
"Meat (to) you-given-the me-give ; that not-is-if rice

a-pia" to ezoa otsok chonrhui khia
me-give" thus having said rice having demanded taking

wocho. Osi emi nchyuachicho "Apfuho-cho
went. But old woman a certain "Apfuho-that

n-kantsila" to tyua oso-chi vasi vanle
(I) not-do trust" thus saying meat-the having kept while was

Apfuho-na owo "Oso i-pio-chi a-pia ; chi
Apfuho going "Meat (to) you-gave-the me-give ; that

n-li-na otsok a-pia" to ezoa chonle
not-is-if rice me-give" thus saying when demanded

emi-chi-na "I-so-chi shi-ka lo" to
old woman-the "Your-meat-the this-indeed look" thus

ezoa hana chu-ro pile Apfuho-na
saying bringing emerging-coming when gave Apfuho

nhyapang-ki ekhosi yicho.
dao handle-with having struck went.

His fellow villagers plotted to get Apfuho burnt to death. So on the day when the jungle on the land to be sown that year was to be fired they persuaded him to go down to the place and climb into a tree. But he saw their plot and kept lopping a few branches off the tree and saying, "Dear me, my *dao* has come out of its handle." Then he would come down and dig away at a hole in the ground. When the villagers set fire to the jungle he came down from the tree and got into the hole and closed the mouth with a flat stone. When the fire had burnt itself out he came out and found the body of a barking deer which had been caught in the flames and burnt.[1] This he carried up to the village path and cut up the meat and hid it in the jungle. Then he lay down in the path on his back and put the entrails of the deer on his stomach and feigned dead. And when the villagers coming up along the path saw him some said, "Poor old Apfuho," and some said, "We have made a good job of Apfuho at last" and passed on. When they had gone Apfuho got up and took the meat which he had hidden in the jungle and went up to his house. To everyone who had said "poor old Apfuho" he gave a piece of good meat as his share and to everyone who had said, "We have made a good job of Apfuho at last" he gave a piece of bone.

Then he waited a day or two until everyone had eaten up their presents of meat and then went round the village and pretended he had sold the meat instead of giving it, and said to each man, "You must give me back my meat, or if that has gone pay me in rice." But there was one old woman who thought to herself, "Apfuho is not to be trusted" so she kept

1 Animals and birds are often caught in these fires.

her piece of meat; and when Apfuho came round asking for his meat, or its price in rice she said, "Here is your meat" and gave it to him. Then Apfuho in anger hit her with his *dao* handle and went away.

17

APFUHO AND THE TIGER

Nkolo kyon tsongora n-tyunta-thang motsü.
Formerly man animals not-separate-time story.

Mharr to na Apfuho to ochen shano
(The) tiger indeed and Apfuho indeed vasts to make

zukhu pankai wotacho. Owo ochen
river having crossed went. Having gone vats

shani vasi, mharr-chi-na Apfuho. "Kotoli
having made having left, tiger-the Apfuho, "How

hamla ?" to engacho. Apfuho-na mharr-chi
do (I) carry ?" thus asked. Apfuho (to) tiger the

"Tonkachho hanakama" to ezoa tonkachho
"Top up carry" thus having said top up

hantokcho. Mbo ochen-chi chenchho hansi
made to carry. He vat-the upside down having carried

otchhü-chi tyenga chucho, Osi mharr-chicho ochen-chi
water-the crossing emerged. But tiger-the vat-the

tonkachho hansi chi-lo otchhü thri otchhü-chi
top up having carried it-in water entering water-the

tyenga chu-na n-chuche, tyenga
crossing emerging-from (did) not-emerge, crossing

chu-na n-chuche to tyenga voale,
emerging-from (did) not-emerge thus crossing while was,

Apfuho-na "A-na i-yicheka" to ezoa
Apfuho "I you-will pull out" thus having said

ochen-chi-lo olung penthechiale na oyak-i
vat-the-in stones throwing and forked stick-with

tyanthechi to tssoa otchhü-ki pfua
having pushed thus becoming water-with floating

yitokcho. Chito-si Apfuho-na mharr-chi tchhitchhianato
made to go. That-after Apfuho tiger-the was dead or not

zeta cho-wole tchhü-tsai pfua chu
to see down-going water-by the side of down stream emerged

vansi mbo hüngale "A-moratsamo-chi shi" to
being him seeing "My-enemy-the this" thus

tyua mbo rhamale. Apfuho-na chi-thang
having said him when seized, Apfuho that-time

tchhü-tsai tsakmen zuncho hünga-chi "A-motzü
water-by bees' nest saw-the "My-grandfather

aiyo züro champo-i-na otyang-shi oyam
I forty *morung*-men drum-this other men

ti-tampitoke to a-zoa otyang-shi
must not-allow to beat thus me-telling drum-this

a-nhyaktokala" to ezocho. Tole mharr-ch-na
me-are causing to watch" thus said. Then tiger-the

"Toka a-na tampile hungo?" to engaio Apfuho-na
"Really, I beating may see?" thus asking Apfuho

mharr-chi "A-metzü, a-na oyi züro
(to) tiger-the "My-grandfather, I going forty

champo-i engasaka; osa. Osi züro champo-i-na
morung-men will ask; stay. But forty *morung*-men

tampi to tyu-na a-n i-zochika," to ezocho.
beat thus say-if I you-will tell," thus said.

Tole mbo-na ekoni-na oyi "A-motzü,
Then he far-from having gone "My-grandfather,

züro champo-i-na tampia to" to ezochicho.
forty *morung*-men beat thus (say)" thus said.

Chisicho mharr-chi-na tampile tsakmen-chiang-na mbo
Then tiger-the beating bees-the him

taktsangi	tsantsansi	tsantsansi	lungrheni-na	ekhangtsangi
stinging	running	running	cliff-from	having fallen

tchhicho.
died.

This is a tale of the olden days when men could understand the talk of animals. Apfuho and the tiger went across a river to hollow out vats out of a log on the other side. When they had finished their vats and the time came to return the tiger asked Apfuho the best way to carry his vat acsoss the river. Apfuho told him to carry it rim upwards, and the tiger did as Apfuho told him. But Apfuho carried his own vat upside down and was able to cross the river, while the tiger try as he would could not cross the river, with his vat rim upwards. Apfuho called out "I will pull you out," but instead of doing so he threw stones into the tiger's vat and pushed him away from land with a forked stick so that he was washed right down stream. Then Apfuho went along to see if the tiger was drowned or not, and found him lower down by the water's edge. When the tiger saw Apfuho he cried "Here is my enemy," and tried to devour him. But at that moment Apfuho espied a bees' nest by the water and said "The men of the *morung* have set me to watch this *morung* drum, father tiger, and see that no stranger beats it." Then the tiger said, "May I beat it and see what it is like ?" and Apfuho replied "I will ask the men of *morung*. You stay here, and if they say you may beat it I will shout and tell you." So he went a long way off and shouted back, "They say you may beat it." Then when the tiger hit the bees' nest all the bees attacked and stung him and he ran and ran until he fell down a cliff and was killed.

18

HOW APFUHO SHARED SOME MEAT WITH THE TIGER

Apfuho ha mharr oni ora-i wotale
Apfuho also tiger they two jungle-in while going

sorachak tyocho. Chisilocho sorachak-chi oni
(a) kill found. Then kill-the they two

chitale, Apfuho-na mbo echi-lo-cho ozu tai
when dividing, Apfuho his own share-in-the meat only

larhui the na mharr echi-lo-cho orru tai larhui
carving setting aside and tiger's share-in-the bone only carving

thei to tssole chi-thang mharr-chi-na
setting aside thus when becoming (at) that-time tiger-the

"Nni ha khiaka; a-po titai a-thea to" to
"You too take; my-own only (for) me-leave thus" thus

ezoa chitatokcho, Tole mharr-chi-na "Apfuho,
having said allowed to divide up. Then tiger-the "Apfuho,

kotoli hantaola?" to engale Apfuho-na
how shall we carry?" thus when asked Apfuho

"Okhyu ezalo nrakai the hana"
"Bamboo basket leaving attached having made putting carry"

to ezoa okhu ezalo nrakatoksi
thus having said basket leaving attached having caused to make

mbo khyu-tong langi nrai oso-chi thei
his basket-tree having cut having made meat-the putting

hanai oki otsok-man yencho. Osi mharr-chicho
carrying home (for) rice-price sold. But tiger-the

oso-chi okhyu ezalo nrakao-chi-lo thei
meat-the basket leaving attached made-the-in putting

hankai zesila n-hankakok-na "Shi-na
carrying away seeing not-could carry awap-because "This one

alo, shi-na alo" to tyua so-khyu ntsang-
is it, this one is it" thus having said meat-pieces on-

ntasanga khichei orru-chi nkaksila is
one taking out bones-the gnawing throwing away

nkaksila si to tsso-tssosi okainacho
gnawing throwing away thus having become-become at-last

orru ntsanga tai n-nkaknhyui oki hansi yicho.
bone one only not-gnawed home having carried came.

Apfuho and the tiger came upon a kill in the jungle, They set to divide it between them, but Apfuho cut off and laid aside nothing but meat for his share and gave the tiger nothing but bone. The tiger only said, "Take plenty yourself. Do not give everything to me," and let him go on dividing up the meat. Then said the tiger, "How shall we carry it, Apfuho?" Apfuho replied "Split a bamboo and make a basket of it, but do not cut it free from the root. Then put the meat in that and carry it up." So the tiger made a basket without cutting the bamboo off at the root, but Apfuho cut his own bamboo off when he made his basket, and put the meat in that and carried it home and sold it. But the tiger put his meat in his basket without cutting the basket free and tried in vain to carry it. "It must be this, it must be this" he kept saying as he took out the pieces of meat one by one and gnawed the bones and tnrew them away, till he had eaten all the meat and at last only had one piece of bone left to carry up to the village.

19

AFUHO AND THE OLD WOMAN

Nchoka emi-na otsi rukachi vasi penching
One day old woman rice cooking having kept oil seed

chena vanle, Apfuho-na 'yam phurro
pounding when remaining, Apfuho another's dog

tatsangi hansi owo chi-chi
having killed carrying coming (to) old woman-the

"I-tsi-chi elakchyala" to ezocho. Tole
"Your-rice-the is boiling over" thus said. Then

emi-chi-na otsi-chi ze-lo thria-thang-na Apfuho-na
old woman-the rice-the see-to enter-time-the Apfuho

phurro-chi hanao tsamboku-i thechi vaisi,
dog-the carrying pounding table-on placing having kept,

"Emi, i-penching-chi phurro-na tsoalo" to
"Old woman your-oil seed-the (a) dog is eating" thus

ezocho. Ole emi-chi-na yungachi zesi, Apfuho-na
said. Then old woman-the running having seen, Apfuho

phurro tatsangi hanao tsamboku-i thechi
dog having killed carrying pounding table-on placing

vai-ochi erhapthechicho. Osi chisicho Apfuho-
put-the struck. But then Apfuho

emi-chi ezocho "Hayo, hayo, n-na 'yam
(to) old woman-the said "Alas, alas, you another's

phurro tatsangta-kama i-woko-chi a-m-piocho a-na
dog have killed-because your-pig-the me-not-giving I

'yam ezoka" to ezocho. Tole emi-chi-na
the other man will tell" thus said. Then old woman-the

"A-woko-chi i-pika ; oyam ti-zo" to
"My-pig-the you-will-give ; the other man do not-tell thus

ezocho. Tole Apfuho-na mangsa-thang woko-chi khi-lo
said. Then Apfuho evening-time pig-the fetch-to

woa-tang olan-i mi-lon elamo rena nchakarhui
going-time path-on fire-torches many arranging having lighted

vasi owo, "Emi, n-na i-woko-chi
having put going "Old woman, you your-pig-the

a-m-pi-na 'yam hetata olan-i mi-lon penrasi
me-not-give-if villagers so many path-on fire-torches carrying

tsaka, zeta" to ezole emi-chi-na "A-woko-shi
are coming, look" thus when said old woman-the "My-pig-this

i-pika ; "ti-ro" to owo ezoa to ezole
you-will give ; "do-not-come" thus going say thus when said

mbo-na owo mi-lon-chiang tamhekhani sisi
he going fire-torches-the having put out having thrown away

oyi woko-chi rhamai khicho. Osi woko-chi hankata-tahang
coming pig-the seizing took. But pig-the carrying-time

mbo-na "Emi-tacholam" to tyua hankale,
he "Old woman-food" thus saying when carrying,

emi tsoi-chi-na "A-pvü, shi-na
old woman's daughter-the "My-mother, he

'Emi-tacholam' to tyuala" to opvü ezocho.
'Old woman-fool' thus says" thus (to her) mother said.

Apfuho-na zoi "Ei nungria 'acho' to
Apfuho hearing "Now, now, girl 'all right' thus (I)

tyuna" to nungri-chi ezole opvü na "Ho, ho,
said" thus (to) girl-the when said (the) mother "Ho, ho,

Apfuho-na 'acho' to tyucho" to ezoa mbo woko-chi
Apfuho 'all right' thus said" thus saying her pig-the

Apfuho hansi yitokcho.
Apfuho carrying allowed to go.

One day an old woman set her rice on the fire to boil and went into her outer room to pound oil seed. Apfuho came along carrying another man's dog which he had killed, and called out to the old woman, "Your rice is boiling over." When the old woman went back into the inner room to look at her rice, Apfuho put the dog which he was carrying on her pounding table and called out, "A dog is eating your oil seed, old woman." Then the old woman came running out to see, and hit the dead dog which Apfuho had put on the pounding table. At this Apfuho cried out, "Oh dear, oh dear, you have killed another man's dog. If you do not give me your pig I will tell the owner." So the old woman said, "I will give you my pig. Do not tell the owner." At dusk when Apfuho came to fetch the pig he fixed lighted torches all along the path, and said to the old woman, "Give me your pig. Look how many men are coming with the owner of the dog, carrying lighted torches in their hands." To this the old woman replied. "I will give you my pig. Go and tell them not to come." So he went and put out the torches and threw them away, and came back and took the pig. But as he was taking the pig away he murmured, "What a fool of an old woman." Her daughter heard this and said, "He called you an old fool, mother." But Apfuho heard her say this and replied, "I only said 'oo', girl,"[1] and the mother said, "Yes, yes, Apfuho only said 'oo'." So Apfuho went off with the pig.

1 The play upon the words cannot be reproduced in English. Apfuho really said "*emitacholum*" (What a fool of an old woman !) and then got out of his difficulty by pretending he had only uttered the middle syallable "*acho*", which is an exclamation like the English "Oh !"

20

SITYINGO AND NGAZO

Sityingo ha Ngazo oni oshyu chi-lo
Sityingo also Ngazo the two bamboo rats dig-to

wotacho. Ole Sityingo-cho lamalo chiche, osi Ngazo-cho
went. Then Sityingo-that many dug, but Ngazo-that

engalang chicho oshyu-ro ntsanga tai chichecho.
all day long dug bamboo rat-little one only dug out.

Tole Ngazo-na Sityingo-chi "Aiyo shi tai nno
Then Ngazo (to) Sityingo-that "I this only you

tata chiche" to ezoa echücho. Ole Sityingo-na
so many dug out" thus saying showed. Then Sityingo

Ngazo-chi "Chi ha a-na i-pichoki" to ezocho.
(to) Ngazo-that "That also I you-gave" thus said.

Tole Ngazo-na "A-na engalang chichisi chiche-na
Then Ngazo "I all day digging dug out-after

n-na a-picho-ani" to ezocho. Osi Sityingo-na
you me-gave-in truth" thus said. But Sityingo

"Toka a-na i-picho-mak-na vachi zei" to ezole
"Then I you-gave-not-if letting go see" thus when said

Ngazo-na Sityingo 'yi enga vachicho. Oshyu-
Ngazo Sityingo's words hearing let go. Bamboo rat-

ro-chi loko-i yua thresicho, osi Ngazo-na
little-the ground-in burrowing entered, but Ngazo

oshyu-ro-chi chia chia phanala n-chicheosicho.
bamboo rat-little-the digging digging chasing not-dug out.

Tole Sityingo-na Ngazo-chi "A-na i-picho-mak-na
Then Sityingo (to) Ngazo-that "I you-gave-not-if

n-chicheta to" to ezole Ngazo-na lamm
not-dug out indeed" thus when said Ngazo anger

tsoki oni eyatacho. Ole Ngazo-na Sityingo
getting they two wrestled. Then Ngazo Sityingo's

evung nyalepisicho. Chi-tssoko-na Sityingo-cho poko
neck twisted. This-being-from Sityingo-that one way

tai zechiala, to tyutala. Kyon-na nhungacha
only looks, thus (men) say: Men till now

Sityingo-na zechiyo olantaro mhala osi
Sityingo looking at (them) something get but

Sityingo-na n-zechiyo olantaro ntia
Sityingo not-looking at (them) something anything

m-mhala to tyutala.
not-get thus say.

Sityingo[1] and Ngazo went to dig for bamboo rats. Sityincho caught many, but Ngazo, though he dug all day, only got one. Then Ngazo said to Sityingo, "I have only caught this and you have caught so many," and showed him the rat. Then Sityingo replied : "Even that you only got because I gave it to you." To which Ngazo replied, "What, I have dug out this rat after digging all day and you say you gave it to me !" "Then let it go", said Sityingo, "and see whether I gave it to you or not." So Ngazo let it go as Sityingo said, but the rat burrowed into the ground, and Ngazo, though he dug and dug after it, could not catch it again. Then said Sityingo, "You say I did not give it to you and yet you cannot dig it out !" At these words Ngazo became angry and they fell to wrestling, and Ngazo twisted Sityingo's neck. That is why Sityingo can only look one way. Men say to this day that a hunter towards whom Sityingo looks is sure to get something, but that he from whom Sityingo's face is turned away will get nothing at all.

1 A sort of godling who owns wild animals as men own cattle. He is like a man with very long fingers and spotted all over. Ngazo is practically identical with him.

21

THE CHILDREN WHO TURNED INTO CATFISH

Kyon nchyua-na nungri yenga mbo 'li socho.
Man a children band (to) his fields took.

Ole oli owo chonta-chontasi nshi thangale
Then (to) field going working-working midday-meal at time of

otsi nshitoko tyutacho. Tole opfui-chiang-na nshi
rice allow to eat said. Then owners-the midday meal

n-thang ha to ezoa otsi-chi n-nshitokcho.
not-time indeed thus having said rice-the did not allow to eat.

Chi-icho nungri yenga-chiang-na tsaka-lo wo tyutachei
Then children band-the wash-to going having said

oten topu-na tsaka-lo wokhancho. Osi oten-na "Otsi sito
they all wash-to went off. But they "Rice quickly

e-n-nshitokaka zyümo kamtane," to tyuta
us-not-allowed to eat catfish let us become," thus saying

"Zyümolili, "zymüolili" to khuta zyümo kamayicho.
"We are catfish. we are catfish" thus calling catfish turned into

Ole opfui-chiang-na "Otsi nte nshitokoka, yita"
Then owners-the "Rice you (we) will allow to eat, come"

to ezoa tsale nungri yenga-chiang-na
thus having said when they called children band-the

"Nte-na nthangna e-n-nshitokcho kama, 'yo nhungo
"You just now us-not-allowed to eat because, going now

kyon etso-yu n-ntsi kama n-yi" to
man's food-drink not-knowing because will not come" thus

ezoa zyümo komayicho. Hochi-na nhunga
having said catfish turned into. This-because of nowadays

zyümo-na lechap essa mbao shi nkolo
catfish-on *dao* holder like being this once upon a time

nungri yenga-na lechap hanrasi zyümo kamayicho-
children band *dao* holdcrs wearing catfish turned into-

na heto mbapo tssoala to kyon-na rutala.
because so always is thus men tell.

A man took a band of children down to his fields to work. When they had worked all morning and it was time for the midday meal they asked him to give them their rice. But the owner of the field and his family said it was not yet time and would not give them any rice. Then the children said they were going to bathe and all went off, and said "Then would not give us our rice in time so we will become catfish." With these words they turned into catfish, calling out "We are catfish, we are catfish." The owner of the field called out "Come along, I will give you your rice," but the children replied "You would not give it us before. Now we have forgotten about men's food. We will not come," and off they went in the from of catfish. Men say it is because these children were wearing *dao*-holders when they were turned into catfish that these fish always have a mark on them like a *dao*-holder.

22

HOW CHILDREN TWRNED INTO MONKEYS

Onpoi-na otsoi epue tsaka eloe tsaka to
Man and wife children male one female one indeed

poki vasi eloe-chi tchhicho. Tole epue-chi-na
having got kept wife-the died. Then husband-the

eloe-chi tchhicho silo eloe ethan soa vancho. Ole
wife-the died after wife new marrying remained. Then

eloe ethan-chi-na eloe etchhio-chi 'tsoi-t-oni-chi
wife new-the (of) wife dead-the children-two-the

n-nzam elam to kangshi ntsoshicho. Osi
not-caring much indeed persecution gave. But

nchokacho mbo-na nungri-t-oni "Li-nhyako wota,
one day she children-two "Fields-to watch go,

otsi-cho a-na eng-aku ni-ni hantokmungka,
rice-the I day-every (for) you-two will have carried down,

oki-(i) ti-yitake" to ezoa wotokcho
house-(to) do not-come" thus having spoken made to go.

Chisilo mbo-na otsi kilato ziro-chü
Then she rice calling it (i.e. instead of) rat-dung

hono-chü na maku to tai nkap-nkapi
fowl-dung and husks thus only wrapping-wrapping

nungri-t-oni hantokmungcho. Tole nungri-t-oni-na
(for) children-two had carried down. Then children-two

eng-aku mbo-na otsi kilato ziro-chö hono-chü na
day-every she rice calling it rat-dung fowl-dung and

maku to nkap-nkapi hantokmung-chi
husks indeed wrapping-wrapping had had carried down-the

lanphe-lanphei zesisicho. Chisilocho nungri-t-oni kyon
open'ng-opening saw. Thereafter children-two man's

etso-yu n-chamcheo ora-i tsangti-longpen tai
food-drink not-remembering jungle-in nuts-berries only

hlo-tso-hlo-yuta vancho. Ole nchokacho
picking-eating-picking-drinking were. Then one day

opo-na otsi hansi 'wo "Oyi, otsi tsota" to
(their) father rice bringing going "Come, rice eat" thus

ezoa tsale, nungri-t-oni-na "A-po, eyo
saying when he called, (the) children-two "My-father, we

nhungo kyon etso-yu n-chamche-kama
now man's food-drink not-rembering-having become

yakso kamayiala" to ezoa "Wuwu" to
monkeys are turning into" thus having said "Wuwu" thus

khua yakso kamayicho. Chisilocho opo-na "Toka
crying monkeys turned into. Thereupon (their) father "Then

ni-ni-na yakso kamayina oyan mung-thang
you-two monkeys having turned into village sabbath-time

mangri eli chepya 'yam-li penchümöchü shotsoshoiya
keeping is seeing village-field seeds of all kinds scratching-up

yitake" to ezoa yitokcno. Hochi-na
you shall come" thus saying allowed to come. This because of

nhungaliya yakso-na oyan mung-thang mangri eli chepya
to this day monkeys village sabbath-time keeping is seeing

'yam-li penchümuchü shotsoshoiyala to
village-fields seeds of various kinds scratch up thus

rutala.
(men) tell.

A man and his wife had two children, a boy and a girl. The wife died and when she was dead the husband took a new wife. The new wife took no pity on the children of the dead wife, but used them cruelly. One day she said to the children. "Go down and watch in the fields. I will send food to you every day. Do not come home." With these words she sent them off. But instead of food she sent them down only rat dung and chicken dung and husks tied up in leaves. Then the children opened the leaves and saw that she had only sent them down rat dung and chicken dung and husks instead of food. So the children forgetting all about human food went and picked nuts and berries in the jungle. One day their father brought down proper food and called to the children saying "Come, eat food," but the children answered "No father, we have forgotten all about human food now and are turning into monkeys." Then with a cry of "wu wu" they did turn into monkeys. Then their father said "You have turned into monkeys and when you see that the village is keeping an *emung*[1] day you will go and scratch up seeds and roots in the village fields." With these words he went away. That is why, men say, to this day when they see that the village is keeping *emung* the mokeys scratch up roots and seeds in the village fields.

1 A day of purification when no work may be done.

23

HOW WOMEN WERE TURNED INTO GIBBONS

Nkolo Kimongthang-na[2] mbo echantyoi-chiang
Once upon a time Kimongthang his wife's relations-the

tsarhuiki soko yutoksi ezocho, "A-na
summoning rice beer having given to drink said, I

ozü khio chentong tani vachoka.
sacrificial post to take *chentong* tree having cut have left.

Owo lomo ntsanga tia ti-lhungtokna süsi yita," to
Go leaf one even not-letting fall dragging come," thus

ezocho. Ole oten-na owo sütale otong chi tanvami
said. Then they going when dragging tree-the half dry

vacho kama oten-na sü-na lomo-chi vucho vucho.
was left because they dragging-by leaves-the falling falling

to tssocho. Tole oten-na lomo-chi n-vuchotoko
indeed were. Then they leaves-the not-to let fall

kilato lomo-chiang topu khero-lo shenkakhani vasi
intending leaves-the all twigs-on tying having fixed

sütacho. Toala lomo-chiang topu vukhantsicho. Chisilocho
dragged. Yet leaves-the all fell off. Then

oten-na Kimongthang yikra oyan-i n-yina ora-i-na
they Kimongthang shame village-to not-coming jungle-in-at

2 One version of this story states definitely that Kimongthang was of the Othui clan and that formely men of that clan were forbidden to eat gibbon.

epue-chiango lishung kamkhani "Kyon, kyon" to khua
men-the mynas having become "Man, man" thus crying

yiracho Osi eloe-chiango soko ruo oham
went. But women-the rice beer for making flour

chentokle hochi-na oten 'ton-o esekhansi
having ground this-with their forehead-on having smeared

"Woka, woka" to khuta khuso kamayicho.
"Going, going" thus calling gibbons became.

Once upon a time a man called Kimongthang called his wife's relations together and gave them rice beer to drink and said to them, "I have cut a '*chentong*' tree ready for a sarcrificial post. Go and drag it in for me, but do not let a single leaf fall to the ground." So they went and began to drag the tree, but leaves were half withered and they kept letting them fall. Then they, determined not to let the leaves fall, tied them onto the twigs and set to work to drag the tree again. In spite of this all the leaves fell off. Then they were ashamed to go back to the village and meet Kimongthang. So they fled away into the jungle, and the men became mynas and called "Kyon, kyon." But the women smeared on their foreheads the rice flour they had ground up for rice beer and called out "Woka, woka" and became gibbons. That is why the gibbon now has a white forehead.

24

THE BARKING DEER AND THE TIGER

Nchoka seno to na mharr to
One day (a) barking deer indeed and (a) tiger indeed

olan-i-na oni ntoktacho, Mharr-chi-na
path-on-from they two met. Tiger-the

seno-chi "A-kam, eni ha ocho
(to) barking deer-the "My-friend, we two indeed whose

'ho erowo sana leshüwo-shi etsetakalo"
teeth sharp are tuft of thatching grass-this let us nip off"

to ezole seno-chi-na "A-kam, toka
thus when said barking deer-the "My-friend, then

leshüwo-shi etseta" to ezoa oni
tuft of thatching grass-this nip off" thus having said they two

etsetacho. Ole seno-chicho echongana etse-thang,
nipped off. Then barking deer-the clean nipping off-while,

osi mharr-chicho etse-na n-tse-thang
but tiger-the nipping off-by not-nipping off-while

etse-na n-tse-thang to tai tssocho.
nipping off-by not-nipping off-while thus only became.

Chisicho mharr-chi-na seno-chi elam to
Then tiger-the (of) barking deer-the much indeed

khyua vancho. Tole seno-chi-na tarati tssoa
frightened was. Then barking deer-the a little later being

mharr-chi "A-kam osi a-ho-cho heto ero liya
(to) tiger-the "My-friend yet my-tooth-the so sharp being

heto kaloka, he" to ezoa
so is loose. look" thus having having spoken

lokpia echucho. Chitosicho mharr-chi-na
having felt (his tooth) showed. Therefore tiger-the

seno-chi n-khyuo rhamcho. Ovung-thang
barking deer-the not-fearing seized, Former-time

seno-na tyusora-chi-na nhungacha mharr-na
barking deer foolish speaking-that-from till now tigers

seno rhamala, to kyon-ha rutala. Osi nkolo
barking deer seize, thus men tell. But formerly

seno-na tyua chito otsotso nhungaliya seno
deer saying so really till now barking deer

langtai oho-chi zena ero ha ero na kalok
if kill teeth-the certainly sharp both sharp and loose

ha koloka.
also loose.

One day a barking deer and a tiger met on a path. Said the tiger to the deer "Let us nip off blades of tall grass, my friend, and see which of us has the sharpest teeth." The deer agreed and they both began to bite blades of grass, and the deer nipped the blades clean off, but the tiger, try as he would could not bite them through. This caused the tiger greatly to fear the deer, But a little later the deer said to the tiger "Even if my teeth be sharp they are loose. Look," and as he said this he gripped his long upper teeth in his fingers and showed how they moved. At this the tiger no longer feared the deer and devoured it. It is said that it is, because of these foolish words spoken by the deer so long ago that tigers eat deer to this day. If you kill a deer and look you wlll see that what it said long ago is true nowadays. Its teeth are certainly sharp, but they are loose.

25

THE WILD BOAR AND THE TIGER

Nipong to na mharr to oni okamo
Wild boar inded and tiger indeed they two friends

tssotacho, Oni nchokacho ora-i-na ntoktaiki
became. They two one day jungle-in-at having met

nipong-chi-na mharr-chi "A-kam, e-ni ha ocho-na
wild hoar-the (to) tiger-the "My-friend, we-two both which

ocho tou na ocho-na ocho khyu to tssosana
which defeat and which which fear indeed will become

eyataka ; nno nto hamla"? to engale
let us fight : you what will take"? thus when asked

mharr-chi-na "A-kam, aiyo otsak-o orr phakhai
tiger-the "My-friend, I body-on cane having bound

ham" to nipong-chi ezocho. Tole nipong-chicho
will take" thus (to) wild boar-the said. Then wild boar-the

"A-kam. aiyo etyunchon epfui ham" to
"My-friend, I clay having smeared will take" thus

mharr-chi ezocho. Hetosi "Nchok tirok-o eyataka"
(to) tiger-the said. After that "Days six-in will fight"

to oni tyutacho. Chitosicho nipong-cho nchok tirok-chi
thus they two said. After that wild boar-the days six-the

etyunchon tai epfusila tyingtok tyingtok to epfumung
clay only smearing letting dry letting dry thus smearing

na mharr-chicho nchok tirok-chi orr tai tam-tami phakha
and tiger-the days six-the cane only cut-cutting binding

to tssocho. Nchok tirok-chi pentakale oni eyatacho.
thus became. Days six-the when full they two fought.
Tole mharr-chicho nipong-chi owo nkak-na etyunchon-chi
Then tiger-the wild boar-the going biting-by clay-the
tai ewo aku opang etyeng-tyeng nkakcho, na
only attacking each mouth full-full bit, and
nipong-chicho mharr chi owo nkak-na ewo aku
wild boar-the tiger-the going biting-by attacking each
orr-chi ntsang-ntsang-na nkakchia vanvansi
cane-the one-one-by having bitten through being
orr-chi nkakchikhani mharr-chi rhamsi yile,
cane-the having bitten off tiger the having seized when going.
ticho-na hiyacho. Tole nipong-chi-na
(a) thin bamboo stuck into. Then wild boar-the
"Mharrsamona rhamtak-na nte heto-na a-hiyata
"A great tiger even seizing-after you thus-by me-stick into
to" tyua nkakle ticho-chi-na nli-chi
indeed" thus having said when biting bamboo-the tongue-the
nyahckaki, nipong-chi ha chilo-na tchhicho. Hochi
having cut off, wild boar-the also there-at died. This
mharr thampo-na hungi tsosi chi-tssoko-na
tiger another having seen having eaten this-being-from
nhungacha mharr-na nipong rhamala. Tokatola
till now tigers wild boars seize. Yet
ovung-thang mharr-na nipong n-tou-chi-na
first-time tiger wild boar not-defeating-the-from
nhungaliya choro eni-tham n-kampiocho mharr-na nipongr
till now months two-three not-waiting tiger wild boar
n-rham to tyutala.
not-seizes thus (men) say.

The wild boar and the tiger were sworn friends. One day when they met in the jungle the wild boar said to the tiger, "My friend, let us two fight and see which will get the better of the other and which will fear the other. What will you take to protect yourself?" Then the tiger said to the boar, "I will take cane and wind it round my body," but the boar said, "I shall smear clay all over myself." They arranged that the fight should take place six days later. Then the boar for six days did nothing but smear clay over himself, letting at dry after each coating, and the tiger did nothing but cut lengths of cane and wind them round his body. Then when the six days were up they fell to and fought. Now whenever the tiger flew at the wild boar and bit him, all he got was a mouthful of clay, but the boar, whenever he attacked and bit the tiger, bit through a piece of cane, till he had bitten them all though one by one and killed the tiger. But when the boar was going away after his victory a thin piece of bamboo ran into him. Then he said, "I have killed the tiger. What is this doing running into me?" and seized it in his month. But the thin bamboo cut his tongue off so that he died on the spot. Then another tiger came along and saw the body and ate it. That is why nowadays tigers eat wild boars. Yet it is said that because the tiger could not beat the wild boar at first, a tiger cannot catch one unless he bides his time and stalks it for two or three months.

26

THE SUN AND THE MOON

Ovung-thang-cho nhunga eng-shicho choro na nhunga
(At) first-time-the now sun-the moon and now

choro-shicho eng tssocho. Tole nhunga choro-shi-na eng
moon-the sun was. Then now moon-the sun

tssoa-thang-cho eng elam to woncho. Elong-i
being-time-the sun much indeed shone. Heavy jungle-in

otsang-otong lomo-ḷosü pato laplap tchhikhancho, na
trees-trees leaves-leaves too all died, and

kyon ha ezaptoka phitsangkhancho. Chisicho nhunga
men too causing to suffer burnt up. Then now

eng-shi-na choro-shi tsaiki ezocho "Nno nto-tsso-na
sun-the (to) moon-the calling said "You what-being-from

eng hetata woniki elong-i otsang-otong lomo-losü
sun so much shining heavy jungle-in trees-trees leaves-leaves

mpato tchhitok, na kyon ha heto ezaptoka
too making to die, and men too so much causing to suffer

phitsangala ?" to ezocho. Osi nhunga eng-shi
burn?" thus said. But now sun-the

choro-shi "Nna eng tssocho-cho kyon-tsoi laplap
(to) moon-the "You sun being-the human-race all

phitsangkham na limha-shi ha monsakama
burning up and world-the also because you are destroying

nching-thang-na eng i-n-tssotokla," to ezoa
to-day-time-from sun you-not-cause to be," thus having said

mangsü 'chu-ki choro-shi 'mha-lo etyakaisi eng
cow dung-with moon-the face-on having smeared sun

n-tssotoko, nhunga eng-shi-na eng tssocho. Hochi
not-made to be, now sun-the sun became. This

tssoko-na nhunga choro-lo nyika mbao-shi nkolo
being-from now moon-on black (mark) being-the formerly

eng-shi-na mangsü 'chü-ki omha-lo etyakaio-chi to
sun-the cow dung-with face-on smeared-the thus

kyon-na rutala.
men tell.

At the beginning or time what is now the sun was the moon, and what is now the moon was the sun. In those days when what is now the moon was the sun it was very hot, so that all the leaves and the trees in the jungle shrivelled up and died, and men suffered torments from the heat. Then what is now the sun said to the moon (which was the sun in those days), "Why do you shine so fiercely that you make all the leaves and trees in the jungle shrivel up and die, and cause men to suffer torments from the heat? You by being the sun are making men and leaves to die from heat and the world will be destroyed. Therefore from to day I will not let you be the sun." With these words he smeared the face of what is now the moon with cow dung, and what is now the sun become the sun. Therefore men say that the dark marks on the moon are where the sun smeared cowdung on its face.

27

THE OLD MAN WHO KEPT WILD DOGS

Nkolo mangtham n-ro-thang kyon nchyua
Once upon a time darkness not-come-time man a

vancho. Mbo-na ranfu ekamrucho. Mbo-na ranfu-chiang
was. He wild dogs kept. He wild dogs-the

sopya oso elam to langtai tsocho. Ole chisicho mbo
taking meat much indeed killing ate. Then later he

sontsangi ora-i ote m-pampikokosicho
having grown old jnngle-in them not-could accompany.

Hochi-na mbo-na mbo ranfu-chiang topu
This-because of he (to) his dogs-the all

tsarhui mbo nthango oki-(i) vantokcho. Eson-
having called him near home (at) caused to be. Old

china otsak aku echi epyotosü nnungi vasi
man-the food each share boiled rice having cooked having kept

mbo-na chitayawocho. Osi okhawo-chi epyototsü-chi-na
he divided up. But youngest-the boiled rice.the-with

n-chancho. Chi-thang eson-chi-na ezocho "A-ranfu-
not-reached. That-time old man-the said "My-wild dogs-

ten, aiyo asontsangtaka nhungo nte m-pampikok.
pack, I having grown old now you not-can accompany.

Olia n-chamchetake a-na koto nte nzan na kote
Yet not-do forget I how much you loved and how much

ekamchosana. Osi nte-na kothang oso rhamana chi aku
looked after. But you when meat catch that each

ocho ntsang-ntsang lanrhu-lo a-vaitake." Chi-thang
leg one-one cross roads-on for me-leave." That-time

ranfu-chiang-na yiaisicho. Tole eson-chi-na nto ezochosana
wild dogs-the departed. Then old man-the what said

n-nchamcheosicho. Osi okhawo-chicho omotzü-thangi
not-remembered. But youngest-the grandfather-with

lamm n-tsso vancho. Nto tssole, omotzü-na
heart not-being was. What being, (his) grandfather

epyototsü mbo m-piochi-na. Osi ranfu-thampo-chiang-
boiled rice him not-giving-because. But wild dogs-other-the

na okhawo-chi engacho, "Eson-chi-na ntoko to
youngest-the asked, "Old man-the what indeed

ezochola ?" Mbo-na ezocho "Eson-chi-na ete ezocho
said ?" He said "Old man-the thus said

"Nte-na kothang oso rhamana chi aku ochü lanrhu-lo
"You when meat catch that each dung cross roads-on

a-vaitake." "Hochi-tssoko-na nhungacha ranfu-na lanrhu-
me-leave." "This-being-from till now wild dogs cross roads-

lo tyoalo.
on leave their droppings.

Long, long ago, before the Great Darkness[1] came, there lived a man who kept wild dogs, as men now call them, With his dogs he killed and ate many deer. But at last he got so old that he conld no longer go into the jungle with his dogs. So he called them all to him and brought them to his house. There he cooked enough rice for each to have a share, but when he divided it up it did not go round properly and the youngest dog got none. Then the old man said. "My dogs, I am very old and can no longer go out hunting with you. But do not forget how I looked after you and cared for you, When you kill a deer, always leave a leg (*ocho*) for me

1 It was after the Great Darkness that men and animals became so different that they could no longer talk together.

at the cross-roads." When the dogs had gone away they quite forgot what the old man had said to them. Now the youngest dog was angry with the old man because he had given him no rice. So, when the other dogs asked him what the old man had said he replied, "The old man said, 'Whenever you kill a deer, leave dung (*ochū*) for me at the cross-roads'." That is why to this day wild dogs leave their droppings at the cross-roads.

28

THE GREEN PIGEON AND SQUIRREL

Worowoni zi-cherha n-tyunta-thang
Kinds of birds rats-squirrles not-separate-time

akau-na mbo 'ro-chi chera-thangi khosokhot
the green pigeon his chicks-the squirrel-to nuts

etham man yencho. Akau-na cherha-chi
three price sold. The green pigeon (to) squirrel-the

"Khosokhoti etham a-pisi a-ro-chi khia" to ezocho.
"Nuts three me-giving my-chicks-the take" thus said.

Tole cherha-chi-na khosokhoti ntap ntsanga na
Then squirrel-the nuts without kernel one and

ntsa eni to pisi mbo 'ro-chi khicho.
with kernel two indeed having given his chicks-the took.

Ole akau-na cherha-chi-na khosokhoti ntap
Then the green pigeon squirrel-the nuts without kernal

ntsnaga na ntsa eni to mbo pi-ochi hanai
one and with-kernel two indeed him gave-the bringing

tarapi zele ntap ntsanga na ntsa
breaking when saw without kernel one and with kernel

eni to sakama cherha-chi-thangi ekhilanta-lo wocho.
two indeed was squirrel-the-to take back-to went.

Mbo-na owo cherha-chi "I-khosokhoti khia osi
He going (to) squirrel-the "Your-nuts take but

a-ro-chi a-pia" to ezocho. Chi-thang cherha-chi-na
my-chicks-the me-give" thus said. That-time squirrel-the

akau-ro-chi ethu tyem-tyem zana ria
(of) green pigeon-chicks-the fat fizz-fizz falling roasting

vansi "Toka i-ro-chi khialo" to ezoa mbo picho,
was "Then your-chicks-the take" thus saying him gave,

Ole akau-chi-na hochi zesi n-khilantao "O o,
Then green pigeon-that this seeing not-taking back "O oh,

akau, akau, ou" to khua tya yicho. Hochi-tssoko-na
akau, akau, ou" thus crying calling went. This-being-from

nhungacha akau-na "O o akau, akau, ou" to
till now (the) green pigeon "Oh oh akau, akau, ou" thus

khuala.
cries.

In the days when birds and rats and squirrels could talk to one another the green pigeon sold her chick to the squirrel in exchange for three nuts, The green pigeon said to the squirrel, "Give me three nuts and you can take this chick of mine." Then the squirrel took the chick, but gave the green pigeon two good nuts and one without a kernel. When the grcen pigeon took away the nuts and cracked them he found that two were good and one had no kernel, so he went to give them back to the squirrel, and said to him "Take back your nuts and give me my chick." The squirrel was then roasting the chick, and watching the fat drip hiss, hiss into the fire. And he said to the green pigeon "Here is your chick. Take it," and handed it to him. When the green pigeon saw what had happened to his chick he would not take it, but went away weeping and crying. "O, o, akau, akau ou" That is why the Green Pigeon still cries "O, o akau, akau, ou."

29

THE WAGTAIL AND THE OWLET

Erangi mangtham rocho silo worowoni
At the beginning darkness came after kinds of birds

n-tyunta-thang, nchoka woro topu santhrui tsangon
not-separate-time, one day birds all collecting day

to na zamo to lio tyutacho. Ole woro topu-na
indeed an night indeed being discussed. Then birds all

velongo-chi "N-na tyua" to ezoa tyutokle,
(to) owlet-the "You speak" thus speaking making to speak,

mbo-na "Tsangon toku mang tsangon toku won
he "Days nine darkness days nine light

to tssoka," to tyucho, Chisilocho woro
indeed shall become," thus he spoke, Thereupon birds

topu-na "Chi to mak, chi to mak" to
all "That indeed no, that indeed no" thus

tyuta hepi-hepi-na kurri-lo tyak-tyak mbo
speaking this side-that side-from head-on pat-pat him

tamicho. Chi-tssoko-na nhungacha velongo kurri
smacked. This-being-from till now owl's head

etyaka-la. Osi woro topu-na "Nhungo ocho-na tyula,"
flat-is. But birds all "Now that one let speak,"

to tyutacho. Chi-thang sese-hambong-ro-chi-na "Toka
thus said. That-time wagtail-cock-little-the "Then

a-na tyuka; engata" to tyua "Mang-won-chi,
I will speak; listen" thus speaking "Darkness-light-the,

mang-won-chi to tssoka" to tyucho.
darkness-light the indeed there shall be" thus spoke.

Ole woro topu-na "Hochi to hochi to"
Then birds all "That indeed that indeed

to tyuta hepi-hepi-na mbo nzampicho.
thus speaking this side-that side-from him stroked.

Nkolocho mbo hono hambong tara kama, woro
Formerly he fowl cock equal though being, birds

topu-na mbo nzampicho-na nhungacha heto teria-la.
all him stroked-because till now so small-is.

Long, long ago, about the time that the Great Darkness came upon the earth, all the birds—for in those days the kinds were not as different as they are now—met in council to decide how night should follow day. With one voice they called on the owlet to give his opinion. Then the owlet said, "Let there be nine days' darkness and nine days' light." "No, no," said all the birds, and smacked him on this side of his head and on that. That is why now-a-days the owlet has a flat head. Then all the birds said, "Who will speak now?" And the wagtail said, "Listen to me, then; I will speak. Let us make darkness and light alternately, day by day". "Yes, yes" said all the birds, and stroked the wagtail all over. He used to be as big as a village cock, but because all the birds stroked him so much he is now very small.

LHOTA ENGLISH GLOSSARY

A

a-	I
a	not
a-	out
ā	my
-a	one
acho	hallo
acho	all right
aiyo	I
aka	child's
akau	green pigeon
aku	all; every; each
alo	is it
apikachilana	hand it up again
apykaicho	crawled
aria	so much
asontsangtak	having grown old
ato	thus
atalo	like
ayo	dear me

B

ba	are

C

cha	worm
chu	cast
chakeha	whisk
cham	brand
chamcheo	remembering
chamchoya	lift off

chamchetake .. .. .. do forget
chamchak .. .. .. rags
chami .. .. .. prepared; made
chamkachele .. .. .. putting on to boil
champo .. .. .. morung
chan .. .. .. to relish; to like; to reach
chani .. .. .. viewing
chan-shi .. .. .. vegetable
chang .. .. .. bundle
changa .. .. .. to tie up; to wrap up
changi .. .. .. gave the
changricho .. .. .. vegetables
changram .. .. .. leaves
chapya .. .. .. running backward and forwards
chena .. .. .. pounding
cheni .. .. .. companion
chenle .. .. .. striking
chenchi .. .. .. to set tasks
chenchicho .. .. .. made to work
chenchisi .. .. .. having made to work
chencho .. .. .. threw his spear
chenchho .. .. .. up side down
cheni .. .. .. companion
cheni .. .. .. brothers
chentokle .. .. .. having ground
chentsangcho .. .. pierced
chepile .. .. .. when pushed
chepya .. .. .. seeing
cherha .. .. .. squirlres
cherhaloma .. .. .. vegetables
cheta .. .. .. watching
chetha .. .. .. secretly watching
chetheiki .. .. .. recognising
chhani .. .. .. (from) fan
chhũo .. .. .. having
chi .. .. .. it; this; that; there
chi .. .. .. her
-chi .. .. .. the

chi .. .. .. digging
-chiang .. .. .. -the
chiang .. .. .. they; them
chiangcho .. .. .. (of) them
chiangki .. .. .. them
chiango .. .. .. saying
chibu .. .. .. clan
chicho .. .. .. that one
chicho .. .. .. the
chicho .. .. .. that
chilo .. .. .. here; there
chisi .. .. .. later
chisicho .. .. .. then; after that; afterwards; later
chisilo .. .. .. then;
chisilocho .. .. .. after this; later, then
chitaka .. .. .. will share
chilala .. .. .. hit
chilo .. .. .. there
chitale .. .. .. when dividing
chitlatokcho .. .. .. allowed to divide up
chitayawacho .. .. divided up
chithechiake .. .. .. would deceive
chito .. .. .. so
chito .. .. .. thus
chitosicho .. .. .. therefore; after this; after that
chiwo- .. .. .. by the side of
cho .. .. .. dawn
cho .. .. .. those
cho .. .. .. down
-cho .. .. .. the
-cho .. .. .. that
cho .. .. .. leg; foot
cho .. .. .. sister-the
choi .. .. .. descending
choi .. .. .. to fall down; to come down; to go down
chok .. .. .. shut
chok .. .. .. to pick; to pluck
chon .. .. .. to cultivate; to demand

chonche .. .. .. cultivating
chonchia .. .. .. open
chonchicho .. .. .. opened
chong .. .. .. up
chongi .. .. .. in; into
chong .. .. .. plucking
chongi/chongo .. .. going up
chonta .. .. .. working
choro .. .. .. moon; months
choro .. .. .. coming down
chorotsakao .. .. .. bathing
chow .. .. .. down
chawo .. .. .. downward
chu .. .. .. out
chũ .. .. .. dung
chu .. .. .. emerging; coming out
chung .. .. .. bottom
chüo .. .. .. being
chungi .. .. .. coming up
chungo .. .. .. climbing
chungra .. .. .. bird trap
chüro .. .. .. coming out
chuwo .. .. .. going out

D

drako .. .. .. hitting

E

e .. .. .. out
ẽ .. .. .. we
ẽ .. .. .. us
e .. .. .. oh
e .. .. .. ho
ei .. .. .. oh
ei .. .. .. now
echakaro .. .. .. a little
echam .. .. .. picking up; seizing
echham .. .. .. oath

echan .. .. .. back
echanala .. .. .. are called
echangpisila .. .. .. having pruned a little
echantyoi .. .. .. wife's relations
echekpya .. .. .. smoothing
echen .. .. .. blood
echhama .. .. .. swearing
echi .. .. .. share
echoi .. .. .. having cut and trimmed
echongana .. .. .. clean
echoroi .. .. .. cutting into small pieces
echü .. .. .. showing
echüla .. .. .. behaves
echunga .. .. .. once upon a time
echunga-na .. .. .. once by
ehitsangi .. .. .. crushing with his nail
ehraktsanga .. .. .. spluttering
ekam .. .. .. live
ekamocho .. .. .. when alive
ekamoche .. .. .. to keep
ekamchosana .. .. look after
ekhab .. .. .. picking
ekhamsi .. .. .. brought up
ekhangtsangi .. .. .. having fallen
ekhentsangchü .. .. were anxious
ekhentsangra .. .. fearing
ekhilanta .. .. .. take back
ekhoma .. .. .. will abuse
ekhosi .. .. .. having struck
ekhui .. .. .. cooking
ekhutsangi .. .. .. coughing
ekok .. .. .. valley
ekoni .. .. .. afar
ekyung .. .. .. king; chief
elak .. .. .. bubbled
elaka .. .. .. bubbling; boiling
elam .. .. .. much; very; many
elampya .. .. .. twitching
elang-chü .. .. .. to cut-off

elani .. .. .. again
elhampiu .. .. .. moving
elhungtheo .. .. .. falling
elhechei .. .. .. opening
elhichi .. .. .. opening
eli .. .. .. is
eloe .. .. .. woman; girl; female
elong .. .. .. heavy jungle
emaicho .. .. .. mocked
emangoti .. .. .. at dusk
emenopang .. .. .. councillor
emerapsi .. .. .. having snapped
emhokta .. .. .. surprised
emi .. .. .. old time
emi .. .. .. old woman
emunga .. .. .. spinning
enato .. .. .. slowly
eng .. .. .. wife
eng .. .. .. sun; day
eng-ya-thang .. .. .. sun-rising time
enga .. .. .. listening; hearing; asking; obeying
enga .. .. .. one day
engana .. .. .. one day
engalang .. .. .. all day long
enghyia .. .. .. pushing
engo .. .. .. day
engyhitechi .. .. .. having pushed off
enhyui .. .. .. remaining
eni .. .. .. we two
eni .. .. .. two
enno .. .. .. ears
enthakala .. .. .. if hurts
epanthang .. .. .. to kill
epo .. .. .. holes
epfu .. .. .. lines
epfukai .. .. .. wrapping
epfusila .. .. .. smearing

epi	fence
epo	torn
epopya	groping
epue	man; male; husband: boy
epvu	to take on credit
epyotosü	boiled rice
era	wax
eramo	elder
erasmi	having put on
eran	old
eran-na	ancestors
eran-ren	old time
erangi	at the beginning
erhua	roaring
erhansola	to break
erhapthechi	to strike
erhyu	pounding up
eria	rolling
ero	sharp
erowo	sharp
errü	entrails
esana	one
esangaro	a little later
esekhansi	smearing
eshoi	pouring
esi	long
esi	threw away
esoktaka	has come out of its handle
eson	old (man or woman)
essa	like
esükha	shipping off
esütchu	tears
etamo	looking
ete-tso	out-food
etchhio	dead
etehüthechi	deceiving
ethakhana	closing
etham	three
ethan	new

ethon	struggle
ethu	fat
ethungtheo	falling
ethi	growing
ethu	strength
ets	being
etsa	name
etse	nipping off
etsai	called
etseta	nip off
etsi	staff
etsia	washing
etso	food
etsoi	child
etsolo	daughter
etsong	wife
etsso	building
etssoi	being
etyaka	flat
etyancheki	touching
etyou	anxious
etyunchon	clay
evamo	lair
evao	put
evung	heck
ewo	attacking
ewo	bamboo shoot
exoa	having spoken
etyaka	to smear
etyeng	full
etyunchon	clay
eyata	to fight
eyia	proceeding
eyikacho	wound round
eyo	our
ezalo	leaving attached
ezaptoka	causing to suffer
ezho	pool
ezhutsak	pool

ezo .. .. .. to say; to reply
ezosi .. .. .. having said
ezung-pfui .. .. .. Ezung-woman

H

ha .. .. .. load
ha .. .. .. also; even; too; indeed; both; also
he .. .. .. now
he .. .. .. look
ho .. .. .. tooth
hambong .. .. .. cock
hamla .. .. .. will take
hamlo .. .. .. to carry
hamo .. .. .. carrying in womb
hamponi .. .. .. relish
hana .. .. .. taking; carrying; bringing
hanasi .. .. .. wearing
hau .. .. .. no
havcho .. .. .. carried
hayo .. .. .. alas
hepi .. .. .. hither; this way
hepi-hepi .. .. .. this side-that side
hepicho .. .. .. here
hepina .. .. .. this way
hetata .. .. .. so much
hetala .. .. .. so many
heto .. .. .. this
hetonacho .. .. .. so much
hilo .. .. .. here
hiya .. .. .. to slick into
hlaplanchi .. .. .. having closed
hlo .. .. .. picking
hlo-hloi .. .. .. pick-picking
hloiki .. .. .. picking
hing .. .. .. wish
hochi .. .. .. she; her
[illegible]euun .. .. .. new
hochi .. .. .. that; this

hochi	that place
hochiang	they
hochiang	they
hoki	watery
honokhui	outside
honkhu	outside the house
honkhui	outside
hono	fowl
hano-hambong	fowl-cock
hono-hanki	fowl-house
hono-khuala	calling of the fowl
hung	seeing; catching

I

-i	by; on; in; to; at; for; from
inamphyo	twitching
is	throwing away

K

ki	with; by house
ka	indeed
ka	child
kalok	loose
kam	turning into
kam	friend
kama	being
kama	because
kama	if able
kami	becoming; turning into
kamo	friend
kashak	crow
khalanchi	shut up
kham	shade
khamki	at the head
khamo	becoming
kampiodo	waiting
kangshi	persecution

khang	falling
khantsaug	back of house
khe	hand
khero	twigs
khethangkheri	sweeping
kheta	(one) hand
khi	fetching; getting; taking
khichei	taking out
hhikai	picking up
khilani	fetching again
kho	head
khokai	having lifted up
kholok	grass heap
khongkho	cotton
khontala	quarrel
khosokhot	nut
khu	hole
khua	crying; saying; calling
khyu	fear
khyu	frightened
khulichotan	marriage meat
khusi	having opened side
khuso	gibbons
khyno	fearing
-khyu	peace
ki	house
ki	through; with
kilato	intending
kiya	for nothing
kni	take
knogken	orange tree
ko	any
koi	where
kok	bends
kakai	piling up
komayo	to turn into
konrossu	little girl's skirt
koremyoi	brambles
kote	how much

kothang .. .. .. sometimes; when
kothanga .. .. .. ever; sometimes
koti-koto .. .. .. where-where
koto .. .. .. in any way; as
koto .. .. .. how much
koto .. .. .. where
kotoli .. .. .. how
kotoli .. .. .. in any way
kotolui .. .. .. how possibly
kotyoh .. .. .. thorns
kazu .. .. .. swing
kozuta .. .. .. swing
kuk .. .. .. hole
kulo .. .. .. where
kupi .. .. .. behind; underneath; inside
kurr .. .. .. head
kurr .. .. .. ashes
kurri .. .. .. head
kurria .. .. .. becoming weak
kyon .. .. .. people
kyon .. .. .. man; human being

L

lo .. .. .. at; in; on; into
lo .. .. .. look
li .. .. .. field
lammsi .. .. .. wanting
lamphei .. .. .. having undone
lamphei .. .. .. having opened
lan .. .. .. path
lange .. .. .. having cut
langta .. .. .. to kill
langtatarai .. .. .. having cut other to pieces
lanphe .. .. .. opening
lanrhu .. .. .. cross road
larhui .. .. .. carving
lanrhu- .. .. .. cross roads
lanyi .. .. .. meet
lamm .. .. .. preference

lak	bubble
lamalo	many
lamm	love; liking
lamm	anger
lamm	heart
lamma	desiring
lap	grave
lap lap	all
lechap	daoholder
lenkasi	having thrown
lenthei	striking the earth
lenroi	scratching over
lepok	dao
loran	servant girl
lenpya	tapping
leshu	thatch
leshuwo	tuft of thatching grass
lhampio	moving
lhungtokna	letting fall
li	field
li-ki	field-edge
li.lan	field-path
li-tsa	field-edge
lia	even
locho	rich
limha	world
lishu	thatching
lishu	thatching grass
lishung	mynas
livero	dry sand
liya	being
loala	never-the-less
loko	ground
lokpia	having felt
lom	some
lomo	leaf
lomo	grass
lon	torches
long	and all

longpen	barries
laran	servant girl
loroe	girls
loreo	girl
losu	leaves
lsotyatale	not getting to eat
lui	doing ; making
lung	rock ; stone
lung	among
lungrhen	cliff
luo	doing

M

m-	not
-mpom	un-split
ma-	not being
mi	fire
-mo	father-in-law
mo	no
mak	no
man	price
manku	back
mang	darkness
mangri	keeping
mangsu	cow
mangtham	darkness
mbao	being
mbata	remaining
mbo	he; his; him
mak	not
maku	husks
mangsa	evening
manku	back
mang	corpse
mehm	beard
men	price
menchoi	earth opening
menzhuisicho	were engulfed
mezeni	to kill

mha .. .. .. face
mhala .. .. .. get
mharr .. .. .. tiger
mharrsamona .. .. a great tiger
mhatongina .. .. .. in front of
mhenkhani .. .. .. ripened
mhom .. .. .. beautiful
mhom .. .. .. well ; good
mhon .. .. .. good ; fine
mhona .. .. .. very good
mhonkhango .. .. .. very good
mhonkana .. .. .. well ; good ; handsome
mhyekchung .. .. .. blind
milani .. .. .. evening
mma .. .. ,. stomach
mmena .. .. .. stomach
momo .. .. .. hairy caterpillar
moratsamo .. .. .. dirty
mori .. .. .. pot
motsu .. .. .. story
'motzu .. .. .. grand father
mpanga .. .. .. climbing
mpato .. .. .. also
mpato .. .. .. upto
mpato .. .. .. too
mpensi .. .. .. earring
mpia .. .. .. even
mphoi .. .. .. hinding
mpho .. .. .. sole
mpongki .. .. .. wind-house
mua .. .. .. forbidden
mugtoi .. .. .. collecting
mukuku .. .. .. pipe
mung .. .. .. sabbath
munga .. .. .. sitting place
munga .. .. .. sitting
'myang .. .. .. name

N

ni	two
na	if
na	from ; to
na	and; in
n-	you
n-no	you
n	not
na	by ; with ; because of
no	on
nathango	hear
neha	spittle
nehai	tucking
nchama	feeling
nchama	understanding ; thinking
nchamchei	remembered
nchokacho	one day
nchuna	hearth stones
nchurang	before
nchyua	a
nching	to-day
nehingk	to-day
nchingo	today
nchok	day
nchoka	one day
nchokacho	one day
nchokopen	every day
nchokania	a few days later
nchorang	before
nchu	hearth
nchunko	always
nchurang	before
nchyu	one
nchyua	one
nchyuachicho	a certain
nchyueni	two
ndri	slaves
ndrindran	orphan

ndrru	snake plant
ndrrutsu	snake
nfua	floating
ng	wife
ngaiche	fulfilling
ngarhang	pregnant
ngaro	child
ngarohang	pregnant
ngo	and such like
ngo	boy
ngo	younger brother
ngo	fish
Ngo-rham	fish-catcher
ngokung	dried fish
ngoyi	fresh fish
nhunga	anew ; again
nhungcha	still ; till now ; to this day
nhungacho	yet
nhungaliya	till now
nhungati	just now
nhungo	now
nhya	swallow
nhyaka	waiting
nhyako	to watch
nhyakcho	awaited
nhyanchap	cobra
nipong	wild boar
nkak	biting
nkaksila	gnawing
nkap	bundle ; parcel ; wrapping
nkapchochi	nipping off
nkho	fence
nko	legs ; feet
nkola	once upon a time
nkolo	before
nkolo	where
nkolo	former ; formerly
nkolocho	formerly
nkoto	what kind of

nlapia .. .. .. flourishing
nlhaneha .. .. .. spittle
nli .. .. .. tongue
nnoki .. .. .. crushing
nnungi .. .. .. having cooked
nnyo .. .. .. top
nnyunkai .. .. .. top
noa .. .. .. urinating
noa .. .. .. enticing
nohok .. .. .. pain
noni .. .. .. days
narakai .. .. .. killing
nrhonroi .. .. .. rotting
nrokthechi .. .. .. scattering
nsangkangu .. .. .. a little later
nshi .. .. .. mid day meal
nshioroi .. .. .. tearing in pieces
ntante .. .. .. so far
ntap .. .. .. without kernel
ntchhio .. .. .. not-being dead
nte .. .. .. you ; your
nte .. .. .. your
nteno .. .. .. you
nthangna .. .. .. just now
nthangi .. .. .. near
nthang .. .. .. real
nthang .. .. .. just now
nthango .. .. .. near
nthikoro .. .. .. on his back
nti .. .. .. anything
nti-ntila .. .. .. any-any way
nita .. .. .. something
nita .. .. .. what ; anything
ntia-si .. .. .. outstretched arms-long
ntila .. .. .. anywhere
nto .. .. .. what
ntonchochia .. .. .. picking and throwing down
ntongi .. .. .. upright
nto .. .. .. what

notki	having met
ntoko	what
ntokoto	what kind of
ntoku	what
ntonsito	about
ntsa	with kernel
ntsaila	knowing
ntsang	on
ntsanga	clean
ntsanga	one ; a
ntsangatai	one only
ntsso	becoming
ntyakai	sprinkling
ntyazhua	sprinkling
nungowo	younger
nungra	sad
nungri	children
nungri	boy
nungaria	girl
nungriten	children
mungtso	believing
nyahchaki	having cut off
nyalepisicho	twisted
nyana	chanting
nyika	black (mark)
nyimtyep	nail
ntyiorhui	having split pieces off
nzam	comfort ; caring
nzana	loving
nzua	year
nzui	swallowed

O

o	for ; at
och	leg
ochak	food
ocham	end
ochang	who

ochen	rat
ochen	vasts
ochi	the ; that
ochiang	they
ochicho	that (woman)
ocho	which
ocho	tomorrow
ocho	who ; whoever ; whose
ocho	leg
ocho	next day
ochoa	next day
ochoa	tomorrow
ochoata	next day
ochoto	next day
ochü	dung
oha	load
oham	flour
okaiti	at last
okainacho	at last
okame-cho	(when) alive
okamo	friend
okhawo	younger
okhu	scratch
okhyu	basket ; bamboo basket
oki	house
oki	home
olampem	idle
olăn	path ; road
olantaro	all
olantaro	something
ole	then
oli	field
olia	but
olong	tree
olung	stones
om	wife's father
oman	marriage price
omang	corpses

omha	face
omholi	fields
omhyek	eye
omi	fire
omo	father-in-law
ompoi-na	man and wife
omoyzü	grandfather
omu	bamboo strip
omyek	eyes
onche	(of) brothers
ongo	fish
ongo	younger brother
onhyan	carrying band
oni	the two
oni	the two ; both
ono	poison
ono	fish poison
onpoi	couple
onte	those two
ontyai	brother and sister
opang	mouth
opfui	owners
opo	father
opoang	(to) parents
opoyang	parents
opvü	mother
ora	jungle
orai	jungle
orano	leprous
orapvü	husband
orapvü 'ki	husband's house
orhak	louse
oro	coming
orotsakatara	washing
orr	cane
orru	bones
osa	fish trap
osham	committing adultery
oshom	friends

oshyu .. .. .. bamboo
osi .. .. .. but
oso .. .. .. meat
ostan .. .. .. hair
osu .. .. .. track
ossu .. .. .. cloth
ota .. .. .. elder brother
ote .. .. .. them
otchhu .. .. .. water
oten .. .. .. they; all
otong .. .. .. trees
otsak .. .. .. all
otsak .. .. .. food
otsak .. .. .. bees
otsak .. .. .. body
otsan .. .. .. hair
otsang .. .. .. wood ; trees
otsap .. .. .. bamboo spoon
otsi .. .. .. rice
otso .. .. .. spear
otsoi .. .. .. child ; son
otsok .. .. .. rice
otsolo .. .. .. daughter
otsotso .. .. .. true ; really ; truly
otyang .. .. .. drum
otyon .. .. .. ugly
otso-tso .. .. .. true-truly
otyon .. .. .. very
ovung .. .. .. first ; former
owo .. .. .. going
oyak .. .. .. forked stick ; forked stick
oyam .. .. .. villagers
oyam .. .. .. the other man ; some one else
oyamo .. .. .. villagers
oyan .. .. . village
oyeng .. .. .. thread
oyi .. .. .. coming
oyi .. .. .. going
oyo .. .. .. mother

oyo .. .. .. leaves
oyochi .. .. .. having arrived
ozu .. .. .. meat
ozu .. .. .. sacrificial post

P

pampikok .. .. .. can accompany
pato .. .. .. too
pang .. .. .. top
pang .. .. .. door
pang .. .. .. mouh
pankai .. .. .. having crossed
panthi .. .. .. having got up
panthiki .. .. .. getting up
peleta .. .. .. strong
pelang .. .. .. bed
pen .. .. .. places
penchochi .. .. .. picking up
penching .. .. .. oil seed
penchumuchü .. .. .. seed of various kinds
penkoko .. .. .. being able to hold
peno .. .. .. fly
penrasi .. .. .. carrying
densi .. .. .. holding
penthechiale .. .. .. throwing
peta .. .. .. squeezing in
pfua .. .. .. down stream
pfua .. .. .. floating
pufi .. .. .. wiping
pfukacho .. .. .. against
phakhai .. .. .. having bound
phaksa .. .. .. binding
phami .. .. .. roasting
phana .. .. .. driving away ; pursuing; chasing
phanpimuhgcho .. .. always accompanied
phari .. .. .. carrying
phayao .. .. .. catching

phencheta .. .. .. pull out
phenchekok .. .. .. can pull out
phendran .. .. .. last year's field
phiro .. .. .. tops
phitsangkham .. .. burning up
phurro .. .. .. dog
pi .. .. .. giving
pi .. .. .. flat top
pikhu .. .. .. fortification
pipo .. .. .. wearing
pipo .. .. .. ornaments
pipotoksi .. .. .. having made to put on
po .. .. .. own
po .. .. .. father
poang .. .. .. parents
poe .. .. .. different
poki .. .. .. being born
poki .. .. .. begetting
poko .. .. .. one way
pomtsangi .. .. .. swelling
pongi .. .. .. taking off
pongkarai .. .. .. one after the other
pongpi .. .. .. wander
poni .. .. .. on the top
poni .. .. .. mating
popo .. .. .. own
potsocheni .. .. .. relations
potsowo .. .. .. sky
pochung .. .. .. generations
poti .. .. .. alone
pukiro .. .. .. little-fish
pulasasi .. .. .. having picked up
pvü .. .. .. mother

R

racho .. .. .. the day after tomorrow
rachotoli .. .. .. the day after
raho .. .. .. out-stretched arm

raki .. .. .. peeling
ramelhram .. .. .. scent
ramo .. .. .. remember
ranfu .. .. .. wild dogs
rangsotacho .. .. .. pulled apart
ranki .. .. .. shed
ranoi .. .. .. leprous
rena .. .. .. arranging
reta .. .. .. desiring
rham .. .. .. to seize; to catch
rhamai .. .. .. seizing
rharoi .. .. .. cutting up
rhoncheo .. .. .. digging
rhui .. .. .. leaving
ri .. .. .. burning
ria .. .. .. roasting
ria .. .. .. about
richlale .. .. .. while burning
rikab .. .. .. belt
rinyu .. .. .. heating red; hot
ro .. .. .. chicks
ro .. .. .. coming
rong .. .. .. to burn
rong .. .. .. fire
roro .. .. .. little
rosi .. .. .. having come
rro .. .. .. son in law
rru .. .. .. bones
rrūa .. .. .. tracking
rua .. .. .. following
ruchokchicho .. .. .. followed up to
rukachi .. .. .. cooking
ruo .. .. .. for making
rutala .. .. .. to tell ; to say
rutamangala .. .. .. (men) tell the tale

S

sa .. .. .. trap

sakama	because
sakama	being
samlo	cloths
samona	even
samphio	wandering
samsam	beautiful
san hoto	thus so
sana	all using
sana	that
sangalia	the sangalia creeper
sangchok	bound up
sangchochicho	having let down
sani	all
santhrui	collecting
sapocho	was long
sau	clothes
sen	white
sena	white
seno	baıking deer
sese	wagtail
senthan	cornelian beads
setya	spreading apart
sha	destroyed
shake shakc	picking up
shakai	having spread
shamcohia	throwing down
shano	to make
shenkakhani	trying
sheriti	red barries
sheyu-lo	plantain tree
shi	this
shi-tai	these-only
shicho	this one
shilap	untidy
shilo	hither
shio	buying
shishang	shishang ceremony
shishotaka	trade
shitok	allow to buy

shochei	digging up
shoisia	scrapping over
sho-mo	that only
shomo	gourd
shongi	growing
shothe	buried
shotshoiya	scratching up
shukchocho	fail
sia	throwing away
sicho	after
silamo	last
silo	after
sio	taking
sisi	leaving
sis	throwing away
sitakna	having been lost
sito	quickly
so	meat; flesh
soa	bringing
soa	seizing
soa	marrying
soa	taking
soalo	hold
socho	took
sochota	having taken each other (i. e. eloping)
sokhansi	taking
soko	rice beer
solana	bringing out
songdra	spearing through
sonhyasi	having taken
sontsangi	having grown old
sonyhasi	having taken with
sopiya	taking
sopya	taking
sorachak	(a) kill
sosi	bringing
sosi	holding
sotyemo	to hunt

soyingiki .. .. .. having begun
su .. .. .. tracks
sü .. .. .. dragging; taking
suchei .. .. .. dragging out

T

ta .. .. .. sister; elder brother; elder sister
tachoq .. .. .. extra
tacholam .. .. .. food
tai .. .. .. only
taka .. .. .. weaving
takhui .. .. .. inside
taki .. .. .. stinging
tam .. .. .. nice looking
tami .. .. .. cutting
tamicho .. .. .. smacked
tampoe .. .. .. (to) another place
tampoi .. .. .. others
tara .. .. .. equal
tata .. .. .. so many
taktsangi .. .. .. stinging
tamhekhani .. .. .. having put out
tampi .. .. .. beat
tang .. .. .. time
tanvami .. .. .. half dry
taratia .. .. .. a little only
tarapi .. .. .. breaking
taratssosi .. .. .. a little later
tarati .. .. .. little later
tata .. .. .. much
tatsangi .. .. .. having killed
tchii .. .. .. dying
tchhu .. .. .. river
tchuthechicheo .. .. to be deceived
tehha .. .. .. stream
tehhu .. .. .. water
tehhukha .. .. .. spring

tehhufo	water spirit
ten	pack
tena	small
teni	picking
tham	three
thamacho	for nothing
thampo	another; others
thampoi	laying aside
thang	time; which
thangi	from
thanle	when split
thangale	at time of
thangi	with; to
thei	putting
thiphyi	drip
thyaki	sharpenning
thri	having entered
thri	sinking
thria	entering
thro	down; in
thrua	going round; swarming
thrrupya	walking round
thryu	to bark
ti	must not
ti	not
tia	even
tia	a single
ticha	thin bamboo
ticho	thin bamboo
tiloran	sand and powder (i. e. magic powder
tirok	six
titai	only
tiza	eight
to	at
to	indeed; thus
to	whatever
toala	but
toala	yet

toala	nevertheless
toka	then
toka	really
tokatola	tokatola; yet
toku	nine
tole	then
ton	forehead
tona	then
tong	tree
tong	setter
tonga	going straight
tong-pen	setting-place
tong-tonga	ping-ping
tongcho	set up
tongtacho	exchanged
tonkacchho	top up
topo	through
topu	all
tosi	indeed
tosi	having put
tou	defeating
tou	defeat
toyu	all
trangang	tinkle-tinkle
tsa	bank
tsa	calling
tsai	by the side of
tsai	by
tsaiki	calling
tsak	food
tsak	body
tsaka	wash
tsakmen	bees
tsamboku	pounding table
tsampi	touching
tsan	hair
isan-pfui	hair-owner
tsana	escaping; fleeing
tsanchi	hair

tsang	wood
tsanga	miserable
tsanglapkakana	very bright
tsangon	sunbird
tsangon	day
tsangtasi	pulling
tsangti	nuts
tsangthi	fruit
tsanka	top
tsangkai	getting up
tsanthei	entering
tsantsansi	running
tsantyani	cooking
tsantyani	meal
tsapo	big
tsarhui	having called
tsaya	supposing; thinking
tse	nipping off
tseni	wrapping up (i. e. in a leaf)
tsi	rice
tsia	knowing
tsirhi	rat trap
tsiro	mithun
tsirochonglong	shuttle
tso	eating
tsoi	son; daughter
tsok	pierce
tsoka	jumping up
tsokchok	jump
tsoki	piercing; pricking
tsokpya	nopping
tsozhu	husks
tsolo	daughter
tsong-rong	ho-ho
tsongora	animals
tsoni	cutting down
tsopelak	long bladed spear
tsopo	big
tsoren	generations

tsoronichen .. .. .. descendants
tsotyungo .. .. .. son
tsoyao .. .. .. getting to eat
tsso .. .. .. being
tsso .. .. .. becoming (settled)
tssoa .. .. .. being
tssoka .. .. .. becoming; happening
tssoka .. .. .. being
tssoko .. .. .. being; happening, having been
tssoliya .. .. .. for
tsunga .. .. .. along when
tsu .. .. .. grandmother
tung .. .. .. seven
tungi .. .. .. infront of
tungli .. .. .. peak
tya .. .. .. calling; weeping; crying
tyai .. .. .. brothers
tyak .. .. .. pat
tyak .. .. .. flat
tyak .. .. .. plop
tyanthechi .. .. .. having pushed
tyatcho .. .. .. to say
tyem .. .. .. fizz
tyemstu .. .. .. guardian
tyeng .. .. .. full
tyenga .. .. .. crossing
tyengla .. .. .. friendly
tyengramo .. .. .. wireless man
tyentao .. .. .. being friendly
tyingsorok .. .. .. dry place
tyingtok .. .. .. letting dry
tyoa .. .. .. having defeated
tyoi .. .. .. finding
tyoka .. .. .. easing herself
tyoka .. .. .. fishing
tyokha .. .. .. fishing
tyoivale .. .. .. defecting
tyontana .. .. .. deserting
tyosora .. .. .. speaking

tyozhu	.. .. .. fish
tyua	.. .. .. saying
tyunkai	.. .. .. having melted away
tyunta	.. .. .. separate
tyuo	.. .. .. to say
tyutala	.. .. .. (they) say

V

va	.. .. .. putting; leaving; keeping
vachi	.. .. .. letting go
vachia	.. .. .. release
vampen	.. .. .. lair
van	.. .. .. (is) born
van	.. .. .. remaining
van	.. .. .. village
vana	.. .. .. staying
vana	.. .. .. living
vanchole	.. .. .. failing
vanpen	.. .. .. lair
vansi	.. .. .. having remained; remaining
vansi	.. .. .. being
vanta	.. .. .. to marry
vansansi	.. .. .. being
vasi	.. .. .. having put; having kept
vasi	.. .. .. keeping
velongo	.. .. .. owl
venya	.. .. .. cover
venyake	.. .. .. cover up
vuchotoko	.. .. .. to let fall
vunga	.. .. .. first

W

wo	.. .. .. going
wo	.. .. .. leaf
woa	.. .. .. going
woi	.. .. .. half

wok	pig
woka	going
woke	(a) pig
won	birds
won	light
woni	going
woni	having beheaded
woniki	shining
woro	bird
worowoni	kinds of birds
wotoko	letting come
wowokaka	(is) able to go
wuzu	pond

Y

ya	rising
ya	(to) come
yai	among
yaka	piercing
yakso	monkeys
'yak	forked tree
yaki	piercing tree
yam	village
'yam	the other man
yampile	marrying
yar	village
yana	seeking
yanal	search
yanchei	having got
yonkitam	old dao
yantsai	poor
yanpia	marrying
yanyo	searching
yekrho	wild taro
yenga	band
yanle	searching
yanri	village-enemy
yantheng	long dao

yenki .. .. .. basket
yengki .. .. .. carrying basket
yengkok .. .. .. spoon
yenpya .. .. .. hawking
yi .. .. .. words
yia .. .. .. coming; going
yicheo .. .. .. pulling in
yina .. .. .. coming
yinga .. .. .. party
yingdro .. .. .. fingers
yingto .. .. .. quietly
yingtovansi .. .. .. remaining quiet
yip .. .. .. sleeping
yip .. .. .. as asleep
yipa .. .. .. sleeping
yipa .. .. .. laying down
yipayisi .. .. .. having gone to sleep
yipi .. .. .. lying down
yiple .. .. .. going to sleep
yipo .. .. .. sleeping
yonchok .. .. .. iron
yontsi .. .. .. spear butt
yu .. .. .. drinking
yungachi .. .. .. running
yungai .. .. .. running
yutoksi .. .. .. having given to drink

Z

zai .. .. .. standing
zamo .. .. .. night
zana .. .. .. shedding
zana .. .. .. falling
zanzhya .. .. .. sprinkling
zaptoke .. .. .. to come to harm
ze .. .. .. to see
zena .. .. .. certainly
zizo .. .. .. rat
zenthe .. .. .. fixed

zenthei	fixing
zo	to tell
zoa	telling
zoi	hearing
zowoti	zowoti fruit
zowoti-tong	zowoti-tree
zei	(to) see
zua	give it to suck
zukhu	zukhu river
zuncho	nest
zuro	(the) forty
zurozuiya	breeze
zyumo	cat fish